# THE PHILOSOPHICAL POSSIBILITIES BEYOND DEATH

THE PHILOSOPHICAL POSSIBILITIES BEYOND DEATH

Exploring the Evidence from Psychical Research

BROOKE NOEL MOORE PhD

Afterworlds Press

Santa Fe, New Mexico
www.afterworldspress.com

The Philosophical Possibilities Beyond Death

Original Copyright © 1981 by Charles C. Thomas Publishers.
Copyright © 2023 by Brooke Noel Moore. All rights reserved.

Published by Afterworlds Press; an imprint of White Crow Productions Ltd.

The moral right of the author has been asserted in accordance with the Copyright, Design and Patents act 1988.

No part of this book may be reproduced, copied or used in any form or manner whatsoever without written permission, except in the case of brief quotations in reviews and critical articles.

For information, contact White Crow Books by
e-mail: info@whitecrowbooks.com.

Cover Design by Astrid@Astridpaints.com
Interior design by Velin@Perseus-Design.com

Paperback: ISBN: 978-1-78677-240-4
eBook: ISBN: 978-1-78677-241-1

Non-Fiction / RELIGION / Comparative Religion /
BODY, MIND & SPIRIT / Afterlife & Reincarnation

www.afterworldspress.com
www.whitecrowbooks.com

To my father, Ralph J. Moore,
for his dedication to clarity
of expression and honesty of thought.

PREFACE FOR A NEW CENTURY

Two aspects of death receive much attention in literature and philosophy: its inevitability, and its irrevocability.

The inevitability of one's own death generally takes a while to register. For much of life one's mind mostly is elsewhere; for many people (though apparently not all), their own demise is abstract, remote, and almost impossible to picture.

This changes by degrees, as personal fragility becomes undeniable, and one begins noticing how most of the memorial services they attend are no longer for people older than them.

Death's irrevocability, by comparison, registers from almost the first time a friend or pet or loved one dies. There is an unescapable realization that their silence is forever. Never again will you see, hear, hold, hug, or talk to them, and never again will they see, hear, hold, hug, or talk to you. The reassurance that you will meet again in a perfect hereafter will perhaps strike those who aren't religious as unfounded and unconvincing, as trying to make bad news good news.

Obviously, many other things disappear from our lives, both inevitably and irrevocably. But when your computer stops working, as eventually it must, you don't exactly fall into a state of mourning. If a family member were to move permanently to another country which made it impossible for either you or they to see each another except via Zoom, the sadness felt would be of a different variety from that felt if they died. Nothing is as valuable to us as those we cherish, and their irrevocable loss can leave us inconsolable.

Whether it's one own's death or the death of another, it's difficult to imagine what consciousness after physical death could be like. The dark glass of death blocks every attempt to glimpse another world. We do know that sensation and perception depend on a living brain: could a departed entity experience happiness without seeing, feeling, hearing, tasting, or smelling anything, or doing so in an unrecognized body, perhaps not even of human form? Could it be anything more than a passive center of consciousness of an unimaginable sort, powerless to effect change? Should we hope for a close family member or friend, or ourselves, to be in such a state, possibly for all eternity? Such questions, among many others, are explored in this book independently of religion.

It is fair to say I have a fuller appreciation of my own inevitable mortality than I did when I wrote this book more than 40 years ago. If I were to rewrite it now, perhaps this newer perspective would influence my words in subtle ways. Yet, when I read the book again now, I find the conclusions I reached then still accurate and convincing.

Brooke Noel Moore
December, 2022

PREFACE

Cebes said to Socrates, "But surely it requires a great deal of argument and many proofs to show that when the man is dead his soul yet exists, and has any force or intelligence."

"True, Cebes," said Socrates; "and shall I suggest that we converse a little of the probabilities of these things?"[1]

Before and since Socrates people have conversed much about "these things." Philosophers, theologians, dramatists, and poets grapple perennially with the question of "life after death" as well as with the problems of life here and now. The widespread interest in the possibility of afterdeath existence is reflected in the everyday talk of ordinary people and in best-selling books about the hereafter.

In this book I continue the age-old conversation on life after death. I do so philosophically in the light of data of the last one hundred years that have aroused considerable popular and professional interest as possibly confirming the reality of an afterlife.

True, no living person can be absolutely certain either that there is or that there is not an existence after bodily death. This is unfortunate for those who want certainty now, as many do throughout life or when confronting the hard inevitability of death in terminal illness or old age.

Though we cannot have certainty, we can, like Socrates, consider the probabilities. It is my objective to do just this: to determine what will probably be our destiny after biological death.

The book has four parts. In the first part, the various theories of the possible nature of survival beyond death are explained, and the assumptions that are basic to my subsequent discussion of afterdeath existence are set forth. In Part II, I consider whether these theories are subject to antecedent philosophical refutation. In the next two parts of the book I examine the data accumulated

---

[1] B. Jowett (trans): *The Dialogues of Plato*. New York, Random House, 1937, Vol. I. p. 453.

during the past one hundred years, which are the most compelling of belief in life after death. At the end of Part IV, I contemplate what conclusions reasonably may be made as to "the probabilities of these things."

Should my conclusions be questionable, my reasoning erroneous, or my treatment of factual matter defective, the fault is not that of those who have helped me to complete this book, and to whom I owe much. I wish to express my gratitude to Professors John Bash, Kirk Monfort, Joyce Norman, Robert E. Thomas, Richard Parker, and Kent Tiedeman, as well as to Chris Steiner, who read drafts of various parts of the book; to William Lawson, Denise Pasetta, and Kirby Smith, who helped with research; to my wife, Linda Ely Moore, and my children, Sherry and Bill, for their patience while I spent long hours in my work and for unwavering support in many forms; to the members of the Philosophy Department at California State University, Chico, for helping me to discharge my duties as department chairman while writing this book; and to Nancy Riley, my knowledgeable typist.

Most especially, I thank my father, Ralph J. Moore, for generously contributing much time and his skill from long experience as a legal editor to the editing of the manuscript.

Finally, I gratefully acknowledge permission to reprint and use copyrighted material, and thank those giving me that permission for their courtesy and cooperation.

B. N. M.

CONTENTS

                                        Page

Preface for a New Century .... *vii*
Preface .... *ix*

PART I: INTRODUCTION

Chapter
1. Personal Survival 5
2. Theories of Survival 12
3. Scientific Survival 15

PART II: PHILOSOPHICAL REFUTATIONS

4. Refutations of Disembodied Survival 25
5. Can the Mind Be Nonmaterial? 29
6. Two Views of Self and Disembodied Survival 44
7. It Isn't Chess Without the King 53
8. Refutations of Reincarnation 63
9. Resurrection and Identity 69
10. The Description of Astral Bodies 74

PART III: THE EARLY EVIDENCE

11. Religious Evidence 79
12. The Ultimate Mediums 82
13. Difficulties With the Piper and Leonard Cases 91
14. Cross-corresponding Communications 102
15. Drop-in Communicators: Runolfur Runolfsson 115
16. Gauld's "Drop-ins" 121
17. Apparitions 127
18. Proof or Corroboration? 131

Chapter	Page

PART IV: THE LATE EVIDENCE

19. Visions at the Brink of Death.........................135
20. Other Studies of Near-death Experiences............145
21. Out of Body Phenomena.............................153
22. The Electronic Voice Phenomenon..................159
23. The Reincarnation Cases............................165
24. Xenoglossy..180
25. Reincarnation Workshops...........................192
26. What Are the Probabilities?........................200

Bibliography..206

Index..215

THE PHILOSOPHICAL

POSSIBILITIES

BEYOND DEATH

PART I

INTRODUCTION

CHAPTER 1

PERSONAL SURVIVAL

It's a shocker! Everyone will come back to life someday. Regardless of your race, religion, age or social status, you will return.
— Ralph Wilkerson, Beyond and Back[1]

... it is rational to suppose that mental life ceases when bodily life ceases. The argument is only one of probability, but is as strong as those upon which most scientific conclusions are based.
— Bertrand Russell, Why I·Am Not a Christian[2]

The Question

The controversy over life after death continues. The primary purpose of this book is to examine this controversy and to help resolve it. *Shall I survive the death of my body?* This is the principal question addressed in this book, and I hope that what is written here will contribute to an intelligent and well-reasoned answer to it.

Shall I survive the death of my body? It is important to understand what this question is not. As treated here, except briefly in Chapter 3, this question is not whether my chemical constituents or genetic code will survive the death of my body. Nor is it the question whether my name or fame or accomplishments will live on after I am gone. Certainly the flow of one's particular germ plasm through his progeny gives him an "afterlife" of sorts; and clearly great statesmen, composers, and scientists enjoy immortality through the unending memory of their achievements. But these are not the kinds of life after death with which I am here

---

[1] New York, Bantam Books. 1977, p. 1. Copyright 1977 by Ralph Wilkerson. Reprinted by permission of Bantam Books. Inc. All rights reserved.

[2] New York, Allen and Unwin, 1957, p. 51. Copyright ° 1957 by Allen and Unwin. Reprinted by permission of Simon and Schuster, a Division of Gulf and Western Corporation.

concerned. Instead, my concern is with what in philosophy is called *personal* survival or survival of *self*: Will I, myself, this very *person*, exist after this body is dead and gone?

No doubt some will regard it as pointless to trouble much over a question to which we'll not learn the certain answer until we die. While we shall not have certainty in the matter until we die, and shall have it then only if we do in truth survive, it is clearly worthwhile to attempt to determine what, when everything is considered, is the most reasonable opinion that a still living person might have about this question. For our opinions as to the possibility and nature of a next life may well affect our management of this life.

Assumptions

Ordinarily certain fundamental assumptions are made in discussions of life after death, and will be made in this book as well. It is important to be aware of these assumptions, for they underlie the validity of any discussion in which they are made. What follows is a list of the most important of these fundamental assumptions. The peculiar thing about these assumptions is that, from the standpoint of common sense, they all seem so obvious as not to be worth mentioning; yet from a philosophical standpoint several of them are highly controversial.

I begin with two assumptions, not about survival, life, death, or persons, but about *minds*. That I begin here should perhaps not be too surprising since, as will shortly be seen, the notion of the mind is implicit in the concept of the self or person.

(1) *Minds are countable*. The first assumption is that minds are countable. Whatever their ultimate nature, whether they are really just brains or are something immaterial, there is a difference between one mind and two minds. Minds are like tables and people and ghosts in that they are the sort of things of which there can be one, a few, or many. Another way to express the fact that minds are countable is to say, simply, that minds are things. And I shall assume, along with common sense, that minds, whether tangible or intangible, as the truth may be, are indeed things.

(2) *Minds are conscious*. The second assumption is that minds are

conscious things. Perhaps they are not conscious all of the time. Perhaps when one sleeps, or is anesthetized, one's mind may be said not to be conscious, but a thing totally without consciousness is not really a mind. The very intimate connection between minds and consciousness is shown by the fact that frequently a person's mind is referred to as his "consciousness."

(3) *Persons have minds.* The third assumption is about persons or selves (I equate the two): persons have minds. Other things too may have minds, but this need not be assumed. I assume merely that to be a person, it is essential to have a mind; and thus a being without a mind cannot be a person (though of course it could formerly have been a person).

(4) *There are as many minds as there are persons and as many persons as there are minds.* Not only do I assume that persons have minds, I also assume that each person has one and only one mind, and I assume that mind is a *complete* mind. Further, the mind that a person has is a mind that he alone, and no other person, has. I assume, in other words, that the number of persons and the number of minds are identical: one person, one mind; two persons, two minds.

Now there are certain reasons for calling into question assumption (4): during the 1940s, the brains of certain individuals suffering from severe cases of epilepsy were bisected—the fibers which connect the right and left hemispheres of the brains of these individuals were surgically severed. After the operations, the patients functioned normally enough under ordinary conditions. But under certain exceptional conditions, conditions produced in laboratory experiments in which stimulation to one hemisphere of the brain was segregated from stimulation to the other hemisphere, the patients behaved, in the opinion of some investigators, as if each hemisphere was a separate and independent center of consciousness.[3]

---

[3] For example, the two different hemispheres of a patient's brain could be fed conflicting instructions with the result that the patient's hands, each of which is controlled by its own hemisphere, would behave in independent and contrary ways. For an interesting and accessible discussion of these "split-brain" cases, see Thomas Nagel: Brain bisection and the unity of consciousness. In John Perry (Ed.): *Personal Identity.* Berkeley, University of California Press, 1975, pp. 227–245. Nagel's article can also serve as a guide to further readings on the subject.

Some philosophers and neurophysicians believe that it is more plausible to describe the patients under these exceptional experimental conditions as each having two minds, or as not having minds countable in whole numbers at all, than it is to describe them as having one mind. Indeed, under these circumstances it is not clear to everyone just what counts as a single patient!

The reader should be aware, in the discussion that follows, that, depending on the outcome of the controversy over how to describe these split-brain cases, assumption (4) may be questionable to some extent. I shall nevertheless make the assumption in this book and limit my subsequent discussion to human beings with normal, i.e. nonbisected, brains, for assumption (4) is ordinarily made by people who discuss life after death, and by most other people, too. We do not ordinarily find it even intelligible to suppose that a person might really have two minds, or a third of a mind, or that Alexander Hamilton and Thomas Jefferson might have had only one mind between them. We ordinarily count minds in whole numbers in accordance with the rule: one person, one mind; two persons, two minds, etc.

(5) *In a case of personal survival, what survives the death of a person's body is the person himself.*[4] This assumption will seem even more obvious, from the standpoint of common sense, than the first four. When one supposes that there is personal survival, one assumes that the entity that survives the death of Mr. Jones' body is in fact Mr. Jones. Let us refer to the surviving entity simply as a survivor. Thus, another way of putting the assumption is to say that the survivor of the death of a given person's body is the same entity as formerly was that person.

Here again is an assumption which, though it sounds virtually self-evident to "common sense," is philosophically controversial in some respects. Suppose, for example, that there exists after the death of A's body some conscious individual, B, who at that time is not, and never before had been, A. But suppose further that the states of consciousness (i.e. experiences) which belong to A before his body dies have come to belong, after his body has died, to the

---

[4]Those of the remaining assumptions in which I refer to personal survival and "survivors" should not be construed as implying that personal survival is an established fact. They should be understood as meaning that such-and-such is true, *if* there is personal survival.

past history of B.[5] Will this be a case of A surviving his body's death? In a sense it will, for the series of conscious states to which A's conscious states belong will have continued to exist after A's body has died; but in a sense it won't, because the individual, B, who will exist after A's bodily death will not be, and will not have been, A.

Now, some philosophers have constructed hypothetical cases which they insist should be viewed as instances of A's conscious states having come to belong, after A's death, to some other person's, B's, past history. Such cases, they say, could be regarded as cases of "survival." But while a case like this (in which, though A has not survived, the series of conscious states to which his present conscious states belong has survived) may constitute some sort of "survival," it is reasonable to deny that it constitutes a case of the *personal* survival of A. For, in such a case, he who would live after A's death, though having had A's experiences, would not be A.

So I shall assume, as is generally done, that in a case of personal survival, what survives the death of Mr. Jones' body is Mr. Jones himself; or, in the language of philosophers, what survives the death of Mr. Jones' body is an individual who is numerically identical with Mr. Jones.

(6) *A survivor and a formerly living person are numerically identical if and only if the survivor has had that person's conscious states.* To be the survivor of Mr. Jones, the conscious states had by a survivor cannot be merely exactly similar to the conscious states Jones had before death, they must be the selfsame conscious states. If indeed it is Jones' conscious states that a survivor had, then that survivor is the survivor of Jones, and not the survivor of any other person.

Given this assumption, those hypothetical cases referred to immediately above as counterexamples to assumption (5), in which one person's conscious states are hypothesized to have come to belong after his death to some other person's past, are obviously impossible. While assumptions (5) and (6) would thus be questioned

---

[5]Until recently, most philosophers would have regarded this supposition as self-contradictory. However, now many philosophers are not so sure. For a discussion of the issues touched upon in this and the next paragraph, see the articles by Derek Parfit: Personal identity. In John Perry, *ibid.*, pp. 199-223; and : Lewis, Perry, and what matters. In A. Rorty (Ed.): *The Identities of Persons*. Berkeley, University of California Press, 1976, pp. 91-107. Both articles contain references to other discussions of these issues.

by anyone who thinks that such hypothetical cases are possible, both assumptions are very much in keeping with common sense and most discussions of life after death, and I shall make them both in this book.

(7) *In a case of personal survival, the survivor is conscious.* Mr. Jones has a mind, and his mind is a conscious thing, so Mr. Jones is a being with consciousness. I assume similarly that if Mr. Jones were to survive his physical death, his survivor would be a conscious being too.

(8) *The survivors of bodily death are countable.* Survivors, like people and minds, are assumed to be countable entities: There is a difference between one survivor and two survivors, just as there is a difference between one person and two persons. Indeed, according to assumption (5), survivors *are* persons.

(9) *The survivors of bodily death are countable on the basis of the persons they formerly were.* Just as Mr. Jones and Mr. Smith count as two things and not one, and just as Mr. Jones' mind and Mr. Smith's mind count as two things and not one, so do Mr. Jones' and Mr. Smith's survivors count as two things and not one. In other words, the assumption is that survivors are to be individuated on the basis of the persons they formerly were: one former person can have but one survivor, and each survivor can be the survivor of but one former person. So Mr. Jones' survivor and Mr. Smith's survivor could not be one and the same, and Mr. Jones could not, after death, survive as two entities. (Indeed, the assumption of countability of survivors on the basis of their countability as persons before death logically follows from the previously discussed assumptions.)

Here again is an assumption that is entirely obvious from the viewpoint of common sense, but not wholly free of philosophical controversy. Suppose, for example, that my brain is bisected, and the two halves are then transplanted into two new bodies. Presumably a person can live with half of his brain destroyed. So, if a transplant of this sort could be arranged, then perhaps we should wish to say that under the circumstances I, in fact, have *two* survivors. Or suppose again that the halves of my brain given to these recipients are subsequently removed from them and reunited in some third body. Perhaps we should wish to say that, under these circumstances, a single individual is the survivor of two persons.[6]

Of course, such transplants of the human brain have not occurred, but nevertheless, to the extent they are imaginable, they raise philosophical questioning as to the universal validity of assumption (9). So here again my discussion will rest on this common-sense assumption which is to a minimal extent philosophically controversial.

(10) *Bodily death occurs upon irreversible cessation of brain, respiratory, and circulatory activity.* The question, "When is a human dead?", has assumed enormous ethical and legal importance in this age of transplantation biology. Fortunately, it is not necessary to become involved in the controversy surrounding this question. For when we wonder whether or not we shall survive the death of our body, what we are essentially wondering is whether or not, when our body is *completely, irreversibly,* and *undeniably* dead, we shall somehow manage to live on. Thus the following definition of bodily death is satisfactory for my purpose:

The death of the body consists in the irreversible cessation of (a) all cerebral functioning as monitored by an electroencephalograph, and (b) the spontaneous functioning of the circulatory and respiratory systems. In other words, when the activity of one's brain, heart and blood, and lungs, has irreversibly ceased, one's body has died.

These, then, are assumptions that will be made in the discussion. They are all reasonable though philosophically controversial in abstruse and recondite respects which are of some, but not much, concern to adequate treatment of afterdeath survival. The assumptions delineate what most people assume in discussion of their survival after death. Their importance to my discussion will be evident.[7]

---

[6] Problem cases which challenge assumption (9) can be constructed without invoking split-brain examples. A modification of John Perry's "brain rejuvenation" example could be used in this regard. See: Can the self divide? *Journal of Philosophy,* 69: 463–488, 1972.

[7] Many philosophers lay out their assumptions at the outset of a discussion, as I have done here. In *Body and Mind,* Keith Campbell states three assumptions that he makes concerning the nature of the mind. I am indebted to Mr. Campbell for his "Assumption of Individuality," the essence of which I have incorporated in my Assumption (4), above. See *Body and Mind,* New York, Anchor Books, 1970, pp. 6–7.

CHAPTER 2

THEORIES OF SURVIVAL

When it is supposed that a person survives or might survive the death of his body, what exactly is supposed? These are the four basic theories of personal survival:

Disembodied Survival

The most widely accepted theory of survival, at least in western societies, is that of "disembodied" or "discarnate" survival. According to this theory, before the death of the body a nonphysical, noncorporeal entity known as the soul (or mind, self, personality, or consciousness) resides in or is imprisoned in the body; upon the death of the body, the soul is released from the body and continues to exist in a disembodied state. Often people will refer to the disembodied soul as a "spirit," to distinguish it from the souls that you and I and other living people have. It is important to note that, according to this theory, the soul essentially is the person; unless Mr. Jones and his soul are one and the same, the fact that Mr. Jones' soul survives the death of his body would not constitute a case of Mr. Jones' surviving the death of his body.

Reincarnation

The second theory is reincarnation. According to this theory, the surviving Mr. Jones has a physical body, but it is not the body he has in this life. According to the theory of reincarnation, Mr. Jones' present body dies, but Mr. Jones, nonetheless, manages to survive because he has acquired a new body, i.e. has been reincarnated. According to some versions of the theory, Mr. Jones exists between reincarnations in a disembodied state; according to other versions, he goes directly from one body to another.

In any case, much of the fascination of this theory doubtlessly lies in the fact that, according to it, we might have lived *before*: we might actually *be* some historically identifiable person such as the former John Paul Jones or Joan of Arc or Abraham Lincoln. The possibility that we have lived before is, I suppose, more intriguing to some people than is the possibility that we might live again because the details of the future are so very vague and "unreal" in comparison with the concrete history of the past.

Survival Of An Astral Body

According to the third theory, the surviving Mr. Jones again has a body, but his body is not the ordinary flesh-and-blood body that I or anyone who has been reincarnated has. Rather, the surviving Mr. Jones has an "astral" body, a body that apparently has some sort of location and shape (usually very nebulous), but has neither mass nor solidity nor tangibility (flesh-and-blood hands purportedly pass right through astral bodies). This body is ethereal, transparent, and ghostly enough to escape detection by ordinary empirical means, though under certain circumstances some individuals have claimed to be able to "see" astral bodies. Interestingly enough, "astral survivors" are sometimes seen wearing clothes, which seems difficult to understand unless astral clothes are available to astral bodies.

Resurrection

The final theory of personal survival is known as the theory of resurrection. According to this theory, the surviving Mr. Jones has the body he formerly had, but the body he formerly had has been resurrected, and, according to most versions of the theory, in the process of being resurrected has been "transfigured," "idealized," or "spiritualized," to some extent or other. It is usually thought that at the very least the resurrected body has had removed whatever physical conditions led immediately to the death of the body, for if you resurrect a man in the final stages of terminal cancer just as he was, what you get is a man in the final stages of terminal cancer. Nevertheless, as John Hick has pointed out,[1] the resurrected body might, in a new realm, be subjected to a process of healing

---

[1] John Hick: *Death and Eternal Life*. New York, Harper and Row, 1976, p. 294.

which returns it to a healthy or even younger state. So it would evidently not be necessary for the resurrected body to have been "transfigured" much at all.

At the same time, at the other extreme, there are versions of the theory according to which the resurrected body has very little indeed in common with this flesh-and-blood body it formerly was: it will have no sexual characteristics, will not suffer from indigestion or other maladies, will be neither young nor old, neither fat nor thin nor tall nor short. In fact, according to some versions of the theory of resurrection, the transformed body will have lost so many of its physical characteristics as to be virtually indistinguishable from an astral body.

It is worth noting that sometimes the term *spirit* is used to refer to survivors who have astral and resurrected bodies as well as to survivors who have no bodies at all. (Of course, if Jones' spirit has *any* sort of body, then Jones' spirit is not totally disembodied.) This means that, when people talk about Jones' spirit, it is not always clear whether they regard Jones' spirit as a disembodied entity, or as an entity that has an astral or resurrected body.

While these are the four traditional theories of personal survival of bodily death, recently, due to developments in contemporary medical science and biology, there has been widespread speculation that certain other forms of survival are, or at any rate shortly will be, possible. Just what is the truth behind this speculation?

CHAPTER 3

SCIENTIFIC SURVIVAL

Certain journalists and news commentators have speculated upon (and played up) the possibilities of survival offered by medical science and biology. The primary sources of this speculation are (1) cryobiology, (2) cloning and genetic engineering, and (3) transplantation biology. The rumors are impressive. But what are the facts?

Cryobiology

Cryobiology is the field in which low temperature environments are employed to study living organisms. As is well known, low temperatures can be used both to destroy and to preserve living cells. Investigation of the causes of cell-death due to freezing has led to development of methods of circumventing these causes, so that techniques of freezing can now be used to store living cells and tissues. These techniques, which involve using liquid nitrogen to reduce temperatures throughout a mass of cells quickly and evenly, have made it possible to preserve blood, blood cells, animal sperm, and other matter as long as desired, without cellular damage.

However, when large aggregates of cells are to be preserved, it is more difficult to avoid damaging or killing the cells in the freezing process. Present technology thus does not allow long-term storage of more complex organs such as the heart or the liver. So, while it is perhaps theoretically possible to put a human being into "cold storage" without hurting or killing him, the day when this can be done is nowhere near being here. Accordingly, we cannot presently hope for preservation by cold storage. Nor, for that matter, should people in the future hope to survive through such methods, unless they are extremely rich or very powerful.

Furthermore, and most importantly, preservation through freezing would in any case not constitute a way of *surviving* bodily death but rather a way of *postponing* it. As fascinating as cryobiology may be, it does not in actuality afford any genuine possibility of personal survival.

Cloning And Genetic Engineering

A clone is a group of organisms, or a member of this group, produced from one individual through a nonsexual process that does not involve the interchange of genetic material. In one cloning technique, the nucleus of a cell from the body of a given organism, a nucleus that contains a full set of the chromosomes belonging to that organism, is implanted into an egg cell whose nucleus has been removed: the result, if things go right, is the triggering of the reproductive process of the unified cell. This cell will then divide and redivide, just as does an ordinary fertilized egg cell, giving birth ultimately to a clone, an individual or group of individuals genetically identical to the individual from which the original body cell is derived.

The process has been successfully worked with certain vegetables and with some animals, and, if David Rorvik is to be believed,[1] a human clone has already been secretly produced. Even if Rorvik's report is not to be accepted, and the total lack of corroboration of his report makes one skeptical, it well may be that the day of successful human cloning is not far off.

However, it would be a great mistake to regard cloning as offering any promise of personal survival after bodily death. The result of the cloning process is an infant genetically identical to the donor of the body cell, an infant identical twin, so to speak. This infant may have all of the genetic characteristics of its parent-donor, but it is not *literally identical* with its parent-donor any more than identical twins are literally one person. Should this infant survive its donor-parent, as due to its youth would normally happen, its doing so would no more constitute a case of the personal survival of the parent than would an individual's outliving his identical twin constitute a case of personal survival of the deceased twin. Speculation to the contrary to the effect that, through

---

[1]David Rorvik: *In His Image.* New York, Lippincott, 1978.

telepathic communication between an individual and his clonal offspring, an individual's consciousness might extend beyond his own death appears to be entirely a product of wishful thinking and is, of course, wholly without empirical support.

However, cloning is but one technique employed in what is now loosely referred to as "genetic engineering," i.e. the manipulation of genetic material to achieve desired ends, whatever those may be. There can be no doubt that the "genetic revolution" is upon us, and that it is every bit as momentous in its implications as the atomic revolution. What is at stake in this revolution is nothing short of mastering the basic processes of life itself. "Genetic engineering is essentially man's attempt to take command of the biological controls," writes Robert Cooke, "to take command of this fragile living enterprise and, like a captured ship, steer it off in new directions."[2]

The possible outcomes of genetic manipulation are staggering. Genes are in essence the control-room of all cellular reproduction and thus of life itself. By rearranging the biochemical "masterplans" that govern the operations of this genetic control-room, biologists could actually redesign human beings. The basic techniques have already been used to rearrange the genes of viruses and bacteria. Who really could say that biologists, with the power in hand to redesign human beings, could not steer the "ship of human life" away from the shoals of death?

To take some of the more obvious examples, many agents harmful to human existence seem susceptible to elimination by genetic manipulation. Targets of this sort already under attack include cancer, heart disease, and hereditary diseases such as hemophilia, sickle-cell anemia, and Tay-Sachs disease. Conditions that make old age burdensome, e.g. rheumatism and arthritis, could theoretically be removed. The very machinery of aging itself might conceivably be altered. For example, there is apparently some reason to think that aging is connected with the slowing of genetic mechanisms that correct radiation damage: these mechanisms might very well be modified through genetic tampering. The body's cellular immunological response system might also be

---

[2]*Improving on Nature: The Brave New World of Genetic Engineering.* New York, The New York Times Book Company, 1977, p. 24.

strengthened to resist infections; or it might temporarily be disconnected so that the body is able to receive organ transplants. At the very least, better medicines and more nutritious foods, with their ability to help sustain life, will result from current biological research.

These are only the more obvious, "right-around-the-corner"-type ideas. Ideas that are more far-fetched, but which cannot be ruled out, include the breeding of humans who could breathe under water or photosynthesize like plants![3] The point is this: biologists are already introducing alien genes into organisms in which such genes do not occur in nature; scientists are already in effect doing the impossible: hybridizing different species of living things. It is very difficult to speculate at this point on possible outcomes of this sort of experimentation. Clearly human immortality, or very prolonged mortality, might be the result of the genetic revolution.

However, will the methods and techniques of genetic engineering be used to prolong life or to shorten it? While in this book I deal with survival after death, it is appropriate, as within the broader context of this subject, to note too that genetic engineering presents dangers to the furtherance of life. Without question biology offers the most inexpensive, easiest to hide, hardest to defend against, and deadliest weaponry devised by man to date.

In addition, there is always the possibility that a new and lethal—and completely unstoppable—virus or other life form will accidentally (or intentionally) be created and then escape from laboratory confinement. The potential consequences of the escape of some sort of "Andromeda Strain" require no elaboration.

Finally, the social security system notwithstanding, our society has never been overly concerned with the problems of its older members, and very few individuals seem able to grasp the fact that they too will eventually become old. So perhaps the techniques of genetic engineering will be used less to benefit the aged and more to address the problems of the young: perhaps the emphasis will even be on curing such "trifles" as acne, obesity, crooked teeth, awkwardness, pale skin, or premature baldness.

The main point, the essential point, is being by-passed. As

---

[3]*Ibid.*, p. 13.

exciting (or depressing) as the possible outcomes of genetic engineering may be, they are at best going to prolong life, or, what is the same thing, postpone death. As has already been mentioned, there is a fundamental difference between *postponing* death and *surviving* death. It is true that if death can be postponed long enough, the reason for worrying about survival disappears, but it hasn't disappeared yet. In spite of the genetic revolution, at this time the old truism still holds inexorably: all people *are* mortal.

Transplantation Biology

Replacement of diseased, decaying, or malfunctioning bodily components through transplantations remains yet another method for significantly lengthening life. The potential of transplantation biology for the furtherance of life will become especially vast when our knowledge of the processes that control cellular reproduction is more complete.

Each cell of an organism is now understood to contain within it the complete genetic program for the entire organism; because of this, biologists have been able to trick cells from one organ into reproducing cells appropriate for a different organ. Thus it is that scientists may eventually be able to take a sample of healthy cells from a person and, using the techniques of genetic engineering, contrive to have those cells grow into a new heart or kidney that can be transplanted into the person. Because the new organ would be constituted of the tissue that originally came from the patient, it would be less prone to rejection by the body as a foreign invader.[4]

Yet another dramatic form of preservation through transplant biology would involve transplantation of the very center of consciousness, the brain. Let it be supposed that Mr. Jones' body is frail with age, but that his mind is still healthy and alert. Then, on the assumptions that many would deny, namely, that Mr. Jones and Mr. Jones' mind are essentially one, and that Mr. Jones mind and Mr. Jones' brain are either essentially one or are at any rate inseparable, we could preserve Mr. Jones' life by transplanting his brain into the healthier body of a younger individual, perhaps

---

[4]*Ibid.*, p. 31.

one whose brain is damaged but whose body is healthy enough. The operation could be repeated again and again, as long as Mr. Jones' brain didn't deteriorate too greatly, and this deterioration might be avoided or greatly slowed by other medical means. Already an animal brain has been kept intact and alive outside its body by Doctor Robert White. Perhaps, therefore, the day when Mr. Jones could survive a brain transplanting operation is not too far off.

The possibility of brain transplants (or should they be called body transplants?) raises fascinating and important philosophical questions of personal identity, i.e. questions of under what conditions, and in virtue of what, can individual A be said to be the same individual as individual B? An excellent recent compilation of important professional philosophical literature on these questions can be found in John Perry's *Personal Identity*.[5] I shall not just now discuss questions of personal identity, but shall consider whether brain transplants are even possible.

As it turns out, they are not now possible, and will not be for a long time. There are two very basic problems. First, in a brain transplant so many nerves would have to be severed that they could not practically be matched up with the corresponding nerves in the recipient body. Second, even if they could be matched up and attached, there still could be no transmission of nerve impulses because of the fact that nerve tissue does not regenerate itself.

However, there is another possibility: transplant the entire head, and not just the brain! Such a transplant would, in one obvious way, be far less complicated than a brain transplant: none of the cranial nerves would be severed and thus would continue to function normally. Further, this operation, which is called cephalic transplant, has already been performed with some success on laboratory animals, including rats and monkeys. In one case, for example, a monkey with a head transplant survived for almost a week with an artificial respirator for mechanical support. Further, according to Doctor White, "Human cephalic transplants can be done technically . . . it would take a year, no more, to work out the

---

[5]Berkeley, University of California Press, 1975.

surgical engineering involved in such an operation."⁶

To be sure, there are fundamental problems involved in a cephalic transplant. The main problem, as in the case of brain transplants, is that of nonregeneration of nerve tissue. Because nerve tissue does not regenerate itself, the relatively "simple" splice between the two spinal column ends will not transmit nervous impulses from the new head to the recipient body. So, for example, the monkey in the experiment above was, in effect, a tetraplegic; its brain had no nervous control over body motor functions. However, this problem is not in principle insurmountable, or so one would judge in view of the millions of dollars spent annually by the National Institutes of Health on research on ways of regenerating nerve tissue.

For the present, at least, it would seem that neither head nor brain transplants offer much prospect even for prolongation of life (let alone survival of death).⁷

So what, in sum, can be said about "scientific" survival? As has been pointed out, science offers at best only the means to postpone death, not to survive it. This point has not been fully appreciated by everyone, because recent developments in the biological sciences are sometimes misleadingly presented as promising "immortality," or a "second" or "renewed" life, and so forth. Cloning in particular has been thought of as a possible means of "cheating nature," and of actually surviving bodily death.⁸ What goes unnoticed is that the survival that may be made possible by scientific developments is survival only in a most qualified or limited or metaphorical sense; e.g. "survival" through the continuing function of our thought-patterns in the mind of a clone.

The fact remains, however, that the gap between prolonging life and surviving death is fundamental. There is at present no reason to think that science offers anyone the means of bridging it. We may indeed expect our children's lives to be lengthened by medical and biological science. We may even see our own lives

---

⁶A report on Dr. White's surgery, and other cephalic transplants, can be found in Robert Bahi: A new ethical question: head transplants. *Science Digest*, *81*: 76–78, 1977.

⁷It should be remembered, however, that not so very long ago the same thing was said about heart transplants.

⁸E.g. Rorvik, *op. cit.*, p. 34.

lengthened significantly. Even so, one day, whether or not we wish it, our brains and our bodies are going to cease to function. Medical technology will not ultimately prevent it. We thus shall continue to face the question of whether we shall survive this inevitable death. Modern science does not yet obviate the reason for wondering about this question. Nor does it offer any answer to it.

There are thus left only four genuine possibilities of personal survival after bodily death: disembodied survival, reincarnation, survival of an astral body, and resurrection. Are these really *genuine* possibilities? Part II treats the matter.

PART II
PHILOSOPHICAL REFUTATIONS

CHAPTER 4

REFUTATIONS OF DISEMBODIED SURVIVAL

... disembodied survival is logically absurd.
— *Terence Penelhum, Personal identity.*[1]

How we think is the subject of psychology and physiology. The validity of our thinking is the concern of philosophy. I wish now to consider the validity of our thinking about life after death. I am concerned, in particular, with whether there are any conclusive theoretical refutations of the belief in afterdeath personal survival.

Some philosophers, including Epicurus, Lucretius, Hobbes, and, more recently, Terence Penelhum, Antony Flew, and Peter Geach, have maintained that it is quite impossible for a person to survive his bodily death in a discarnate form. Hobbes was particularly harsh in his rejection of the belief in a discarnate afterlife, which he regarded as an "absurdity."[2] Other philosophers, such as Bertrand Russell, while stopping short of saying that afterdeath discarnate survival is totally impossible, have concluded that it is very, very unlikely that we shall enjoy an existence after death in a disembodied state.

An examination of the reasoning of those who view discarnate personal survival with skepticism discloses that the belief in a discarnate afterlife faces three fundamental objections to its validity. One objection is that without afterdeath consciousness there can be no personal survival, and that consciousness depends on the living brain. The second objection is that mental activity is brain activity and ceases when the brain dies. The third is that the idea of personal survival discarnate is not intelligible.

---

[1] In Paul Edwards (Ed.): *The Encyclopedia of Philosophy.* New York, Macmillan, 1967, Vol. VI, p. 106.
[2] Thomas Hobbes: *Leviathan.* Oxford, Basil Blackwell, 1955, pp. 442–443.

Consciousness Depends On The Brain

Certainly, the apparent dependency of mind and consciousness on the brain and its functioning would seem to preclude the possibility of disembodied survival of the conscious person or self. To quote at greater length from the passage by Bertrand Russell that I set forth in opening Chapter 1:

> We know that the brain is not immortal, and that the organized energy of a living body becomes, as it were, demobilized at death and therefore not available for collective action. All the evidence goes to show that what we regard as our mental life is bound up with brain structure and organized bodily energy. Therefore it is rational to suppose that mental life ceases when bodily life ceases. The argument is only one of probability, but it is as strong as those upon which most scientific conclusions are based.[3]

Mental life, for Russell, includes consciousness. Must we agree that mental life ceases when bodily life ends?

If, as Russell says, all the evidence goes to show that mental life is bound up with a living brain and organized bodily energy, then Russell's conclusion is inescapable. However, does all the evidence really show this? The empirical data upon which some people base their belief in discarnate afterdeath survival, if these data truly evidence discarnate survival, would obviously indicate that our mental life is not totally dependent for its existence on the working of our brain. So before Russell's conclusion can be accepted, these data must be examined. This examination is made in Parts III and IV.

Mental Activity Is Brain Activity

According to Russell, mental life, including consciousness, is "bound up with" brain life. By this he means, I think, only that mental life and consciousness *depend* for their existence on the active, functioning brain. Others, known as "materialists," believe that the relationship between the mind and the brain is even more intimate. It is not merely that mental activity is *dependent* on brain activity, materialists will say: it is that mental activity *is* brain

---

[3] *Why I Am Not a Christian.* New York, Allen and Unwin, 1957, p. 51. Reprinted by permission of Simon and Schuster, a Division of Gulf and Western Corporation.

activity. Our mental processes, from thinking to daydreaming, are but so many electrical-chemical processes within the brain, and the "mind" is merely the sum of these purely physical processes.[4]

Materialism, if true, absolutely precludes the possibility of discarnate personal survival. If my mental life is my brain life, it ends when my brain dies, and if anything is left, it is brainless and mindless, and so is not a person, since a mindless thing is not a person.[5] Thus, I, as a person, cannot survive bodily death if materialism is true.

Some people, perhaps most, may regard it as common sense that the mind is nonphysical, so that for them the materialist conception of the mind as a set of physical processes within the brain is radically mistaken. It may therefore surprise some readers to be told that materialism has become, as Daniel Dennet puts it, the reigning orthodoxy in contemporary philosophy.

As will be seen in Chapter 5, it is not without reason that materialism is widely accepted by contemporary philosophers. Nevertheless, while the case for materialism is strong, it is not conclusive, as will be seen, too. Obviously, any possibility of afterdeath disembodied survival depends on the mind being other than a set of physical processes in the brain.

Discarnate Survival Is Unintelligible

In best-selling books about life after death, there are invariably reports of the "dead" walking, talking, peering at people, and so forth. If the dead are truly without bodies, these reports are nonsense, for that which has no body has nothing at all with which to walk, talk, or peer. Though in the best-sellers disembodied spirits are sometimes said to "talk but not in a physical sense," it is very unclear how that is different from not talking at all.

Indeed, some critics of theories of discarnate survival contend that it is just as nonsensical to talk about a disembodied entity wishing, willing, or communicating, as it is to talk about it walking,

---

[4]While Russell's view comes close to materialism, it is inaccurate to call him a materialist. Paul Edwards, William Alston, and A. N. Prior: Bertrand Arthur William Russell. In Paul Edwards (Ed.): *The Encyclopedia of Philosophy*. New York, Macmillan, 1967, Vol. VII, p. 255.

[5]Cf. Chapter One.

talking, or peering. Some say, in fact, that nothing whatsoever can sensibly be said about an entity that has no body: to suppose that it has thoughts, desires, imagination or anything at all is as totally unintelligible as it is to suppose that the number ten has headaches. They in effect deny that there can even be a concept expressed by the terms "disembodied soul," "discarnate personality," "disembodied survivor," or the like. Purported discourse about discarnate souls, they say, is really not discourse at all, but only unintelligible babble.

In Chapters 6 and 7 I shall explain and evaluate these sweeping objections as to the very intelligibility of speculation about afterdeath disembodied survival.

CHAPTER 5

CAN THE MIND BE NONMATERIAL?

... every part of the universe, is body, and that which is not body, is no part of the universe: and because the universe is all, that which is no part of it, is nothing ...
— *Thomas Hobbes*, Leviathan, *Chapter 46*[1]

Materialism And Dualism

In this book I use the term *materialist* to denote one who believes that the entire universe, including people and their minds, is exclusively material. To the materialist, the whole person is nothing more or other than a complex material or physical organism.[2] In his view, a person's mental processes, including thinking, willing, wishing, imagining, and all the rest, are purely physical processes centered within his brain. In the opinion of the materialist, though not all brain activity qualifies as mental activity (e.g., the degeneration of brain cells does not qualify as mental), all mental activity consists of purely physical happenings within the brain. Thus, according to the materialist, a person's mental life is a part or phase of his brain life, and a person's mind is just the sum-total of those brain processes which constitute his mental life.

Obviously, the materialist, who believes in effect that "mind" is only a word for certain happenings and workings of and within the physical brain, must conclude that the person's mind, and hence the person as well,[3] cannot survive the death of the body.

Contrasted with materialism, is the theory that the mind is a

---

[1] Oxford, Basil Blackwell, 1955, p. 440.
[2] I equate the terms *material* and *physical*.
[3] No mindless thing is a person. Cf. Chapter 1.

nonmaterial (immaterial), nonphysical something over and above or apart or distinct from the brain and from every other part, piece, and process of the body, and that mental activity is activity of a nonphysical sort on the part of this nonmaterial mind.

The most widely accepted variant of nonmaterialistic theory is that of *dualism* (or Cartesian dualism, as it is sometimes called, in deference to its most important early modern expositor, Rene Descartes). A dualist maintains that every existing thing, except for abstract entities such as numbers, geometric points, humanity, and the like, is either material (physical) or nonmaterial. Further, according to the dualist, nothing is both material and nonmaterial. The mind and its contents, powers, and processes are, in his view, nonmaterial.

What is a material thing, and what is a nonmaterial thing, and how are they to be distinguished? The dualist and materialist both say that a thing is material if it possesses any physical properties and is nonmaterial if it is devoid of any physical properties.

Physical properties include mass, density, velocity, electric charge, temperature, texture, and the like. Most fundamental of physical properties, however, is occupancy of space. Even electromagnetic fields, antiparticles, and antimatter, since they occupy space, are classified, by dualists and materialists alike, as material entities.

In order to be nonmaterial, on the other hand, a thing must be devoid of any physical properties. So it must therefore have properties other than physical in order to have existence. It is very hard to say, however, what such properties might be, though dualists maintain that nonmaterial entities alone are capable of having conscious states and of exercising volition.

In any case, according to the dualist and the materialist both, although a nonmaterial thing cannot have any of the purely physical properties, there are some properties that both material and nonmaterial things may have. Thus, for example, material and nonmaterial things alike have temporal "position," i.e. if a thing exists, then, whether it is material or nonmaterial, it exists at some time or other, either before, after, or at the same time as other material and nonmaterial things.[4] Also, both material and

---

[4] An exception is sometimes made in the case of God, who some regard as a nonmaterial being who exists "outside" or "beyond" or "above" time.

nonmaterial things may possess "neutral" properties; both, for example, may be complicated, belong to groups, be numerous, and beautiful, etc.

Since materialists think that nothing is nonmaterial, they obviously agree with dualists that nothing is both material and nonmaterial. Dualists, though believing that nothing is both material and nonmaterial, think that one and the same thing may *have* both material and nonmaterial components. Thus, a human being, according to dualists, has both a material body and a nonmaterial mind (sometimes called a soul). In the dualist's view, the termination of biological life in the body does not necessarily end existence of the mind and so does not necessarily preclude personal survival, as the materialist maintains.

So the question is, are there any considerations that rule out the dualistic conception of the mind in favor of the materialistic? For, if dualism is not a viable theory of the mind, if mental life does consist merely in brain activity, then there is no mental life after bodily death, and it would be quite pointless to consider the possibility of discarnate personal survival any further.

Mind-Sharing

Dualism, in the view of some philosophers, must be rejected because it is unable to account for a certain important fact of human existence, *viz.*, that two or more persons never share a mind.

Consider, for example, Mr. and Mrs. Smith. They jointly have a house, automobile, bank account, and the same child, but they do not have one and the same heart or brain; nor do they have one and the same mind, be their minds material or nonmaterial.

These facts require explanation. Why is it that two different people never have one and the same brain, heart, or mind?

The reason Mr. and Mrs. Smith do not have the same brain or heart is that brains and hearts are material objects and occupy space, and it is impossible for one and the same space-occupying object to be in two different places at the same time. Since Smith's brain and heart are within him and Mrs. Smith's brain and heart are within her, the Smiths would have one and the same brain or heart only if that brain or heart were simultaneously in the two different places at which Mr. and Mrs. Smith are, and this is not possible. Now, if a mind is an aggregate of space-occupying, physical brain processes, as the materialist supposes, then the reason the Smiths would not have one and the same mind would be the same as the reason they do not have one and the same brain or heart.

However, if, as the dualist supposes, minds do not occupy space, why is it that Mr. and Mrs. Smith do not have the same mind? It is a fundamental fact about two human beings who are alive at the same time that they do not have one and the same mind. If minds were nonspatial entities, then there would apparently be no reason why two people could not have one and the same mind. Consequently, the fact that they never do would remain an unexplained and seemingly inexplicable mystery.

A dualist might suggest that perhaps two people could conceivably share one mind after all, but then why does this never happen? Why is it that in the case of Mr. and Mrs. Smith and every other husband and wife there are two minds per pair rather than one? Further, if Mr. and Mrs. Smith might in actuality have but one mind, then why should we regard Mr. and Mrs. Smith as two different people and not as just one? Surely the idea that Mr. and Mrs. Smith may not *really* be two people cannot be taken seriously, but if the Smiths did in actuality have but one mind between them, then wouldn't they really be just one person? Consequently, the suggestion that perhaps two people could share one mind is untenable.

How, therefore, is the dualist to explain why it is that two different people never have one mind?

In answer, the dualist might say that the mind is located in exactly the same place as the brain or has exactly the same outline as the brain but has no spatial occupancy, just as, for instance, a boundary occupies no space. Or he might assert that the mind is located somewhere within the person's brain, but takes up no room because it has no dimension, just as geometric points have no dimensions.[5] If minds were to be viewed in either of these two

---

[5] The possibility that the mind, like a point or an outline, might have spatial location but not spatial occupancy, has been suggested by Keith Campbell: *Body and Mind.* New York, Anchor Books, 1970, p. 45.

ways, then we could account for the fact that Mr. and Mrs. Smith do not have one and the same mind in exactly the same way that we can account for the fact that they do not have one and the same brain: one and the same geometric point or "outline" could not be in two different places at the same time.

But, likening minds to points and outlines is of doubtful validity, since points and outlines, unlike minds on either the materialist or dualist theories, are abstract entities. I cannot myself make any sense of the analogy.

Furthermore, even if the dualist could intelligently maintain that the mind has spatial location but does not occupy space, how, then, would he account for another basic fact about a person, namely, that a person has only *one* mind? If minds were bare geometric points or outlines, then there would apparently be no reason why one's skull could not be filled with minds, and thus the fact that it is not so filled would stand in need of explanation.

The dualist might also proffer as an explanation of the fact that two people never share one mind that it is "due to the will of God," or "lies in the nature of things." To say this is, I think, regardless of one's beliefs about God, only to confess that one does not really have an explanation. It is to say that two people never share a mind because "they just never do."

So it seems then that either we must adopt materialism and regard the mind as an aggregation of space-occupying physical processes or we must leave unexplained one or the other of two fundamental facts about human beings (that two humans do not have the same mind and that one human does not have more than one mind).

Now, many things are unexplained, it is true, but this truth is hardly a defense of dualism. If one theory of the nature of the mind (dualism) leaves certain notable facts about the mind unexplained and a second theory (materialism) does not, then in this respect the second theory is more plausible than the first. That dualism leaves it completely unexplained why a human has one and only one mind and a mind that he shares with no other human is thus a shortcoming in the theory, and it is not the only fault in the theory, as will be seen.

Interaction Of Mind And Body

(1) Understanding Mind-Body Interaction

A second consideration bearing on the credibility of one or the other of the opposing views in regard to the nature of the mind is the interaction of the mind with body. The mind decides or directs, and the body and limbs respond with activity or restraint of activity. Or occurrences within or upon the body affect the mind, as when, for instance, a fever produces hallucinations. This indisputable interaction of mind and body accords easily enough with the view of the materialist that mental activity is but a phase of brain activity. The interaction is much more difficult to explain by the dualist, who views mind as non-material and mind and body as separate entities within the human being.

If, for instance, someone claimed to be able to open doors by mental command without any physical intervention, one well could regard the claim with skepticism. Yet, if our minds are nonmaterial, wriggling our fingers (or moving our lips or eyes, etc.) would be no less remarkable than turning doorknobs without intervening physical mechanism.

True, the two cases are not altogether similar. Fingers are parts of our bodies, doorknobs are not. Therefore, between one's fingers and one's brain, and not between doorknobs and one's brain, there is direct neural and mechanical linkage. So, if mental activity is equivalent to brain activity, then one's fingers, unlike doorknobs, have a direct linkage with the center of all mental activity.

If the mind is *nonmaterial*, does the fact that one's fingers, but not doorknobs, are linked neurally to one's brain mean that one's fingers are more closely connected to one's mind than are doorknobs? It would seem not. For, if the mind is nonmaterial, then there is no clear sense in which even one's brain is more closely connected with one's mind than are doorknobs. Possibly the clearest sense in which one's brain might be said to be close to one's mind is a spatial sense: i.e. doorknobs are to a greater or lesser extent removed from me whereas my brain seems right on top of me, so to speak. If the mind is nonmaterial, then a doorknob is no further removed from my mind than is my brain. For if the mind is nonmaterial, then it quite literally is not at any place at all.[6] It has naught to do with the principles appropriate to space-occupying things, and hence is neither close to nor far from any spatial object.

So, turning doorknobs through mental command and without touching them would, if the mind is nonmaterial, in principle be no more remarkable than activating one's brain neurons through mental edict, or willing one's hands to move or one's mouth to open or to stay shut. If skepticism is justified as to opening doors solely through an exercise of the nonmaterial mind, then it is also justified as to moving one's fingers through mental edict.

The underlying problem is that, if, as the dualist supposes, the mind belongs to an entirely different "realm of being" than does the body or any of its components, then it is difficult to see how the body and the mind could interact. This difficulty is best perceived only when the effort is made to picture the mind interacting with something other than "its own" body. Since the interaction of mind with body is a common occurrence of everyday life, no attention is paid to it; thus few notice how amazing this interaction would have to be *if* the mind and the body really did belong to different realms of being. But perhaps the fact that interaction between the body and the mind is so commonplace really shows only that it is unreasonable to regard the mind as non-material.

(2) Categorizing Mind-Body Interaction

The difficulty of understanding how a nonmaterial mind could interact with a material brain and body should be fundamentally disturbing to an exponent of dualism. Some philosophers suppose there is a further problem for the dualist in that he cannot *categorize* the interactions between a nonmaterial mind and a material brain and body.[7]

The supposed problem is said to arise because interactions between an entity of type X and an entity of type Y apparently

---

[6]This is true unless sense can be made of likening minds to such abstract entities as points or perimeters, which have spatial location but no spatial occupancy.

[7]Gilbert Ryle, for example. See: *Concept of Mind.* New York, Barnes and Noble, 1949, pp. 12–13.

cannot themselves be classified either as X-phenomena or Y-phenomena. Thus, for example, the interactions between a wooden bat and a leather ball cannot themselves be said either to be wooden or to be leather. The interactions between X and Y apparently belong to some larger category, as, for example, the interaction between the bat and the ball belong to the larger category of "physical interactions."

The supposed problem is, therefore, that, because the interactions between the nonmaterial mind and the material body cannot themselves be categorized either as nonmaterial or as material, dualism involves a search for a third category to which these mind-body interactions belong. Beyond the material and the nonmaterial, there is no third category and cannot be. By ordinary definition, material and nonmaterial are categories mutually exclusive and jointly comprehensive of all things. Either something is in space or it is not in space, and if it is in space, then by definition it is material.

Thus, it is reasoned, a dualist, in answer to the question, "What *kind* of thing is interaction?", must in effect concede that it is no kind of thing.

However, this supposed difficulty in categorizing the interactions of mind and body is not really fatal to dualism. To deny that interaction between a nonmaterial mind and a material brain or body is any kind of thing is *not* equivalent to denying that such interaction exists. X-type things and Y-type things can interact, I believe, without there being a third, Z-type category of thing, to which the "interactions" themselves belong. The interactions between two different kinds of thing are not themselves "things" in the first place. To say that X and Y interact is, I think, only to say that changes in X produce changes in Y and that changes in Y produce changes in X. To speak of the "interactions" between X and Y is thus not to speak of things of a certain type or category; it is merely to make reference, elliptically, to the fact that changes in X bring about changes in Y and vice versa.

If I am correct, then, although there is still difficulty in understanding *how* a nonmaterial mind could interact with a material brain and body, that they could interact is not *a priori* precluded by the impossibility of the categorization of the "interactions" as a kind of thing.

Interaction And Physiology

(1) The Locus of Interaction

A further difficulty confronting dualism is that of determining the precise point at which the nonmaterial mind and its activities become involved with those physical processes which are known to be the cause of all bodily activity.

Consider this example of the difficulty. I decide to close my fist and do so. The closing of my fist is an action of my body; my decision, on the other hand, is an act of my mind, regardless of whether the decision is nonphysical or is mere physical activity on the part of my brain, as the materialist theorizes. Although my mind, through its act of decision, brings about the closing of my fist, it does not do so directly, for the immediate cause of my fist's closing is a contraction and shortening of the muscle fiber in my forearm.

Further, the immediate cause of the contraction and shortening of the muscles is not my mind or some mental event. The change in the muscle fiber is caused by energy released from chemical reactions involving a substance, adenosine triphosphate, known more simply as "ATP." And the chemical reactions involving ATP are in turn the result of nerve impulses reaching the muscle fiber. The nerve impulses consist of electrical transmissions within the nerve cells and of chemical reactions at the junctions, or synapses, of the nerve cells. These impulses move from the Betz cells of the motor cortex area of the brain, and are transmitted via the corticospinal tract down through the basal regions of the brain, through the medulla, along the pyramidal tract, and into and through the spinal cord to the nerve fiber, which contacts the appropriate muscle fiber.

The chain of electro-chemical reactions that constitute this entire sequence, which terminates in the closing of my hand, is exceedingly complicated, but the essential point is that the entire sequence is almost fully explainable by physiology, which, indeed, assumes that in time the process will be fully so explainable. There seems to be no room for the operation of "nonphysical forces" anywhere in the sequence. Physiology mostly makes no attempt to consider any nonmaterial thing within or acting upon the process, and its journals contain little, if any, "research" into a nonmaterial mind and its relationship to brain and body. It does not occur to physiologists even to think about where, to borrow an expression from Daniel Dennet, the nonphysical soul bangs on a synapse.[8] Not only would it probably seem *arbitrary* to the physiologist to select some point as *the* point the nonmaterial mind involves itself in this purely physical sequence, but also it would probably seem *unnecessary* to suppose that a nonmaterial something is involved anywhere in the sequence.

In spite of the impressive detail of the physiological explanation of human bodily behavior, most of us, as a result of our philosophical heritage, believe that not all can be explained by mere gross matter. To many, there is something imperfect or even corrupt in mere matter unrelieved and unelevated by a nonmaterial causative intelligence, an intelligence that in its incorporeality is one with God or the original creative force. Most of us take these sentiments seriously and respectfully, and none should scoff.

On the other hand, rejection of these sentiments should also be respected. It need not be assumed unworthy of God to have made us out of the same elements as animals, plants, rocks, and soil. Indeed, what a magnificent achievement it would be for material particles through God to have been assembled in such an utterly complex way that humans look in on themselves and out at their universe to the darkest horizons of space and the beginning of time and act so inventively in adjustment to the world around—though we hope not fatally to themselves in the end!

Yet, moved perhaps by considerations of the necessity to find a nonmaterial being diffusing and elevating us above the grossness of mere dust, some philosophers, scientists, religionists, and others

---

[8]Professor Joyce Norman, a physiologist, tells me that "it would be safe to say" that physiology journals contain *no* research into a nonmaterial mind or its relationship to brain and body. Sir John Eccles, a prominent British neuroscientist, laments the widespread acceptance by neuroscientists of materialism and their failure to "bother about how the mind may interfere in their neurophysiological investigations." (See Cerebral activity and consciousness. In Ayala and Dobzhansky [Eds.]: *Studies in the Philosophy of Biology*. Berkeley, University of California Press, 1974, p. 90.) Of course, *outside* the context of their professional journal work some physiologists, including Eccles, will speculate as to the possibilities of nonphysical influences in human physiological processes.

have at times made highly ingenious efforts to specify a plausible niche for the activity of a nonmaterial mind in the sequence of physical happenings that ultimately result in our bodily behavior.

C. D. Broad, for example, theorized that perhaps the nonmaterial mind influences bodily movement by raising and lowering the resistance of the synapses so as to direct nerve currents.[9] That such efforts are made is hardly surprising since, as one commentator put it, "When all is said and done, dualism is the only position on the relation of mind and brain which is not counterintuitive to the western mind."[10]

(2) Eccles' Dualism

Sir John Eccles, a British neurophysiologist, is another who has specified a niche of interaction.[11] Although Eccles mostly does not use the term, *nonmaterial mind*, he is a self-avowed dualist,[12] and it is very clear that what he calls the "conscious self" (or, in some writings, the "self-conscious mind") is the equivalent in his own terminology of what I have been calling the nonmaterial mind.

Eccles in effect philosophizes that the conscious self may exert its influence not *within* the physiological sequence that ends with the movement of the hands, arms, lips, etc., but rather at the very beginning of the sequence. He notes that the motor nerve activity that produces bodily behavior is ultimately caused by the discharging of neural "columns," which are large populations of neurons in the cerebral cortex. He theorizes that the patterns of discharge of these neuron populations may be affected by the firing of certain "critically poised" groups of neurons within the cortex and that these critical groups may in turn be activated by the firing of individual neurons within the cortex. Thus the nonmaterial mind or "conscious self" may act on *individual* neurons

---

[9]C. D. Broad: *The Mind and Its Place in Nature.* New York, The Humanities Press, 1951, p. 113.

[10]Gordon G. Globus, Grover Maxwell, and Irwin Savodnik (Eds.): *Consciousness and the Brain: A Scientific and Philosophical Inquiry.* New York, Plenum Press, 1976, p. 123.

[11]See, e.g. (1) The brain and free will. *Ibid.,* pp. 101–119; (2) Cerebral activity and consciousness. In Ayala and Dobzhansky, *op. cit.,* pp. 87–107; (3) *The Self and Its Brain* (with Karl Popper). New York, Springer International, 1977.

[12]*Ibid.* (*The Self and Its Brain*), p. 355.

in the cortex, and these then will act synaptically on the critically poised groups of neurons. By acting in this way on a great number of individual neurons through the cortical neural network, the "conscious-self" will have "influenced" the patterns of discharge of the neural columns and thus will ultimately have directed our bodily behavior.[13]

Eccles may be right in this, but one cannot avoid the suspicion that he has determined in advance that the nonmaterial mind ("conscious self") must be involved somewhere in human behavior, and that he finds a place for it in his account of physiological activity, not because specific happenings in the brain require reference to nonphysical agency, but for *a priori* reasons.[14] Such items as Betz cells and synapses, by contrast, clearly make their way into explanations of human behavior because of certain specific discoveries about the nature and functioning of the human nervous system. It seems altogether different in the case of Eccles' "conscious self," and it is too easy to think that the conscious self is brought into the picture not as a result of some specific theoretical physiological need but rather as a result of the psychological need of Sir Eccles to bring it in.

Further, the same difficulties confront Eccles' theory that face any dualism. For instance, the theory leaves it completely unexplained *how* the nonmaterial mind (conscious self) acts on individual neurons. That my nonmaterial mind could act on individual neurons within my brain in this way would be just as inexplicable a mystery as would be my mind's acting on the atoms in my office door. In other words, the theory represents no advance with respect to the important question of how something from a wholly different and nonphysical realm could interact with a physical thing in the first place. As C. Wade Savage has put it, in criticism of Eccles' theory,

> Does the soul [Savage's word for Eccles' "conscious self" or the nonmaterial mind] act on a neuron in the way that one neuron acts on another? If so, the soul is something like a neuron—a material, spatial agency. Does the soul act on a neuron in the way that a cosmic ray might act on a neuron to cause it to discharge? If so, the soul is something like a cosmic ray (or the sun that emits the ray) and is a material, spatial entity. Does the soul act on a neuron in a manner quite unlike those mentioned? If so, the action of the

---

[13]Cerebral activity and consciousness. In Ayala and Dobzhansky, *op. cit.*, p. 100.

[14]Eccles might say that such magnificent creations as scientific theories, works of art, tools, and social institutions could only have been the work of nonmaterial minds. However, while there is ample proof in our works that we are a creative and intelligent species, I see only *a priori* reasons for inferring the nonmateriality of our minds from our capacity for intelligent creation.

soul is utterly mysterious and inexplicable. This is precisely the unsatisfactory state in which Descartes left the problem of interaction.[15]

Furthermore, Eccles' own writings suggest that it is not even necessary to refer to a non-material mind in an explanation of the physiology of human behavior, as Professor Savage has pointed out. According to Eccles, the mind, i.e. "conscious self," acts on the neurons in the cerebral cortex of the *dominant* hemisphere of the brain. Yet, in the opinion of Eccles, the *minor* hemisphere is capable, *without* the activity of the "conscious self," of carrying out "immense and complex operational tasks such as the decoding, synthesizing, and patterning" of, e.g. musical data.[16] Thus, as Dr. Savage notes, on Eccles' own account, "it is easy to suppose that thinking can be carried out by the cortex without the activity of the conscious self. For understanding language can be compared to understanding music, and understanding language is thinking. Why doesn't Eccles face it: The brain can think, and can do so without the soul [i.e. nonmaterial mind]."[17]

Eccles may be correct as to the conscious self or mind acting on the neural system in the manner he envisions, but his exposition does not justify believing that he is.

Conclusion

There are objections, other than those I have dealt with, to viewing the mind as nonmaterial. However, these other objections I regard as of less importance. It has been claimed, for example, that a nonmaterial mind cannot act upon a physical body because for it to do so would involve a violation of the principle of conservation of energy. It has also been suggested that

---

[15]An old ghost in a new body. Reprinted by permission of Plenum Publishing Corporation and Professor Savage. In Globus, Maxwell, and Savodnik, *op. cit.*, p. 131. Eccles himself concedes the mystery of interaction: "When thought leads to action," he writes, "I am constrained, as a neuroscientist, to postulate that in some way, completely beyond my understanding, my thinking changes the operative patterns of neuronal activities in my brain." See: Cerebral activity and consciousness, in Ayala and Dobzhansky, *op. cit.*, p. 98.

[16]*Ibid.* (Cerebral activity and consciousness), p. 97.

[17]In Globus, Maxwell, and Savodnik, *op. cit.*, p. 136. Reprinted by permission of Plenum Publishing Corporation and Professor Savage.

the emergence of a nonmaterial mind either within the development of an embryo into a fully formed person or within the evolution of humankind from one-celled organisms is ruled out by the continuousness of the processes involved. These and lesser criticisms of dualism are quite answerable, in my view.[18]

Numerous criticisms of materialism have also been made, but, since here it must be determined only whether there are any decisive refutations of dualism, whether there are any considerations which preclude the possibility that the mind is nonmaterial, it is not necessary to examine criticisms of materialism.[19]

Is dualism a tenable theory as to the nature of the mind? The materialist thinks not:

First, dualism leaves it unexplained and perhaps inexplicable why a human being has only one mind, a mind which is shared with no other.

Second, dualism leaves unexplained and seemingly inexplicable how the nonmaterial mind, which is conceived of as belonging to an entirely different category of being from that to which belongs the material body and brain, could interplay causally with that body and its brain and neural processes.

Finally, bodily activity is the result of physiological processes in which there is no known nonphysical intervention. True, certain aspects of the working of the body are but dimly comprehended, and may ultimately require explanation by reference to nonphysical agency, but, in the opinion of the materialist, there is at present no reason to suppose that this is so. At one time every aspect of bodily activity was but dimly comprehended, and even though now much has been explained, it has not yet proved necessary to refer to nonphysical forces in the explanations. It is reasonable to infer that those aspects of bodily activity that are not understood now will themselves come to be explained in purely physical terms.

My own view, however, is that none of these considerations is *absolutely* decisive as to the unsoundness of dualism. Indeed, few

---

[18] For answers to these and other objections to dualism, with references to the literature on the subject, see, especially, Jerome Shaffer: The mind-body problem. In Paul Edwards (Ed.): *Encyclopedia of Philosophy.* New York, Macmillan, 1972, Vol. V, pp. 336–346; and Keith Campbell, *op. cit.,* pp. 41 ff.

[19] For criticisms of materialism, see Eccles and Popper, *The Self and Its Brain.* New York, Springer International, 1977, pp. 51–99.

materialists contend that dualism is a totally impossible theory, though some would claim that the absence of any really clear characterization of a nonphysical property makes the theory virtually unintelligible. Most materialists hold merely that dualism raises more questions than it answers and is in any case an unnecessary theory. There are no genuine reasons, materialists say, no reasons beyond those given by religious conviction, cultural outlook, or sheer speculative introspection, for believing that a nonmaterial agent or self or mind is somewhere involved in human activity.

Yet it seems to me that acceptance or rejection of dualism and of its concept of a nonmaterial mind depends in part on whether there is any convincing evidence of personal survival after biological death. If there is, then this would indicate that a person is not merely a material or physical organism. On the other hand, apart from such purported evidence, there is not, in my opinion, sufficient reason to postulate the existence of a mind as a nonmaterial component of a person.

Whether or not materialism constitutes the best theory of the nature of mind and person thus cannot be determined prior to an examination and evaluation of the supposed evidence of personal survival. Great importance attaches in contemporary philosophy to the nature of the mind. In view of the significance to this issue of the purported evidence of afterdeath personal survival, it is surprising that so little attention has been paid to that evidence by contemporary philosophy.

CHAPTER 6

TWO VIEWS OF SELF AND DISEMBODIED SURVIVAL

... to speak accurately I am not more than a thing which thinks, that is to say a mind or a soul...
—*Rene Descartes,* Meditations II[1]

For my part, when I enter most intimately into what I call myself, I always stumble on some particular perception or other... I never can catch myself at any time without a perception, and never can observe anything but the perception.... I may venture to affirm of the rest of mankind, that they are nothing but a bundle or collection of different perceptions...
—*David Hume,* A Treatise of Human Nature, *Book I, Part IV, Section Six*[2]

Subjects And Bundles

It is widely believed among philosophers that there are only two conceivably acceptable views of the nature of the self or person. Critics of the belief in discarnate personal survival,[3] such as Antony Flew, have argued that under neither of these views is it intelligible to suppose that a person or a self could survive the death of its body.[4] I, however, am not fully persuaded by the

---

[1] E. S. Haldane and G. R. T. Ross (trans): *The Philosophical Works of Descartes.* Cambridge, Cambridge University Press, 1968, Vol. I, p. 152.

[2] Edited by L. A. Selby-Bigge. Oxford, the Clarendon Press, 1968, p. 252.

[3] I use "person" and "self" interchangeably, and equate "personal survival" with "survival of self." Cf. Chapter 1.

[4] See Antony Flew: Is there a case for disembodied survival? In Wheatley and Edge (Eds.): *Philosophical Dimensions of Parapsychology.* Springfield, Thomas, 1976, pp. 330–347.

argument.

The two views of the self are those of Descartes (1596–1650) and of Hume (1711–1776). Descartes regarded himself as an individual subject that *has* thoughts, feelings, perceptions, and other conscious experiences, which, until such time as Descartes' body would cease to function, would be "infused" in that body.[5] "I, the thinker," wrote Descartes, "am distinct from my own thought."[6]

Hume, on the other hand, found himself quite unable to detect within himself anything remotely resembling Descartes' "thing which thinks," i.e. subject of experiences. Every time Hume focused his attention inward, in an effort to observe this subject, he could discern only some idea, thought, feeling or other conscious experience, and could never catch even a glimpse of the subject which, according to Descartes, was distinct from these various conscious experiences and was supposed to *have* them. Accordingly, Hume concluded that his essential self could really be "nothing but a bundle or collection of perceptions" (for Hume, "perceptions" correspond to what we would call "conscious experiences").[7]

Hume and Descartes were not themselves primarily interested in the question of life after death (Hume did not regard disembodied survival as a conception worth "hearkening to"), but their theories as to the essence of the living person are of importance here because, in the opinion of most philosophers, a living person or self, and whatever survives of him discarnate, if anything does, must either be an individual subject which has conscious experiences or the continuing series of conscious experiences itself. He must either be like a baseball *player* (a person who *has* certain abilities and characteristics) or like a baseball *game* (which is simply a series of events of a certain sort).

Are there really no other acceptable views as to the nature of the self? I, at any rate, can conceive of no others, for the Hume and Descartes theories seem to me to represent the only possible relationships between the self and its conscious experiences: either the self is the subject which has those experiences, or it is just simply equivalent to the series of experiences itself.

---

[5]See, especially, Descartes' *Meditations II* and *VI*.

[6]Haldane and Ross, *op. cit.*, Vol. II, p. 65.

[7]Hume, *op. cit.*, p. 252.

Of course, those who accept the Cartesian theory of the self as a subject of experiences may still differ as to whether the self so conceived is material or non-material; likewise, those who regard the self as a bundle of experiences can still disagree as to the nature of the experiences. I expressed my opinion in Chapter Five that we need not necessarily accept materialism and regard a person as a purely material entity. Certainly, if there is such a thing as discarnate personal survival, the surviving "person," whether "subject" or "bundle," must be incorporeal and nonmaterial.

Is the belief in a discarnate survival of the self intelligible under either of these theories of the self, or is Flew correct in believing that it is intelligible under neither? For reasons I shall now explain, I agree that a self or person could not survive the death of its body as a discarnate *bundle* of conscious experiences. I do not, however, agree that it is unintelligible to think that a self or person could survive bodily death as a discarnate *subject* of experiences.

Survival As A Discarnate Bundle Of Experiences

Certainly the theory that I am naught but a bundle of conscious experiences runs counter to common sense. From the common sense point of view Hume is mistaken: there cannot be a bundle of experiences without an experiencer, i.e. a subject of some sort. "Experiences without experiencer" is nonsense: experiences cannot simply exist unattached and ownerless. From the point of view of common sense, to conceive of a group of ownerless experiences is as illogical as to conceive of a group of employerless employees or faceless grins or parentless progeny.[8]

However, that a theory runs counter to common sense is not a decisive objection to the theory, or we would still think the world flat and Columbus would never have set sail. But the theory of the self as a stream or bundle of conscious experiences also suffers from a fundamental *theoretical* difficulty. Hume himself was very aware of the difficulty and indeed could find no solution to it

---

[8]As Descartes said, "...no qualities or properties pertain to nothing...where some are perceived there must necessarily be some thing or substance on which they depend." Haldane and Ross, *op. cit.*, p. 223.

which he felt was satisfactory. The difficulty is this:

Without a tie there can be no bundle. Without a set of rules which define which of the happenings on a playground belong to a baseball game and which do not, there is no baseball game. The difficulty in the bundle-theory of the self, as Hume himself realized, is that it provides no tie, no rule or principle which can serve to establish which experiences belong to one bundle or stream of consciousness, and which do not.[9]

To relate this difficulty to the question of whether a disembodied survivor could be but a stream or bundle of conscious experiences, suppose that at two o'clock tonight I die in my sleep and that my death is followed by the occurrence of numerous conscious experiences, i.e. by experiences which are not "had" by any underlying subject or "owner." Are these experiences then *mine*? Do they all belong to one and the same stream of consciousness, that stream, namely, that is I? Or do they belong to several different bundles or streams of consciousness? Is a feeling of rapture that occurs at, let us, say, 2:05 AM, a member of the *same* bundle as a mental image of a sunset experienced a little earlier, or is it a member of a *different* bundle? If these experiences are asserted both to be members of the same bundle, what is it that entitles us to make this assertion? What is the thread that unites them to each other, and, moreover, binds them in turn to the experiences *I* had while I was living?

An exponent of the Cartesian view of the self would cite an underlying subject or "owner" of experiences as the source of the unity of a series of successive experiences. To the question, when are experiences that occur on different occasions parts of the same stream of consciousness, he would reply that experiences are parts of the same stream of consciousness when they belong to one and the same subject or "owner" of the experiences.

However, the exponent of the bundle-theory of the self cannot cite a subject of experiences as that which unites certain experiences, and not others, within the same stream of consciousness. Is there any other factor that he might cite as a source of unity

---

[9] In the Appendix to Book I of his *Treatise*, Hume expressed dismay that he could not "explain the principles" that unite the experiences within a single bundle and that he was unable to "discover any theory, which ... [gave him] satisfaction on this head." Hume, *op. cit.*, pp. 633–636.

among the experiences of a bundle?

If experiences exhibited some kind of unique identifying characteristics, if they had "branding marks," so to speak, then possession by several experiences of the same characteristic or "brand" would serve to unite those experiences within the same bundle. However, as far as anyone has ever made out, experiences have no "marks" by means of which they might be grouped.

It is sometimes said that memory serves to tie together different experiences into one and the same bundle. Thus, for example, the mental image of a sunset might be regarded as belonging to the same stream of consciousness as the earlier feeling of rapture because the image is accompanied by a remembrance of the rapturous feeling. Both the image and the feeling might be regarded as belonging to *my* stream of consciousness (and not yours) because they are both accompanied by remembrances of experiences I (not you) had prior to death.

The trouble with viewing memory as the tie that binds together the experiences that belong to one bundle is that memories are themselves experiences. Some further tie is therefore required to bind the memories themselves to the other experiences of a bundle. Since according to the bundle-theory there is no unifying subject of experiences, what could this further tie be? What would settle whether a given memory goes together with *these* experiences or whether it goes together with *those* experiences?[10]

In short, the bundle-theorist in effect asks us to play a game like checkers with pieces of random colors, and this cannot be done. For one does not know which pieces go with which other pieces and so cannot say which pieces belong to which side. In fact, the mention of a "side" is without meaning in these circumstances. Just as a "side," to exist at all, must be composed of certain pieces and not others, a survivor, to exist, must be composed of certain experiences and not others. The theory of survival as a discarnate bundle of conscious experiences does not provide a principle for determining which experiences go with which other experiences

---

[10]True, there is a causative connection between a given experience and a later memory of that experience, and this connection would, I think, suffice to "tie" a given experience to a later remembrance of that experience. However, the causative relationship between an experience and a memory of that experience would not serve to tie a remembrance to an experience that was concurrent with that remembrance.

to form one survivor; so mention of a "survivor" is meaningless.

Consequently, if it is intelligible to believe in discarnate survival of the self, it is only because it is intelligible to suppose that a discarnate self conceived of as a subject of conscious experiences might survive the death of its body.

Discarnate Subjects Of Experiences

Various names are used for a subject of experiences, including "soul," "mind," "self," "spirit," "person," and, sometimes, "personality," but when the subject is viewed as existing apart from a body, it is commonly called a "spirit." Henceforth, by "spirit" I shall mean, "discarnate subject of conscious experiences."

Some critics of the belief in survival as a spirit maintain that so little of what is sayable about a self or person is sayable about a spirit, that a spirit cannot logically qualify as a surviving self or person. In the next chapter I shall consider the reasoning of these critics, who include, notably, Peter Geach.

Other critics, and I think Antony Flew and Terence Penelhum would wish to be counted among them, hold that there is *no such conception* as that of a "discarnate subject of experience." They maintain, in effect, that *nothing* at all is sayable about such things; they believe that discourse about "spirits" (or "souls" or "minds" or any other equivalent to "discarnate subjects of conscious experiences") is in actuality unintelligible gibberish. Are they correct? I think not, but much needs to be said by way of explanation.

Terms and Reidentification

Spirit is meant to be a term for a nonmaterial (and consequently nonspatial), but still time-occupying thing, but is the term really intelligible? For any given term, "T," which is supposed to stand for a thing, T, to be intelligible (regardless of whether T is material or nonmaterial), discourse about the same T must be clearly different in meaning from discourse about different Ts.

Consider the term *table*, for instance. If there were no clear difference in meaning between discourse about the *same* table and discourse about *different* tables, then *table* would not be an intelligible term.

Or consider the term *god*. If he who spoke of the actions of the same god said nothing different in meaning from he who talked of the actions of different gods, then *god* would certainly not be an intelligible term, and conversation about gods would be incomprehensible.

The same principle holds with respect to the purported term *spirit*. For *spirit* to be an intelligible term, there must be a clear difference in meaning between discourse about the same spirit and discourse about different spirits.

Now, unless it could be determined, at least in principle, whether or not a table encountered on one occasion is the same table as was encountered earlier, then there would be no clear difference in meaning between the expression, "this is the same table" and the expression, "this is a different table," i.e. there would be no clear difference in meaning between talk about the same table and talk about different tables, and so *table* would not be an intelligible term.

Further, the fact that a table is a material thing and that a spirit is, supposedly, nonmaterial, makes no difference as to this requirement of reidentifiability as essential to intelligibility. If there is to be a difference in meaning between talk about the same spirit and talk about different spirits, then spirits must, in principle, be reidentifiable.

The view that discourse about spirits is unintelligible rests on the premise that it cannot be determined whether a spirit which exists at one time is the same spirit as that which existed earlier. If this cannot be determined, i.e. if spirits cannot be *reidentified*, then *spirit* is not an intelligible term.

The reasoning proffered in support of the premise that spirits cannot be reidentified is as follows:

> Since a spirit is supposedly a discarnate, nonmaterial afterdeath subject of experiences, it could not occupy space or possess any space-implying characteristics like scars or fingerprints. Spirit A, which exists at one time, and spirit B, which exists at a later time, would thus not be the same or different by virtue of having occupied, or having failed to occupy, the same positions.
>
> By what other index might they be said to be the same or different? The only other conceivable index is an "experience-index": for spirit B to be the same as A, it is necessary and sufficient that B and A have had the selfsame experiences. That is, B must have had A's experiences and not merely experiences like A's. But what settles whether B has had A's experiences? That B thinks

it has had those experiences obviously does not prove that it has. Even B's "remembering" having had A's experiences does not entail that it had them, for the "memories" might be erroneous, as they sometimes are.

If B and A are living, embodied persons, we would say that, whatever it might take to settle whether B had A's experiences, to have had A's experiences B must have been in a position to have had them; i.e. B must have occupied the place occupied by A when A had his experiences.

It must, therefore (according to the proffered reasoning), be the same with surviving persons, i.e. with spirits. To have had spirit A's experiences, spirit B must have been in a position to have had them. So, for it to be determinable whether B had A's experiences, B and A *must* occupy spatial positions. But spirits are discarnate, and do not occupy positions. And so it could not be settled whether spirit B had spirit A's experiences or thus whether B is the same spirit as A.

If the proffered reasoning is sound, and I am not convinced that it is, then, since it would not be determinable whether a later spirit is the same as an earlier spirit, talk about the same spirit would not be clearly different in meaning from talk about different spirits. This in turn would mean that *spirit* is not an intelligible term.

Is Spatial Occupancy by Spirits Necessary for Their Reidentification?

As I have already indicated, I am not persuaded by the reasoning proffered to the effect that *spirit* is unintelligible. I do *agree*, however, that for later spirit B to have been earlier spirit A, B must have had A's experiences. The question is, can it be determined that B had A's experiences, given that neither B nor A, as spirits, occupy spatial positions?

My answer is that I am not certain that it could be determined that spirit B had spirit A's experiences (given that spirits by definition do not occupy space), but, more importantly, I am also not convinced that it could *not* be determined. True, that B "remembers" that it has had A's experiences does not prove that it has, assuming that the memory of spirits is as fallible as our own. How then could the correctness of a spirit's memory be established?

One possible answer is that correctness may be proved by identifying the causative relationship between a spirit's past experiences and its present memories of these experiences. There obviously is a causative relationship between an *embodied* person's past experiences and present memories of those experiences, a relationship that obtains only between the experiences and memories of the same person.[11] If, therefore, it could be shown that spirit B's "memories" of having had spirit A's experiences were in fact caused by A's experiences, then B, I think, would have to have been A.

It is, of course, possible that a causal relationship between A's experiences and B's memories can be established only if B and A occupy spatial positions, but, if this is so, it is not self-evident that it is so, and I do not think that anyone has ever demonstrated that it is so.

Because the theoretical possibility of the reidentification of spirits has not, to my knowledge, been eliminated, I am not persuaded that *spirit* is an unintelligible concept. I am not persuaded, that is, that it is unintelligible to suppose that a subject of conscious experiences might exist discarnate.

So, while I think that survival of myself as a discarnate *bundle of conscious experiences* is not really intelligible, I am not convinced that my survival as a *spirit* is unintelligible. However, as I indicated earlier, some critics of the belief in discarnate survival, while apparently conceding that a discarnate subject of conscious experiences, i.e. a spirit, is a conceivable thing, hold that such a thing could never qualify as a surviving self or person, because too little of what can be said about selves or persons can be said about such a thing. This is a matter that I treat in the next chapter.

---

[11] Efforts to provide an analysis of the causative relationship between an *embodied person's* past experiences and present memories have been made. See e.g. John Perry: Personal identity, memory, and the problem of circularity. In Perry (Ed.): *Personal Identity*. Berkeley, University of California Press, 1975, pp. 135–155. Also see John Perry: The importance of being identical. In A. Rorty (Ed.): *The Identities of Persons*. Berkeley, University of California Press, 1976, pp. 67–90.

CHAPTER 7

IT ISN'T CHESS
WITHOUT THE KING

... my soul is not I; and if only souls are saved, I am not saved, nor is any man.
— *Peter Geach,* God and the Soul[1]

Antony Flew has likened disembodied survival to kingless chess.[2] The implication of the analogy, if the analogy is valid, is not difficult to see. A game played with all the chess pieces except the king, though it might superficially resemble chess, certainly would not be chess. Similarly (the analogy implies), a subject of experiences without a body might resemble a self or person (again, I equate the two), but it would not really be a self or person.

If the analogy is valid, then even if there did exist discarnate subjects of conscious experiences, i.e. spirits, these would not be selves or persons and thus would not be surviving selves or persons, just as, if there were games played with all the chess pieces but the king, these games would not be chess. If what survives my death is my spirit (or "soul," as Geach terms a disembodied subject of experiences) then *I* do not survive my death.

The reason that has been put forth, notably by Geach,[3] for saying that if subjects of experience were removed from the body then they would no longer be persons or selves is that so little of what is sayable about a person or self is sayable about a bodiless subject of experiences that no such subject could qualify as a person or self.

---

[1] New York, Schocken Books, 1969, p. 22.
[2] A New Approach to Physical Research. London, Watts and Company, 1953, p. 80.
[3] Geach, *op. cit.*, pp. 17-29.

Existence as a Spirit

Can one successfully imagine *himself* as a spirit, i.e. a bodiless subject of experiences? Or is what is imagined so alien as not to qualify as oneself?

First of all, a spirit would be unable to receive any information from the physical senses. It would experience neither lightness nor darkness, not even the "darkness" that occurs when we close our eyes or look about on a pitch-black night. It would be without a sense of smell or taste, and in a state neither of sound nor of silence, not even the silence of a totally soundproof room. All further sensations, too, would be absent, including tactile sensations and those internal sensations that tell incarnates whether their legs are moving, their stomachs are empty, they have had enough sleep, and so forth. It would, thus, be unable to experience warmth or coldness or the beating of a heart. No sensation would signify to it that it was standing, floating, lying, or running; it would have no sense of being either right side up or upside down, of having wiggled a finger or of having shaken a leg. Not even a transitory hunger pang would punctuate the sensationless void.

Second, a spirit could not *do* anything that requires use of a body. It could not read, laugh, crawl, cry, hide, hum, or hurry. A brief consideration of human activity will disclose how very little a spirit could do.

Indeed, perhaps the only thing a spirit might purposely do would be to change its thought, imaginings, and memories; i.e. to decide to think one thing and not to think another, or to choose to remember or imagine one set of experiences and not another. However, it is difficult to comprehend what the difference would be between a spirit's purposely or voluntarily changing its thought and its thoughts simply changing involuntarily.

Could a spirit dream? If so, how might it distinguish a dream from a "waking" experience, given the lack of sensory equipment?

Finally, what would the passing of time be like to a spirit? No sensations would measure time's lapse. Unless it had ESP (a possibility that is discussed later) it would have no access to external, objective standards, such as clocks, by means of which to measure the length of thought or reverie. So, it might well misjudge a momentary thought as lasting longer than one that had, in fact, endured much longer. It might take thirteen seconds to count to ten on one occasion, and, on another occasion, take thirteen minutes and yet be completely convinced that it was counting more slowly on the first occasion. Whether it were discarnate for minutes or for years would be something it could never really determine (unless it were equipped with ESP).[4]

Given, then, what "existence" would apparently be like to a spirit if its existence were unrelieved by ESP,[5] it is easy to understand Geach's remark to the effect that if it is my spirit that survives my death, then *I* do not survive my death. A thing which sees naught, hears naught, tastes naught, smells naught, feels naught, and has no sensations of any sort whatsoever, a thing which cannot act physically or communicate sensibly, a thing which cannot distinguish dreams from reality and cannot even determine how long it has existed cannot be I, Geach would say. At best such a thing, if it survived my death, would be a mere psychological remnant of myself, a mere nonphysical remainder or fragment of the former me, which could no more be myself than a game without a king could be chess.

Nevertheless, though I can see how others might accept Geach's contention that survival of one's spirit is not survival of oneself, I do not agree with it. No doubt discarnate existence, if unelevated by some kind of ESP, would be no more desirable than would total paralysis of the body through injury or disease, but I do not agree that, because most of the things that can be done by an embodied person cannot be done by a spirit, it necessarily follows that a

---

[4]The average dream, we have been told, lasts only a second or two from start to finish in spite of the fact that, to the dreaming individual, the dream seems to last much longer, and in some cases seems to cover the span of several weeks or even years. In a similar way, a stream of "experiences" thought by a discarnate entity to have lasted a long time might in fact have lasted for only a brief moment. Since the briefest experience could be thought by a discarnate to have lasted an aeon, even momentary discarnate survival after death might answer one's craving for eternal life.

[5]For other depictions of disembodied afterdeath existence, the reader may wish to consult H. H. Price: Survival and the idea of another world. *Proceedings of the Society for Psychical Research, 60:* 1–25, 1953; or Michael Grosso: The survival of personality in a mind-dependent world. *Journal of the American Society for Psychical Research, 73:* 367–380, 1978. In chapter fourteen of *Death and Eternal Life* (New York, Harper and Row, 1976), John Hick treats the important question of the extent to which a disembodied survivor might be capable of exercising volition or able to develop his character.

spirit could not qualify as a former person or self. What matters is whether or not a spirit can do what is *essential* to existence as a person or self.

The Necessity of Self-Awareness

For a spirit that exists after my death to qualify as I, myself, the person who I am, and not be merely a lingering psychological fragment of me, it must, I think, comprehend itself as distinct and different from other things, just as I do. It must thus be able, as I am, to distinguish the reality that is external to, and independent of, its own mind from its beliefs, conjectures, and hopes about that reality: it must in principle be able, as I am, to determine the validity or invalidity of its beliefs about this external reality.

To be I, a spirit that exists after my death must also comprehend itself as a conscious being separate and distinct from other conscious beings, and must therefore be able, as I am able, to recognize others as others, to distinguish among them, and to communicate with them.

Should it be thought that discarnate personal survival does not entail that a spirit have these various capacities to distinguish itself from what it is not, I would reply that I have these capacities and consider them essential to my awareness of myself as a conscious being, and that I cannot conceive of myself surviving if I do not survive with these capacities.

Now, obviously, beings without bodies cannot use physical apparatus to perceive the external world (i.e. the world external to and independent of their own minds), or to verify their various beliefs about that external world. Obviously, too, they cannot communicate with each other or anyone else by sensory means. How then could disembodied and non-sentient spirits be aware of the external world? How, also, could they recognize other discarnate beings or distinguish one discarnate being from another, or communicate with them?

It is often suggested that a spirit, though devoid of body and sensory equipment, may have and may manifest a unique personality by which it can be recognized and distinguished from all other spirits. Indeed, spirits are frequently referred to as "disembodied personalities."

But what kind of personality traits could spirits have, since they have no bodies? I find it impossible to conceive of a bodiless entity as generous, for example, or as kind, selfish, or gracious. I cannot conceive of a bodiless being as promiscuous, austere, or restrained. Similarly, it makes no sense to me to suppose that a discarnate being might be stern, ruthless, or studious; prim, priggish, or princely. In fact, I find it difficult to conceive of discarnate beings as having any of the traits of personality that living, embodied persons have. If I picture an acquaintance whose personality is striking and then attempt to picture his personality apart from his facial expressions and bodily gestures and spoken words, etc., I find that I cannot do so. Bodiless "personalities" thus seem to me to be very difficult, if not totally impossible, to conceive of. The "personalities" of spirits must at least be very different from our own.

Furthermore, even if spirits do possess unique personalities, could they manifest, exhibit, or display their personalities? Given that they would have no apparatus for the emission of light, sound, radio wave, or other physical signal, it is difficult to think that, even if they had unique personalities, they could exhibit or display and thus be recognized by their personalities.

However, could spirits recognize or be recognized by other discarnates by using ESP?[6] Could they also use ESP to communicate with others and to acquire knowledge about the external world, the world outside and independent of their own conscious states? If they could, then they could comprehend themselves as distinct from other things and other spirits.

Knowledge Through ESP

Suppose that Smith has recently been killed in an air accident and has passed on as a spirit. Actually, to suppose that it is *Smith* who has passed on and not merely a component of Smith begs the question whether a spirit is really Smith and not a mere surviving fragment of Smith. I shall nevertheless, for the purpose of discus-

---

[6]Obviously, if by "ESP" is meant perception through an extra *physical* sense, then discarnates could not have powers of ESP. But I am not using the term in this book in this narrow way, but instead include within its scope perception or awareness through a completely nonphysical mode.

sion, continue for the moment to refer to the spirit which exists after Mr. Smith's demise as "Smith." But it must be kept in mind that it is still unsettled whether or not this spirit is complete enough to be Smith or is merely a surviving Smith-fragment.

If the discarnate "Smith" should ask himself whether or not Mrs. Smith died in the accident too, he might, after pondering the question, suspect that she had not. Of course, Smith cannot just look around and see if Mrs. Smith is living or dead since, having no eyes, he cannot really see anything. Nor can he ascertain the fact by any sensory mode. So if he is to determine whether Mrs. Smith is still alive, it can only be through ESP, i.e. through clairvoyance or through telepathically reading the mind of someone else (including Mrs. Smith) who knows about Mrs. Smith.[7] Let us consider these two possible sources of information, clairvoyance and telepathy, in turn.

Knowledge Through Clairvoyance

Such experimental evidence as is available relative to the existence and nature of clairvoyance strongly indicates that a belief founded on supposed clairvoyance cannot be confirmed or disconfirmed except through use of the normal senses. For example, in card-calling tests for clairvoyance, the "clairvoyant" who correctly calls an unseen card does not, at the time he makes his call, know whether or not he is correct. He may *believe* very strongly that his call is correct, but he does not *know* that it is until he sees the card or has been told. Smith is in the same position, with one important difference: he has no way of obtaining the required sensory follow-up information concerning the correctness of his belief that his wife is still alive. He must therefore remain uncertain (unless he is informed through telepathy, a possibility I discuss below) as to whether his belief is correct.

Any other belief Smith might have, and any other conjecture he might make, about the states of affairs external to or independent of his own thoughts would be equally as uncertain and incapa-

---

[7]Whereas telepathy is extrasensory mind-reading, clairvoyance is an extrasensory awareness of facts, where such awareness does not involve telepathy. If I can tell what cards you are looking at by reading your mind, that is telepathy. If I can tell what cards you are looking at by extrasensory perception of the cards themselves, that is clairvoyance.

ble of confirmation or disconfirmation through clairvoyance alone. But could Smith receive confirmation or disconfirmation of his belief that his wife is dead through some other entity, either a spirit or a living person, by telepathy?

Knowledge Through Telepathy

It is doubtful that Smith's belief that his wife is alive could be confirmed or disconfirmed through Smith's receiving a telepathic communication from some other being, incarnate or discarnate. For Smith would have no way of distinguishing a telepathic communication from one of his own thoughts. A consideration of card-calling tests of telepathy makes this clear:

In such tests one person looks at or thinks of a card, and the card thought of or seen is recorded by the experimenter. The subject calls out his identification of the card thought of or seen by the other person, and his identifications are compared with the experimenter's record. It is only after several thousand identifications have been made and scored, and the subject's correct identifications have been found to exceed chance, that the subject can expect us to credit him with a telepathic faculty. But even then he does not know *which* of his correct identifications resulted from telepathy and which were mere lucky guesses.

Now Smith, unlike the card-calling subject, cannot have his "calls" scored. He has no access to the "record." He thus cannot tell whether a given instance of possible telepathic communication about his wife's condition is genuinely a case of telepathy, or is really just a conjecture on his part. Smith will not, in short, have any way of distinguishing a telepathic "confirmation" of his belief (that his wife is still alive) from a thought of his own.

I think, therefore, that if Smith, or any other spirit, is able to obtain knowledge through ESP of any facts "outside his mind," it must be through powers of ESP unlike any that embodied persons are known to have. It is perhaps not logically impossible that discarnates might have such powers, but it is, I think, rather pointless to speculate as to what they might be like, though I would think that they would have to be as numerous and as diverse as are our own physical senses, if they are to serve spirits in the ways that our sensory powers serve us.

Communication to Others

Difficulties too will be encountered by a spirit in attempting to communicate his thoughts by ESP *to* others, whether or not they are embodied. If the others are *disembodied*, they will be as unable as the disembodied Smith was to distinguish a telepathic transmission to them from their own thoughts. If the others are *embodied*, i.e. still living, transmission to them will suffer from a similar problem:

Suppose, for instance, that the Smith-spirit attempts to transmit a telepathic message to his still-living wife. If Mrs. Smith thinks that she has received a telepathic communication from Smith-the-spirit, she could not really know whether the "message" was a genuine telepathic communication or a thought generated purely by her own mind. For what further information might there be that could serve to establish what the origin of the "message" really was? Subsequent "messages" from Smith could not enlighten Mrs. Smith as to the origin of the first "message," for their origin would be as uncertain as that of the first.

If, however, the "message" from her husband came to her through the spoken or written words of a medium, then there would be no difficulty in distinguishing it from her own thoughts. But can the disembodied Smith appropriate, through some nonphysical means, a medium's speech organs and use them to talk to Mrs. Smith? Elsewhere, I shall treat communication through mediums and shall only say here that the difficulty, if not impossibility, of a disembodied Smith, who sees, hears, tastes, touches, and feels nothing, taking charge through nonphysical causation of the speech organs of a medium are obvious. How would the disembodied Smith recognize whether or not he had been successful in his efforts at appropriating the speech apparatus of the medium? Certainly such an appropriation would be entirely unlike anything he (or you or I) had done in this life.

Nevertheless, it is not logically impossible or conceptually absurd that the surviving discarnate Smith might take control of some living person's speech organs and use them to communicate his identity and thoughts to the living. If he could do this, then he could certainly also take control of the person's eyes and ears and other sensory organs as well, and so could gain full contact with the world outside his mind.

Furthermore, if Smith could in this way communicate his existence and identity to Mrs. Smith, then in theory he could also communicate his existence and identity to another spirit who had in a similar way appropriated the sensory apparatus of some other living person, and who could thus see, hear, and respond to the body controlled by Smith.

Conclusion

I have stressed that continuation of self-awareness is essential to the disembodied survival of the identical person or self as lived before death. If what survives my death does not possess the capabilities that are essential to comprehension of self as distinct from other beings and things, then what survives is not I.

On the other hand, if after my death a spirit should possess these capabilities, then, if that spirit truly remembered having had any of my experiences, it would be I.

Spirits by definition would not have the sensory powers of the bodies they leave, and thus would require extrasensory means of distinguishing themselves and their mental states from external reality, of disproving or confirming their beliefs about external reality, and of communicating with other conscious beings.

Spirits would lack not only the sensory but all physical powers of the body, and, therefore, would be unable to do most of the other things embodied persons can do. However, the capacity to do these other things is not, in my view, required for existence as a person or self, though it may well be required for better than "vegetable" existence.

The experimental evidence as to the existence and nature of ESP indicates that beliefs founded on clairvoyance cannot be confirmed or disconfirmed except through use of the normal senses and that telepathic messages from other beings cannot be known to be such without follow-through sensory information.

I therefore conclude, on the basis of this chapter and Chapter 6, that personal survival without the body is not necessarily like "chess without the king." One could, theoretically, survive the death of his body as a spirit, provided that two conditions are met.

First, spirits must be reidentifiable (if they were not, then it would be unintelligible to talk about them). In Chapter 6 it was seen that to be reidentifiable, spirits must either have infallible memory or, if their memory is fallible, then it must be determinable, in spite of the fact that spirits lack spatial occupancy, whether or not a later spirit had an earlier spirit's experiences.

Secondly, spirits must have a nonphysical capability of "perceiving" the world beyond their thoughts and of communicating with other things. The capability must either be through some form of ESP unlike that reported to be possessed by living persons, or through a supernatural utilization of the body of a living person. Obviously, being able so to utilize a living person's body would come very close to being *not* disembodied at all.

CHAPTER 8

REFUTATIONS OF REINCARNATION

> ... *if the nature of the soul is immortal and makes its way into our body at the time of birth, why are we unable to remember besides the time already gone, and why do we retain no traces of past actions? If the power of the mind has been so completely changed, that all remembrance of past things is lost, that, methinks, differs not widely from death; therefore you must admit that the soul which was before has perished and that which now is has now been formed.*
> —*Lucretius*, **de Rerum Natura**[1]

Personal survival through reincarnation, i.e. through rebirth of oneself in a different body, has been said to be impossible for an assortment of reasons.

Does Reincarnation Involve Disembodiment?

It is sometimes said that to be reincarnated a person must exist in a discarnate state while between his lives in different bodies and that therefore the theory of reincarnation is liable to refutation through disproof of discarnate survival. However, as I have indicated, in my opinion, discarnate survival is not itself subject to conclusive disproof.

Further, there are versions of reincarnation theory that are predicated on the assumption that the person may be transferred from one body to another without disembodiment. For example, according to the religion of the Tibetan Lamas, when the Dalai Lama dies, his spirit is immediately reincarnated as a newborn

[1] H. A. J. Munro (trans). Cambridge. Deighton Bell. 1886. Book III, lines 670–678.

infant, without existing for any time in a discarnate state.

The view that reincarnation presupposes disembodiment stems, perhaps, from an unnecessary assumption that the "self," to terminate existence in one body and begin it anew in a later body, must travel through space from the first body to the second. Since travel takes time, the self must exist discarnate while in transit.

There is no necessity to liken reincarnation in this way to a missile speeding from silo to target. A more appropriate analogy may be that of two television sets, one of which is turned off simultaneously with a second's being turned on. If the television sets are tuned to the same station, then, the same program will disappear from the first set at the same moment that it appears on the second. For all that we can imagine to the contrary, the self, like the program, may appear in a second body simultaneously with its disappearance from a first.[2]

Fluctuations in Population

It is sometimes said reincarnation cannot satisfactorily explain changes in the world's population, for, should the population increase, then some future persons would not be reincarnations of presently living individuals; should it decrease, then some presently living individuals would fail to be reincarnated.

One proffered explanation of these population changes is that persons need not be reincarnated as human beings. Should the human population decrease, then some persons would be reincarnated in the bodies of other creatures, frogs and birds perhaps; and should the human population increase, then some persons formerly dwelling in the bodies of other creatures would be reincarnated as humans.

Another suggested explanation is that there is a "reservoir" of human spirits: upon the death of a human body, each human

---

[2]Though the analogy between the self and the program is not altogether perfect. A television program is what philosophers call a "universal," and a self a "particular": the same program can be carried simultaneously on a million different sets, but a given self cannot simultaneously exist in a million different bodies. Further, one can speak of the moment at which a television set is turned on. It is not clear that one can speak of *the* moment at which a body is "turned on," i.e. the moment at which a self or person commences inhabitation of a body. Still, we know that there is an end and a beginning of bodily existence even if we don't know or cannot agree just when.

spirit enters the spirit realm to await his turn to be reinstalled in a human body. Should the number of human bodies continue to increase, then the spirit reservoir would diminish until the trend in the population reversed itself. Should the world's population through atomic war be reduced by billions, there would be billions of spirits in the spirit realm who would have to wait for centuries after the catastrophe for reinstallation. (And perhaps even then they would have to settle for installation in idiots and monsters who resulted from the atomic pollution of the human germ plasm.)

Yet another proffered explanation is simply that if the human population decreases, some human spirits will cease to exist. If, on the other hand, the human population increases, then some new human spirits would have come into existence.

The trouble with these explanations and others like them is that they only force the reincarnation theorist to make further explanations of, for example: why some human spirits are reincarnated and others are not; why some persons are reincarnated as human beings and others as lesser creatures; why some humans are reincarnated as another species such as frogs, and other humans as a different species such as birds. In order to provide these further explanations, many versions of reincarnation incorporate complicated metaphysical, theological, and ethical theories about the purposes of human existence, divine objectives, the nature of virtuous behavior, and so forth. Unfortunately, the more complicated a theory of reincarnation becomes, the more it strains the available empirical evidence to support the whole theory.

Nonetheless, it is one thing to say that a fully developed theory of reincarnation accounting for population changes would have to be very complicated and quite another to say that a complicated theory could not be true. So while changes in the world's population constitute a theoretical difficulty for the reincarnationist, this difficulty does not absolutely require one to abandon belief in reincarnation.

Heredity and Environment

Is a person totally the result of his heredity and environment? If my *physical* being is completely determined by my genetic heritage and my *psychological* being is entirely the result of the interaction of my physical being with my environment, then the speculation that I am a reincarnation of some formerly existing person or will become reincarnated in some future human body is meaningless.

In reality, the contention that a person is completely the result of heredity and environment exceeds the warrant of the current physiological and psychological evidence.[3] Though many of one's psychological characteristics no doubt result from an interplay of various biological and environmental factors, it is an extrapolation from available scientific evidence to presume that all of them do. That is to say, current evidence does not absolutely preclude the possibility that some psychological traits and propensities, perhaps those that define the essential "self," have been brought from a previous life, and may in turn be carried on to future existence.

Reincarnation and Memory

The most cogent of proffered disproofs of reincarnation is predicated on our lack of memory of previous lives. Since I do not remember having been some person who lived previously, it is said by some to be false to suppose that I am. It is said to be false because memory is deemed necessary to personal identity: Mr. A, who lives at one time, can be the same person as Mr. B, who lives at a later time, only if Mr. B remembers having had some of Mr. A's experiences, or if he could so remember except for old age, illness or injury.[4] If Miss Brown is not able to remember having any of Mr. Peter's experiences, and if the incapability is not due to accident, illness, or old age, then nothing would serve to connect Brown with Peters. She could not be the reincarnation of Peters, and a report about Mr. Peters' demise and a report about Miss

---

[3] As Ducasse has pointed out. *A Critical Examination of the Belief in a Life After Death.* Springfield, Thomas, 1974, pp. 229-231.

[4] A more precise formulation of the principle that memory is necessary to personal identity, but one which would complicate the text, is this: A, who lives at one time, is the same person as B, who lives at a later time, only if some of B's conscious states are of type R, where a type-R conscious state is one that contains or could contain either a memory of one of A's experiences or a memory of an earlier conscious state of type R.

When I say in the text that a given person, B, must be able to remember some of the experiences of an earlier person A, I should be understood as meaning that some of B's conscious states are of type R, as defined here.

Brown's later birth would be reports about two different individuals.

Of course, the Deity may use the minerals that compose my body (or the spiritual substance which composes my soul, if I have a nonmaterial soul) over and over again in different persons if He chooses to be economical with these commodities. He may reuse them without my knowledge and without awareness by any future person in whom my constituents recur that these constituents were once mine, but I cannot regard it as the survival of *me* if my material (or nonmaterial) components were to be recycled into another, unless that person in whom my elements came to exist were able to remember some of my experiences. Similarly, should the elements, whether chemical or "spiritual," of some past person by chance or by design of God happen to be those that constitute me, then this, in my opinion, would not make me that person unless I were able to remember some of his experiences.[5]

So, reincarnation viewed as personal survival, of survival of self, in my opinion presupposes that the later incarnation is able to recall some of the experiences of the earlier person, unless the lack of recall is due to illness, injury, or old age. From this it might *seem* to follow, since I have no memory of prior lives in different bodies, that I have not had any such prior lives.

Ducasse, however, takes note of the distinction between lacking memory in the present and having it in the future. So he suggests that, even though I do not presently have any memories of experiences from a "prior life," it is possible that I might at some later date have them.[6] And if, indeed, I did in the future come to have memories of the experiences had by some earlier person, then wouldn't this mean that I was that person? Hasn't Ducasse thus shown that my present lack of memory of previous lives is not a

---

[5]Further, if by "reincarnation" is meant any process by which one's physical (or nonphysical) components reappear in some future person without the latter's being able to recall any of one's life or experiences, then I would regard the question of whether or not I shall be reincarnated as completely unimportant.

[6]The later date might be either in this life or in a future life: A lives and dies. Thereafter B lives and dies, and thereafter C lives and dies. B remembers none of A's experiences. C remembers B's experiences *and* A's. So A, B, and C are the same self. Ducasse, *op. cit.*, p. 225.

logical refutation of the possibility of my having lived before?

I think that Ducasse is right, but there is one difficulty in his counter to the "memory refutation" of reincarnation that must be considered:

People do have fantasies that they were someone in the past, usually Napoleon or Christ or Washington, etc. Thus, if some day I should come to "remember" being Napoleon and to have received my military commission in the artillery in 1785, to have defeated the Austrians at Marengo in 1800, and so forth, how might my "memories" be shown not to be delusions?

Without doubt inability on my part to relate sufficient accurate information about Napoleon would tend to discredit my claim to have been Napoleon and would support those who questioned my sanity and regarded my "memories" as dreams. No doubt too many would remain unconvinced that I was Napoleon even if I could provide highly detailed and accurate reports about Napoleon and his circumstances, but there are still others who would say that it is impossible, even in principle, that my "memories" could be non-fantasies. They would define that which alone could serve to distinguish a genuine memory from a particularly well-developed and highly accurate fantasy as the presence of the "rememberer's" body in the circumstances surrounding the "remembered" experiences, and from this definition it would necessarily follow that I could never truly remember Napoleon's experiences or thus be Napoleon's reincarnation.

However, as noted in my earlier treatment of discarnate survival, if B's "memories" of A's experiences are in fact *caused* by A's experiences, then this entails that B's memory of having had A's experiences is genuine. So, only if my physical presence in Napoleon's circumstances is necessary to establish a causal relationship between Napoleon's experiences and my apparent memories of them, is Ducasse incorrect in thinking that I could someday come to remember Napoleon's experiences.

Is physical placement necessary to establishing a causative connection between A's experiences and B's memories of those experiences? It is possible that this is so, but until it has been proven, I conclude that my present lack of memories of lives in vanished bodies does not necessarily preclude my having had such lives.

CHAPTER 9

RESURRECTION AND IDENTITY

And if time should gather up our matter after our death and put it once more into the position in which it now is, and the light of life be given to us again, this result even would concern us not at all, when the chain of our self-consciousness has once been snapped asunder.
— Lucretius, de Rerum Natura[1]

... if a statue is remade from the same brass, it will not be the same identically. Therefore much less will it be identically the same man if he be reformed from the same ashes.
— St. Thomas Aquinas, Summa Theologica[2]

The theory of survival in a *different* body, i.e. survival through reincarnation, does not seem to suffer from fatal theoretical defect, as I explained in Chapter 8. Is the case otherwise with the theory of survival in the same body, i.e. survival through *resurrection?*

The Problem of Identity

The apparent lack of identity between the resurrected body and the body before death is the main philosophical difficulty confronted by the theory of resurrection. The problem can be illustrated through analogy:

If a child builds a "man" out of pipe cleaners, disassembles it, and then a month later puts the pieces together again just as he did before, has he assembled the selfsame "man"? Many would say that he has not. They would say that he has assembled a second pipe-cleaner "man," one that is just like the first, but which,

---

[1] H. A. J. Munro (trans). Cambridge, Deighton Bell, 1886, Book III, lines 850–855.

[2] Translated by the Fathers of the English Dominican Province. London, Burns, Oates, and Washbourne, 1912, Part III (Supplement), Question LXXIX, Answer II, Objection IV.

though made of the same constituents as the first, is not the very same "man."

The difficulty in the theory of resurrection is that saying that very same human body can or will arise from the dead is like saying that the very same pipe cleaner "man" can be recreated by the child. In the words of St. Thomas Aquinas, "... It will not be identically the same man that shall rise again ... After the change wrought by death the selfsame man cannot be repeated."[3]

Resurrection and Replication

Does resurrection really require, however, that the selfsame *body* be repeated? John Hick, for one, thinks not. What the theory of resurrection requires, Mr. Hick in effect says, is that the *person* be resurrected, and this can be accomplished, he thinks, through a mere *replication* of the person's body, as opposed to a resurrection of it.[4]

For me to be resurrected, Hick says, it is not necessary that the identical physical organism that I now have be reconstituted after my death, but only that after my death all the properties my body has be possessed by another body. While the physical constituents of this second body will not have belonged to the body I now have, the fingerprints, stomach contents, neuron structures, brain cross-connections, and all the other properties of the second body will be exactly similar to what mine are. As the arrangement of the physical constituents of the replica-body will be exactly similar to the arrangement of the constituents of my own body, the replica-person will have all of my memories, Hick thinks.

The oneness of this replica-body with my earthly body will thus supposedly lie not in the fact that both bodies are made out of the very same atoms, which they are not, but rather in the fact that both will exemplify the same "code," to use Hick's term.

However, Hick's theory is really not a theory of resurrection at all but in truth a theory of reincarnation. The only difference between it and the more conventional theories of reincarnation is

---

[3]*Ibid.*, Objection I.

[4]Hick understands St. Paul as possibly conceiving of resurrection as involving replication of the body (though he thinks that the nature of Paul's conception of resurrection is a difficult exegetical question). See *Death and Eternal Life*. New York, Harper and Row, 1976, pp. 278–279.

that, whereas according to the conventional theories Julius Caesar may "come back" in the body of, say, Abraham Lincoln, according to the Hick theory, Julius Caesar may come back in a body exactly similar to his own.

Further, Mr. Hick's theory is, I think, questionable. If one replica of my body could be created, then so could two. In fact, two replicas could be created at the same time and exist simultaneously. If one replica counts as being I, then so do two, but it is logically impossible that two simultaneously existing things could both be one and the same I: two is not one. It therefore follows that even one replica does not count as being I.[5]

So the identity of the former body with the resurrected body must be found otherwise than in the bodies' having a like "code." A resurrectionist cannot maintain that the resurrected body and the body that dies may be numerically different, no matter how alike he envisions them as being. By definition, to resurrect is to bring back to life. One body is not brought back to life by creating a new body. I do not bring my car back to life by buying or building a new car, even if the new car has exactly the same characteristics as my old one.

Resurrection and the Soul

The living body dies and decays back into dust. If its physical elements should later come together, would there then be the same body again? Or would there then be a second body constituted of the same elements as the first, just as there was a second pipe-cleaner "man"?

According to the customary view of resurrection, the resurrected body and the body that after death decays into dust are one, and what gives them oneness is that they both belong to the same person. The "person" is thought to be composed of soul as well as body, and the body is but a part of the person. When the body dies,

---

[5]Mr. Hick is aware of this objection to his theory, and attempts to rebut it. *Ibid.*, pp. 290 ff. (Oddly enough, he raises a very similar objection himself to certain versions of reincarnation. *Ibid.*, p. 364.) The objection is, I think, absolutely irrefutable. For something to be I, its experiences must have been mine. Two simultaneously existing replicas (which Hick concedes could exist) cannot both be I (as Hick also concedes). Therefore, it is true of neither replica that its experiences must have been mine, hence neither replica is I.

the soul persists in a disembodied state until such time as the body is resurrected and restored to it. So, the body that is alive now and the body that is alive after this body dies thus are one and the same in virtue of belonging to one and the same person; this person who is alive now and the person who is alive later are one and the same in virtue of having the selfsame soul.[6]

Thus, according to the customary view of resurrection, just as a person's kidney might cease to function and then later be revived without thereby ceasing to be the selfsame kidney, so might a person's body cease functioning and then later be resurrected without ceasing to be the selfsame body.

However, must the resurrectionist postulate a continuously existing noncorporeal soul to preserve the oneness of the postmortem and premortem bodies? If he must, then his theory is subject to any difficulties that confront the theory of discarnate survival: this must be of concern to resurrectionists unconvinced by my earlier conclusion that discarnate personal existence is theoretically possible.

However, I do not think that it is necessary to postulate a disembodied soul to secure the identity of the resurrected body with the former body. The mechanic who takes apart his ratchet wrench in the evening has not, when he assembles the parts in the morning, assembled a new wrench. London Bridge, when moved in pieces to Arizona and then reassembled, remains London Bridge, and does so without a "soul," discarnate or otherwise. Why, therefore, should a soul be necessary to preserve the identity of a human body the constituents of which are separated by death and decay and are then gathered up and reassembled by God?

I suggested above that a child who disassembles a pipe-cleaner "man" and then later reassembles the very same pieces might be thought not to have assembled literally the same "man," but instead to have created a new "man" exactly similar to the first. The case of the pipe-cleaner man is inconclusive. We can just as easily imagine the child taking the "man" apart each night, laying

---

[6]In the words of St. Thomas: "The necessity of holding the resurrection arises from this.—that man may obtain the last end for which he was made ... And since it behooves the end to be obtained by the selfsame thing that was made for that end ... it is necessary for the selfsame man to rise again; and this is effected by the selfsame soul being united to the selfsame body." Aquinas, *op. cit.*, Objection IV.

the pieces neatly in a box where they will be out of the way, putting them together the next day, and regarding himself, correctly, as having each time reassembled the selfsame "man." If the child regards Wednesday's "man" as the selfsame man as Thursday's, we would not say that he is incorrect or illogical, but then neither would we say that he is incorrect or illogical if he chooses to regard Thursday's creation as a new and different "man." The case of the pipe-cleaner "man" thus cannot settle whether the reassembly of a thing's parts amounts to a reinstatement of the same thing or to creation of a second thing.

In contrast to using pipe-cleaner "men" or other things analogously, imagine that the technological marvels of the thirtieth century include a device that encodes the structure and arrangement of matter in a human being or other living thing, disassembles the same matter (for ease of transportation, perhaps), and then reassembles the very same matter just as it was before.

If Mr. Smith steps into the machine, will it also be Mr. Smith who steps out of it at the other end of the process? Certainly $Smith_2$, who emerges from the "resurrector," will look, think, and act exactly like $Smith_1$, who earlier stepped into it. $Smith_2$ will think himself to be $Smith_1$, and everyone else will agree. He will remember $Smith_1$'s experiences, including that of having stepped into the resurrector. His atoms and molecules and the precise arrangement of them will be exactly the same as $Smith_1$'s.

To insist, under these circumstances, that $Smith_2$ is really not $Smith_1$ but a perfect copy is, I think, to cleave dogmatically and implausibly to the impossibility of resurrection. $Smith_2$ would not be a copy of $Smith_1$ for the decisive reason that the very same bits of matter which composed $Smith_1$'s body would also constitute $Smith_2$'s body; the oneness of $body_1$ and $body_2$ would be established by the oneness of the physical matter composing each.[7]

So resurrection without disembodiment is conceivable, and thus the theory of resurrection is not liable to disproof through any refutations of disembodied survival that I may have overlooked.

---

[7] Further. the oneness of $body_1$ and $body_2$ would suffice to establish $Smith_2$'s memories of $Smith_1$'s experiences as genuine. and to distinguish these genuine memories from the mere "apparent" memories of a Smith-replica.

CHAPTER 10

THE DESCRIPTION OF ASTRAL BODIES

The resurrectionist, as has been seen, must explain how the selfsame body can be brought back after it has died. The exponent of the theory of survival in an astral body, by contrast, does not maintain that the astral body ever dies. Consequently he does not have to account for the continuing identity of the astral body in the face of discontinuities in the life or functioning of the astral body. So he need not, and ordinarily does not, postulate the existence of a soul, disembodied or otherwise.

Nevertheless, the theory of astral survival is sometimes regarded as logically incoherent.

As I noted in Chapter 5, the categories "material (physical) thing" and "nonmaterial (spiritual) thing" are by traditional definition mutually exclusive and jointly exhaustive of all things. A thing is either material or nonmaterial: there is no other possibility.

Astral bodies, though, reportedly occupy space (though apparently not necessarily to the exclusion of other space-occupying objects). Whenever anyone says that he has seen an astral body, he always claims to have seen it at some place or other. This means that astral bodies are, by definition, material.

On the other hand, astral bodies evidently do not behave the way other material things behave. For instance, they are reported to pass through solid objects and to move from one position to another instantaneously, and are sufficiently ethereal to have escaped detection by physicists and indeed by the vast majority of mankind. Their behavior and characteristics thus suggest that astral bodies are nonmaterial.

On the basis of these considerations it is sometimes reasoned that descriptions of astral bodies are perforce unintelligible, that the idea of an astral body is the self-contradictory idea of a thing that is at the same time material and nonmaterial.

However, I do not think that this reasoning is sound. If an

astral body were both a material and nonmaterial thing then the idea of an astral body would be unintelligible, but there is nothing logically incoherent in conceiving of an astral body as occupying space and hence as a physical or material thing that behaves in ways very unlike other material things and possesses extraordinarily subtle and ethereal characteristics.

Thus the theory of astral survival, as well as the theories of disembodied survival, reincarnation, and resurrection, are none of them absolutely precluded by any purely philosophical or logical considerations with which I am familiar. Personal survival after bodily death as envisaged by all of these theories thus remains logically possible.

In closing Part II, I might comment briefly as to why I have limited my attention to possible philosophical *refutations* of personal survival. Are there not philosophical "proofs" of the actuality of survival?

The answer is that it is not self-contradictory to suppose that the person might *not* survive the death of this body (i.e. personal survival is not a logical necessity); and from this it immediately follows that it cannot be *a priori* demonstrated that a person will so survive.

That a person might not be reincarnated or resurrected or survive his physical death as an astral body is clear without argument. Those who, like Descartes, believe that the person is an incorporeal or nonphysical soul, must also concede that it is possible for a person to fail to survive the death of his body. As Descartes himself explains, "the immortality of the soul does not follow from its distinctness from the body, because that does not prevent its being said that God in creating it has given the soul a nature such that its period of existence must terminate simultaneously with that of the corporeal life."[1]

Afterdeath personal survival is thus neither *a priori* impossible nor *a priori* certain. Whether it is likely can only be ascertained through examination of such evidence as bears on the matter.

This examination is undertaken in Parts III and IV.

---

[1] E. S. Haldane and G. R. T. Ross: *The Philosophical Works of Descartes.* Cambridge, The Cambridge University Press, 1967, p. 47.

PART III
THE EARLY EVIDENCE

CHAPTER 11

RELIGIOUS "EVIDENCE"

My primary concern in the remainder of this book is with the empirical data that have frequently been cited as evidence of life after death. I have divided these data as coming from two periods, an "early" period, which extends from the last part of the nineteenth century to about 1961; and a "late" period, which includes evidence gathered since 1961. However, before examining these data, I think that I should comment on religion as a possible source of evidence of survival.

For millions of people, the expectation of life after death is based on faith. They have faith that they will live after death because they have faith that God has so ordained. To these millions, rational deliberation and extensive empirical evidence in the matter are unnecessary. The question arises, however, whether or not religion offers anything that could be viewed as evidence of survival to those who do not or cannot believe in survival on faith alone or by those who can predicate that faith only on rational considerations. Does Catholicism, for example, offer any evidence of afterdeath survival?

In traditional Catholic theology,[1] the belief in personal survival is frequently said to be grounded both on purported historical fact and revealed truth. Interestingly enough, the traditional Catholic doctrine of survival after bodily death, the doctrine which in the traditional Catholic view is "the very keystone of Christianity," is a doctrine that is not that of most contemporary Protestants and even some Roman Catholics, who follow instead the doctrine of the immortality of the disembodied soul. What traditional Catholicism promises is that "there will be a resurrection, that it will be for all men, and that all men will arise in the same bodies they now have."[2]

---

[1] A principal source of my information in this chapter is H. M. McElwain: Resurrection of the dead. *New Catholic Encyclopedia*. New York, McGraw Hill & Co., 1967, Vol. XII, pp. 419–427.
[2] *Ibid.*, p. 425.

The purported fact that stands in support of the traditional doctrine is Jesus' resurrection. Now, some commentators have criticized a belief in universal resurrection that is based on this purported fact on the grounds that Jesus was supposedly divine and thus had "special protection" against permanent death. To count Jesus' resurrection as evidence that we too shall be resurrected would therefore be, according to the criticism, analogous to arguing that because Mr. Smith, who falls out of an airplane and has a parachute, lives through the fall, another person who falls out of the same airplane but has no parachute will fare just as well.[3]

However, from a Catholic point of view the criticism is misguided, for, according to the Catholic doctrine, Jesus promised *us* survival: we thus in effect all share Jesus' divine parachute. If Jesus is the son of God, then his promise would certainly support the Catholic's belief.

Nonetheless, the crucial premises that we all share in the special divine protection of Jesus and that Jesus is the son of God are obviously not simple matters of history analogous to Columbus discovering America in 1492 or Octavius having become the adopted son of Julius Caesar. More importantly, it is by no means certain that Jesus' resurrection itself is a matter of historical fact. As Professor of Religious Studies John Bash says, the purely historical data that bear on the question of the historicity of Jesus' resurrection are so sparse that they would hardly support one doctoral research project. In fact, the principal evidence bearing on the question is the Gospels, and the historical authoritativeness of these documents is open to some question, in part because they were written "by believers for believers."[4] This fact about the authorship of these documents limits their value as historical sources because if one does not have any independent, impartial corroboration of the testimony of the "believers," one cannot rule out the possibility that such sources contain merely uncreditable hearsay information.[5]

---

[3]The airplane analogy is Ducasse's. See: *The Belief in a Life After Death*. Springfield, Thomas, 1974, p. 19.

[4]D. Geels, The resurrection of Christ. *New Catholic Encyclopedia*. New York, McGraw Hill & Co., 1967, Vol. XII, p. 402.

[5]Perhaps evidence bearing on the actuality of Jesus' alleged resurrection that does not come from the Gospels will eventually emerge: the "Turin Shroud," a linen sheet that reputedly contained the body of Christ after his crucifixion and that has been the property of

However, the Church has "in many official pronouncements" made it clear that resurrection is a truth revealed by God.[6] Now if one believes that such pronouncements are the revealed word of God, then one would regard them as sufficient proof in themselves of the reality of survival, and further evidence of its reality would have to be viewed as superfluous. But if one does not know whether or not these pronouncements are the revealed word of God, then clearly one cannot know on their basis whether or not there is survival, and therefore could not logically regard them as providing good or proper reasons for believing in survival.

Remarks similar in substance to these on traditional Catholicism could obviously be made in connection with the purported revelations of any religion. Thus, the question asked at the beginning of this chapter, namely, are there any data provided by a religion that could reasonably be regarded as evidence of survival by those who do not share the faith of the followers of that religion, seems to have this as its general answer. On the one hand, statements of alleged revealed truth can carry no weight with those who do not share the faith. It is of course open to the faithful to contend that others *should* share the faith, but this contention would oblige the faithful to explain *why*, and until such explanation is forthcoming the nonbelievers are justified in withholding belief. On the other hand, alleged specific instances of survival cited by the religion, if any, should be judged solely on their merits, i.e. amount and detail of supporting factual data, credibility of eyewitnesses, etc. The fact that millions may believe that such alleged instances actually occurred cannot logically be regarded as contributing to the likelihood of their occurrence.

---

the Dukes of Savoy since 1453, reportedly bears the negative image of a man who appears to have been crucified, whipped, crowned with thorns, and stabbed in the chest. In the fall of 1978 a thirty-member scientific team headed by Donald Lynn, a Jet Propulsion Laboratory scientist, investigated the shroud. Lynn, an image-processing scientist, believes that the anatomically correct and "truly astounding" image on the sheet could not be created even with presently existing scientific techniques. In fact, according to Lynn, scientists wouldn't now even know *how* to create such an image (UPI News story, August 29, 1978). If the investigation of the shroud supports Lynn, and the shroud truly dates from the time of Jesus (which fact might some day be established by sophisticated scientific dating techniques), then this would tend to support the thesis that *something* unusual, if not miraculous, had transpired at the time of Christ's crucifixion.

[6]McElwain, *op. cit.*, p. 425.

CHAPTER 12

THE ULTIMATE MEDIUMS

Saul put on different clothes and went in disguise with two of his men. He came to the woman by night and said, "Tell me my fortune by consulting the dead, and call up the man I name to you."
—*I Sam. 28:8*

Hauntings, possessions, and other manifestations of "the dead" were reported in great number to the Society for Psychical Research during the last half of the nineteenth and the first part of the twentieth centuries. Those familiar with these numerous reports may be surprised to be told that there is less evidence of survival from this period than since. Yet this is the case. The reports of these unexpected or "spontaneous" manifestations of the dead are based on observations that for the most part were made under conditions that lacked experimental safeguards and that accommodated and encouraged trickery, wishful thinking, exaggeration, inaccurate recording, and errors in perception. As D. J. West, a Research Officer of the Society for Psychical Research, said about the numerous spontaneous cases on record with the Society, "In the light of all the possible objections, and the obvious flaws in testimony of this kind, most of the cases seem worse than mediocre. The best known ... seem dubious on close inspection."[1]

Nor is anything proved by the sheer number of these cases. As someone has said, if one bucket fails because of its design to hold water, ten buckets of the same design likewise will fail to hold water. Even if some alleged sightings of ghosts did really involve genuine ghosts, the mere multiplicity of reported sightings, without regard to mistakes, lies, conditions of observation, and alternative explanations of what was really seen, proves nothing.

---

[1] D. J. West: The investigation of spontaneous cases. *Proceedings of the Society for Psychical Research, 48:* 290, 1948.

A small number of cases, which involved apparent communications from the dead to the living through mediums, should not be dismissed out of hand. Because the cases were closely investigated and held in high regard by certain survival researchers whose views must be respected, they have been narrated in the survivalist literature as often as the settling of Jamestown has been related in the histories of the United States.

Mrs. Piper

The Bostonian, Mrs. Leonore Piper, was perhaps the most carefully studied of all mediums. Those who investigated and reported on her—for over thirty years around the turn of the century—included many notable people: William James, the famous philosopher and psychologist; Dr. Richard Hodgson, the Secretary of the American Society for Psychical Research and a critical psychical researcher who had, among other things, exposed the infamous Madame Blavatsky; Sir Oliver Lodge, President of the Physical Society of London and of the British Association for the Advancement of Science; Professor Romaine Newbold, Professor of Philosophy at the University of Pennsylvania; James Hyslop, Professor of Logic and Ethics at Columbia; Henry Sidgwick, Knightbridge Professor of Moral Philosophy at Cambridge; and others of like repute.

It is customary to attach a great deal of importance in cases like Mrs. Piper's to the fact that the investigators had been persons with "substantial professional reputations," endowed with "keen" or "critical" or "scientific" minds, or the like. It is abundantly clear that neither the integrity nor the competency as observers of such persons as those I have listed would be questioned if their testimony was cited relative to normal matters, even if those matters required great precision of observation.

Nevertheless, critics of mediumistic evidence will say, with some justification, that flawless credentials do not insure unimpeachable observations in regard to the study of mediums. It is not merely that controls in mediumistic cases are typically quite loose. One's observations are affected by his desires and expectations. The desire to find evidence of life after death is deep in many of us and is not necessarily diminished by education, intelligence, experience, or age. Indeed, often it grows with age and nearness to death. It very well might affect the observations even of the astute, the discerning, the impartial, the honest, and of those well known.[2]

In any case, in all the time that Mrs. Piper was under observation, including a period during which she was observed by private detectives hired by Doctor Hodgson, "not one suspicious circumstance was noticed," as William James remarked; not one incident was observed that might have suggested trickery or dishonesty of any sort on her part.

Over the years while so carefully observed, Mrs. Piper communicated[3] to scores of sitters detached and specific information purportedly from dead relatives of the sitters, information that was thought by many to be too trivial or confidential to have become a matter of public knowledge or to have been known to Mrs. Piper in any way other than through communication with the spirits of the dead or through some remarkable form of ESP.

The most impressive of the communications came from a "George Pelham," who purported to be the spirit of one George Pellew, a young friend of Doctor Hodgson who had died a few weeks before the appearance of the "Pelham" communicator. Mrs. Piper is reported to have met Pellew on one occasion only and was supposedly not aware of this fact until much later. In any case, over a six year period "George Pelham" communicated much confidential yet accurate information about Pellew and is reported over the years to have recognized, out of 150 sitters unknown to Mrs. Piper, thirty of Pellew's past acquaintances. Moreover, "Pelham" never "recognized" someone Pellew had not known. The "Pelham" communications were indeed impressive enough to convert to spiritualism Doctor Hodgson, who had previously been a hardened skeptic.

What impressed many observers of Mrs. Piper was not merely

---

[2]Some professional magicians maintain that very intelligent people, especially scientists, are the easiest to deceive. See: *The Amazing Randi: The Magic of Uri Geller.* New York, Ballantine, 1975, pp. 30, 91–92. Too, the person who must protect a reputation for intelligence, integrity, clear-sightedness, and critical acumen may conceivably be less likely than anyone else to admit to himself or to others to having been fooled by a simple trick.

[3]Hereafter, when in regard to mediums I speak of "communications," or say that such-and-such was "communicated" and the like, I am referring only to what the medium reportedly said while in trance, and do not mean to imply that what was said necessarily was communicated by a spirit.

the recondite information that she produced about a particular deceased person, information which some said "could not have been learned even by a skilled detective,"[4] but also the accurate dramatic portrayal she gave when in trance of the entire personality of the deceased individual. At times this dramatic impersonation was so flawless that the astonished sitter apparently could not help but believe that he was in contact with the deceased person himself.

Thus, for example, Richard Hodgson said of the "George Pelham" communicator:

> The continual manifestation of this personality ... with its own reservoir of memories, with its swift appreciation of any reference to friends of George Pelham, with its "give-and-take" in little incidental conversations with myself, has helped largely in producing a conviction of the actual presence of the George Pelham personality which it would be quite impossible to impart by any mere enumeration of verifiable statements.[5]

Some commentators indeed tend to attach as much or more significance to Mrs. Piper's ability to reproduce details of a particular person's past life in the tone and with the mannerisms and distinctive associations of the former person than to the details themselves. This tendency is apparent, I think, in the evaluation of the Piper material by Ducasse.[6]

Mrs. Leonard

Mrs. Leonard, the British medium equivalent to Mrs. Piper in notoriety and impressiveness of accomplishments, also produced within the trance state startling dramatic representations of deceased persons. Though for the most part the communications from the dead to Mrs. Leonard's sitters were through a "Feda," Mrs. Leonard's "control,"[7] sometimes a communicating spirit would purportedly

---

[4] Ducasse: *The Belief in a Life After Death.* Springfield, Il. Thomas, 1974. p. 179.

[5] R. Hodgson: A further record of observations of certain phenomena of trance. *Proceedings of the Society for Psychical Research, 13:* 295, 1897–1898. Reprinted by permission of the Society for Psychical Research.

[6] Ducasse, *op. cit.,* pp. 176 ff.

[7] There are said to be two kinds of communicating spirits, "controls" and "communicators." A control is a supposed departed spirit who controls the body of the medium to exchange information with the living. Most mediums have only one or two controls. Communicators are those purported spirits whose messages to the living are usually relayed by the control.

take charge of Mrs. Leonard's speech organs and talk directly to the sitters, typically in the voice of the deceased.

The broad range of voices that could issue from Mrs. Leonard's mouth was most impressive. In one instance often mentioned, for example, the voice of an elderly Scotsman who had had bronchial asthma was produced, complete with gasping, coughing, and wheezing. That a disembodied spirit of a person afflicted in life would force the healthy body of Mrs. Leonard to cough and wheeze is puzzling and to some extent gives the episode a circus-sideshow character, but, nevertheless, it may be (no facetiousness intended) that the spirit felt that such display would help sitters to identify him.

In any event, as was the case with Mrs. Piper, all of the investigators of Mrs. Leonard, one of whom hired private detectives to observe her, agreed, regardless of their opinion of her accomplishments, that she was totally honest and sincere.[8]

Among the most famous displays of mediumship by Mrs. Leonard were the so-called "book tests," the conducting of which had actually been suggested by Mrs. Leonard's control, "Feda." Typically in these tests, "Feda" would identify a book by location, e.g. the fourth book counting from the left on the second shelf up from the ground on the right-hand side of an upstairs room in such-and-such house; and then would describe the content of a page of such a book or would refer to a given page as containing information from a deceased relative or as holding the answer to a certain question from such a relative, etc.[9]

---

[8]According to one explanation of mediumistic phenomena, the various controls and communicators that manifest themselves at a sitting are really "secondary" or "dissociated" personalities of the medium herself, which emerge under conditions of the trance, and perhaps at other times as well. If this explanation is correct, and there is considerable reason to believe that many controls and communicators are secondary personalities of a medium, then the impeccable character of the medium, to which attention is so frequently called in the most famous mediumistic cases, loses some of its persuasive force. What might be more to the point is information about the character of the medium's secondary personalities. The fact that within her primary or dominant personality the medium is not a trickster is no guarantee that within a second personality she is not a trickster, especially since secondary personalities often display traits in direct opposition to those of the dominant personality.

[9]See Mrs. Henry Sidgwick: An examination of book-tests obtained in sittings with Mrs. Leonard. *Proceedings of the Society for Psychical Research, 31*: 241–400, 1921.

Skeptics, however, are not much impressed by book tests because so many of the passages of so many books could be regarded as appropriate for any number of messages from the "the dead," and because it is easy to frame descriptions of the contents of a given page which in fact are appropriate to many other pages. Further, as Antony Flew has pointed out, often "Feda's" references to books and pages were imprecise.[10]

However, Mrs. Henry Sidgwick, a past President of Honour of the Society for Psychical Research, whose writings in psychical matters were as penetrating and well-reasoned as those of her husband in philosophy in ethics, closely investigated Mrs. Leonard's book-test communications and found that about a third of some 532 instances of these communications were "completely or approximately successful."[11] In a control experiment conducted in 1923, some 1,800 book-tests created solely for experimentation and not generated through mediumistic communications were analyzed: less than 5 percent of these tests were total or partial successes. Though the evaluation of such experiments inevitably involves subjective elements, these findings are cited, I think with some justification, to prove that Mrs. Leonard's book-tests gave results better than those "obtainable by chance." At the very least, some of Mrs. Leonard's book-tests do seem to be, as Flew has put it, "better than just lucky shots."[12]

Doubters will point out, of course, that when stage magicians relate the contents of unopened envelopes and unseen books, etc., their performances also are better than just lucky shots. To claim that a seemingly inexplicable mediumistic occurrence, such as the "Feda" book directions, is evidence of life after death, it does not suffice merely to show that the occurrence cannot be explained by chance. The claimant must also show that it cannot be explained by other factors either.

Another impressive test of the authenticity of the Leonard mediumship was a series of so-called proxy sittings. The purpose of a proxy sitting is to protect against telepathy between the medium and a person, usually a relative, who desires communica-

---

[10] Antony Flew: *A New Approach to Psychical Research.* London. C. A. Watts and Co., 1953. p. 47.

[11] Sidgwick. *loc. cit.*

[12] Flew. *op. cit.*, p. 46.

tion with the deceased, and to protect also against sensory cuing from that person. He is excluded from the sitting, but a proxy for him is present. The proxy knows little, if anything, about the deceased. The intervening link, the proxy, is deemed to increase distance between the medium and the excluded person who desires the communication.

Obviously, the absence from the sitting of the person desiring communication does protect against his sensory cuing of the medium. On the other hand, however, the proxy technique may very well fail its purpose to protect against telepathy: given what is known and accepted about telepathy, it could easily make no difference whether or not the person desiring communication is at the sitting.

Further, from the standpoint of producing evidence of survival, a proxy sitting suffers from the fact that, whatever evidential value dramatic portrayals of deceased personalities might have, the proxy cannot attest to that evidential value.[13]

In any event, Mrs. Leonard's chief investigator, Drayton Thomas, conducted a series of proxy sittings with Mrs. Leonard for various individuals over a period of many years and the results persuaded many that Mrs. Leonard did indeed have avenues of communication with the dead.[14]

One famous case is named after a ten-year-old boy, one Bobby Newlove, the deceased grandson of an individual for whom Thomas

---

[13] There is reason to believe that the number of true statements produced in proxy sittings is substantially lower than it is in standard sittings. Flew, *ibid*, p. 67. Stevenson indeed states that in contemporary research (i.e. since 1960) with its stricter controls, when the medium deals not with the person wanting information but with his representative, "no positive results have been obtained." This certainly suggests that the impressive results sometimes obtained in standard sittings may be due to factors other than communication with the dead. See Ian Stevenson: Research into the evidence of man's survival after death. A historical and critical survey with a summary of recent developments. *The Journal of Nervous and Mental Disease, 165:* 162, 1977.

[14] Thomas, in the opinion of Stevenson, is one of only four people who were both well informed and worth listening to in regard to the early mediumistic evidence of survival. *Ibid.,* pp. 156–157. For Thomas' reports on the Leonard proxy sittings, see: (1) A consideration of a series of proxy sittings. *Proceedings of the Society for Psychical Research, 41:* 139–185, 1932-33; (2) A proxy case extending over eleven sittings with Mrs. Osborne Leonard. *Proceedings of the Society for Psychical Research, 43:* 439–519, 1935; (3) A proxy experiment of significant success. *Proceedings of the Society for Psychical Research, 45:* 257–306, 1939; and (4) A new type of proxy case. *Journal of the American Society for Psychical Research, 31:* 103–104 and 120–122, 1939.

sat as proxy. Via Mrs. Leonard "Bobby Newlove" communicated in a series of sittings with Thomas several statements highly appropriate to Bobby's circumstances when he was alive, including circumstances bearing on the cause of the child's death.

Another case, the "Daisy Armstrong" case, was less credible in that the proxies were friends of Daisy Armstrong, but the case still is noteworthy. The communicator in the case seemed to speak of Daisy Armstrong's adoptive father as dead, which allegedly was not known either to Daisy or to the proxies at the time; and he was indeed dead.

Mrs. Leonard's reputation as an impressive medium had initially been established through her connection with the Lodges. After Sir Oliver Lodge's son was killed in 1915, Mrs. Leonard communicated information seemingly from the son to Sir Oliver and Lady Lodge. The information, which had satisfied the Lodges of the survival of their son after his bodily death, was published in 1916 and made Mrs. Leonard famous.

Because of her fame, in 1918 Mrs. Leonard was persuaded to submit to research by the Society for Psychical Research, and over a period of some three months gave seventy-three sittings to individuals sponsored by the society, under its supervision. In this series of sittings it was observed that the communicators were usually deceased soldiers or, to a lesser frequency, elderly ladies. Thus, many of the recognitions made by the sitters in this series of sittings are not considered to be of great value since at this period in history every British citizen knew either a young man who had been killed in the war or a deceased elderly lady.[15] On the other hand, that the communications tended to be from soldiers and elderly women may have been because a significant percentage of a person's deceased friends and relatives were at this time soldiers and older persons.

Mrs. Piper and Mrs. Leonard were not alone in producing information suggesting communication from the dead to the living through mediums.[16] But the Piper and Leonard mediumships

---

[15]See Mrs. W. H. Salter: A further report on sittings with Mrs. Leonard. *Proceedings of the Society for Psychical Research, 32:* 1–143, 1921.

[16]Other celebrated mediums who have been investigated by reputable persons and agencies include Mrs. Thompson (1868–?), "Mrs. Willett" (Mrs. Winifred Coombe-Tennant, 1874–1956), and Mrs. Eileen J. Garrett (1893–1970). The main reports on Mrs. Thompson may be found

are the most famous and highly regarded. Further, other cases involving mediums are attended by the same problems of evidentiary value as are the Piper and Leonard cases. To these difficulties I now turn.

---

in (1) Vol. 17 (1902) of the *Proceedings of the Society for Psychical Research*; in (2) J. G. Piddington: On the types of phenomena displayed in Mrs. Thompson's trance. *Proceedings of the Society for Psychical Research,* 18: 104–307, 1904; and in (3) F. Podmore: *The Newer Spiritualism.* London, Milner, 1909. For investigations of "Mrs. Willett," see (1) O. Lodge: Evidence of classical scholarship and of cross-correspondence in some new automatic writings. *Proceedings of the Society for Psychical Research,* 25: 113–175, 1911; and (2) G. W. Balfour: A study of the psychological aspects of Mrs. Willett's mediumship. *Proceedings of the Society for Psychical Research,* 43: 43–318, 1935. Mrs. Garrett authored several autobiographies, including, most recently, *Many Voices: The Autobiography of a Medium.* New York, Putnam, 1968.

CHAPTER 13

DIFFICULTIES WITH THE PIPER AND LEONARD CASES

What are we to make of these strange happenings?
We must try to make something of them.
— H. H. Price, Mediumship and
human survival[1]

Elastic Messages

People both informed and generally sympathetic to belief in survival after death are divided as to the evidentiary value and credibility of the Piper and Leonard cases. Their disagreement suggests weakness in the cases as evidence of personal survival.

One major problem is that we cannot now be sure just to what extent the correct and appropriate information communicated by the mediums was derived by them from the hints, clothes, mannerisms and circumstances of the sitter, or from unconscious sensory cuing, e.g. of eye and lip motions, voice changes, hesitations, and the like, and to what extent the correct information was in reality "elastic," i.e. information that though seemingly appropriate to only one sitter, might well be regarded by more than one sitter as appropriate or even unique to his or her own case.[2]

Elastic messages abound even in the communications given through the best mediums, and sitters have been observed to view as applicable to themselves detailed information that is in fact

---

[1] In J. M. O. Wheatley and Hoyt L. Edge (Eds.): *Philosophical Dimensions of Parapsychology.* Springfield, Thomas, 1976, p. 266.

[2] I believe that the term, *elastic message*, was Professor Hornell Hart's. See: *The Enigma of Survival: The Case For and Against an After Life.* London, Rider, 1959.

intended for others. For example, in a famous experiment conducted in 1947 by Denys Parsons, two out of the four women selected found various items in a transcript of a reading given by a medium for some other sitter as applicable to their own circumstances; one woman indeed confirmed almost every detail of the transcript. Parsons concluded: "Even with mediums of the highest quality it is clear that much material may be given which appears at first sight to be exclusive to the sitter, but of which the evidential value must be discounted because it is in fact not exclusive."[3]

It is reasonable, Parsons points out, to suppose that all professional mediums unconsciously become familiar with those items that are most readily accepted by sitters, and that when "psychic inspiration fails" these items will, as Parsons says, "inevitably issue forth."

Statements susceptible to acceptance by many sitters were especially present in the 1918 research with Mrs. Leonard conducted by the Society for Psychical Research. Mrs. Leonard's control, "Feda," tended during the period of research to offer with only minor variations the same picture of a deceased male or female. Mrs. Leonard's (or "Feda's") males are very frequently young, tall, "well-built," with brown (or "between-color") hair cut short at the sides, possessing straight or almost straight noses, which are a little wider at the nostrils, etc., etc.[4]

Occasionally, an elastic description will go on at length, and it is possible that some sitters and commentators mistakenly thought that the length of these descriptions insured their specificity. A good example of a lengthy but nevertheless elastic description of a young male is Mrs. Leonard's description of the Lodges' son, Raymond. The description was part of the evidence that satisfied Sir Oliver and Lady Lodge that their son had survived bodily death:

---

[3]Denys Parsons: On the need for caution in assessing mediumistic material. *Proceedings of the Society for Psychical Research, 48:* 344–352, 1946–49.

[4]See Mrs. W. H. Salter: A further report on sittings with Mrs. Leonard. *Proceedings of the Society for Psychical Research, 22:* 74–85, 1921; and C. E. M. Hansel; *ESP: A Scientific Evaluation.* New York, Charles Scribner's Sons, 1966, p. 228.

Is a young man, rather above the medium height; rather well-built, not thick set or heavy, but well-built, he holds himself up well. He has not been over long. His hair is between colours. He is not easy to be described, because he is not building himself up too solid as some do. He has greyish eyes; hair brown, short at the sides; a fine shaped head; eyebrows also brown, not much arched; nice shaped nose, fairly straight, broader at the nostrils a little; a nice shaped mouth a good sized mouth it is, but it does not look large because he holds the lips nicely together; chin not heavy; face oval.[5]

Now, over the course of the present century, various appraisal techniques have come to be used in the studies of mediums and in the scoring of mediumistic communications for correctness. These techniques are designed to protect against a medium's record of correctness being enhanced through the use of elastic messages and information inferred from sitters' behavior and circumstances, etc. One technique, for example, is to have sitters for whom a given batch of "communicated" material is *not* intended rate the material in order to ascertain the "chance value" of the material, against which the score of the material for the intended sitter can be compared.

Such techniques apparently originated with H. F. Saltmarsh and were refined by Dr. S. G. Soal, Pratt and Birge, and, more recently, by Gertrude Schmeidler and Ian Stevenson. The most meticulous and exacting of these techniques is the Pratt-Birge, which among other things requires that there be no sensory contact between medium and sitter. It is important to note that when this technique has been used, results positive as to survival have been meager.[6]

An important weakness in the Piper and Leonard medium-

---

[5]Sir Oliver Lodge, *Raymond of Life and Death, with Examples of Evidence for Survival of Memory and Affection after Death.* London: Methuen & Co., 1916, p. 125. Reprinted by permission of Meuthuen & Co., Ltd.

[6]See Ian Stevenson: Research into the evidence of man's survival after death. *The Journal of Nervous and Mental Disease, 165:* 162, 1977. Stevenson, however, obtained what he termed significant positive results in an experiment with the Icelandic medium Hafsteinn Björnsson, but the experiment involved less stringent controls than those required by Pratt-Birge (sitters had no sensory contact with the medium but were allowed to be in the same room with him), and attempts to reproduce the positive results of this experiment (which anyway would be thought by some to be attributable to telepathy) did not succeed. *Ibid.*, p. 163.

ships, therefore, is that, since Mrs. Piper and Mrs. Leonard were not subject to these more exacting recent techniques of experimentation and the material they produced in trance was not subject to rigorous methods of analysis, it is difficult to determine the true probative worth of their mediumships.[7]

It is true, nevertheless, that the Piper and Leonard communications contain much striking information that is difficult to explain as having come to the medium through any known physical mode. But, even assuming the information to be of some nonphysical or paranormal provenance, must it have come from persons surviving death?

Survival or "Supertelepathy"?

Mrs. Sidgwick, who made the most extensive examination of all the information given by Mrs. Piper and who was herself sympathetic to the possibility of survival, believed, for excellent reasons, that the Piper-given information was not to be regarded as evidence of survival by spirits who *possessed* the body of the medium.[8] Professor E. R. Dodds effectively summarizes Mrs. Sidgwick's reasons for not believing in the direct possession of Mrs. Piper: the "shiftiness" of even the most veridical communicators, the "habitual lameness" of their answers to pointed questions, their "confident statements" even when they must have been aware of having lied, and "their acceptance of bogus personalities as genuine spirits" all seem inconsistent with direct possession.[9]

---

[7]Although the studies of the Piper and Leonard communications were made without benefit of recent methodology in appraisal of mediumistic phenomena, they are, nonetheless, thorough and cogent, and may be read profitably by anyone interested in the Mrs. Piper and Mrs. Leonard cases. Concerning Mrs. Piper, see especially Mrs. Henry Sidgwick's important works: Discussion of the trance phenomena of Mrs. Piper. *Proceedings of the Society for Psychical Research*, 15: 16–38, 1900; and: A contribution to the study of the psychology of Mrs. Piper's trance phenomena. *Proceedings of the Society for Psychical Research*, 28: 1–652, 1915. The most important studies made of Mrs. Leonard were by Mrs. Lydia W. Allison, Kenneth Richmond, Mrs. W. H. Salter, Mrs. Henry Sidgwick, Troubridge-Hall (Lady Troubridge and Miss Radclyffe-Hall), and, especially, the Reverend C. Drayton Thomas. However, for a sympathetic and accessible overview of Mrs. Leonard, see Suzy Smith: *The Mediumship of Mrs. Leonard.* New Hyde Park, University Books, 1964. Smith's book contains an excellent bibliography on the extensive literature on Mrs. Leonard.

[8]See: A contribution to the study of the psychology of Mrs. Piper's trance phenomena. *Proceedings of the Society for Psychical Research*, 28: 1–652, 1915.

[9]See: Why I do not believe in survival. *Proceedings of the Society for Psychical Research*, 42: 147–178, 1934.

But if the information given by Piper is not explainable as derived through possession by spirits of Mrs. Piper's body, then, assuming that it cannot be explained on a normal, sensory basis, it must be explained on the basis of telepathy. That is, either Mrs. Piper acquired the information through telepathic communication with the spirits of the dead or she acquired it telepathically from the minds of still-living persons who knew the deceased individual and his circumstances.

Both of these explanations of the Piper-given information assume the existence of telepathy, but one, the "survivalist" explanation, also assumes the existence of departed spirits. The survivalist explanation is therefore the more complicated explanation, and, thus, the less acceptable theoretically, provided that the alternative explanation accounts for all the facts of the case.

However, some commentators do not think that all the facts of the Piper case, or of the Leonard case either, can be satisfactorily explained by supposing that the medium derived her information telepathically from the mind of living persons. They think that in some instances Piper and Leonard (and other mediums, too) gave information about deceased persons that was too extensive to have been acquired through the "ordinary" telepathy that reportedly enables sensitive subjects to determine a simple symbol such as a letter or number thought of by another person.[10] This information could not have been in the mind of a single living person, they think, and so to acquire it the mediums would have to have had "super-potent" powers of telepathy, which would have enabled them, in responding while in trance to a question about a deceased person, telepathically to locate the living people who possessed information about the deceased and then telepathically to sift through the contents of the minds of these people to find the precise pieces of information relevant to the question asked. There is no evidence, these commentators maintain, that this "supertelepathy" really exists.

If, though, the lack of evidence of the existence of "supertelepathy" can be given as a reason for rejecting the explanation of the medium-

---

[10]For information about the most important experimental research on extrasensory perception, see (1) K. R. Rao: *Experimental Parapsychology: A Review and Interpretation.* Springfield. Thomas, 1966; (2) J. G. Pratt *et al.*: *Extrasensory Perception After Sixty Years.* Boston, Branden Press, 1966; and (3) R. H. Thouless: *From Anecdote to Experiment in Psychical Research.* London, Routledge and Kegan Paul. 1972.

istic information as coming from the living through telepathy, then lack of evidence of the existence of departed spirits can be given as reason for rejecting the alternative, survivalist, explanation, that the medium's information derives from telepathy with the dead.

Further, is it even true that there is no evidence of the existence of "supertelepathy"? Mediums have been reported to have ascertained a large number of true and recondite details about missing, but not dead, persons from pieces of the person's clothing.[11] Still other mediums have produced information about persons thought to be dead who were in fact alive, and, as will be seen later, in some instances the information produced was similar in nature and detail to that produced in communications with people who were truly deceased. Whatever the explanation of such cases may be, it has nothing to do with the dead, and yet the same explanation would be appropriate for those cases in which a medium transmits facts about some formerly living person.

I therefore think that, on the assumption that the facts revealed by Mrs. Piper or Mrs. Leonard about deceased persons require a paranormal explanation, there is really no sure way of settling whether those facts came from the dead or whether they came from the living through supertelepathy.

In the essay, a fragment of which I used as the epigraph to this chapter, H. H. Price states his conviction that we must try to "make something" of mediumistic communications. By this Price apparently means that we must try to choose between the survivalist and the supertelepathy explanations of these communications. My point is that, if this is indeed the choice, I do not think that we can yet choose. What is required to choose between these two explanations is not further discussion and debate, but rather further data. If further evidence were to emerge that some people have the power to synthesize information gleaned by telepathically scanning the minds of several other people, then this would favor the interpretation of mediumistic communications as the result of telepathic contact between the medium and living persons. If, on

---

[11]For example, Mrs. Eileen Garrett in 1966 produced a surprising amount of correct and quite specific information, including the then totally secret whereabouts of a missing person, merely by examining the person's shirt. See Lawrence LeShan: The vanished man: a psychometry experiment with Mrs. Eileen J. Garrett. *Journal of the American Society for Psychical Research*, 62: 46–61, 1968.

the other hand, there emerges further evidence of human survival after bodily death, then this evidence would lend credence to the explanation of the Piper, Leonard, and other mediumships as deriving from telepathic contact with the spirits of the dead.

Bogus Communicators

A good reason for skepticism in regard to even the most impressive reported mediumships is that on occasion communicators and controls have turned out to be purely fictitious creations of the medium's subconscious mind.

One of Mrs. Piper's chief controls, for example, a certain "Phinuit," who claimed to be a former French physician (but knew practically nothing of French or medicine), evidently was such a fictitious creation. So, likewise, were a group of spirits who communicated through Mrs. Piper under names like "Imperator" and "Rector" matter mostly nonsensical. At another time, the psychologist G. Stanley Hall received through Mrs. Piper communications from a niece, "Bessie Beals," who was in fact a totally imaginary invention of Doctor Hall. (The ultimate decline in Mrs. Piper's ability to go into trance was due, incidentally, according to Mrs. Piper and her controls, to Hall's unsympathetic and sometimes harsh "experimentation.")

Mrs. Sidgwick concluded that, indeed, all the personalities who manifested themselves in Mrs. Piper's trances were probably the fictitious creations of Mrs. Piper. In her extensive review of the Piper communications, Mrs. Sidgwick noted that the assertions and "intellectual calibre" of many of Mrs. Piper's trance communicators were utterly inconsistent with the persons they professed to be, and that the lapses, limitations, and other implausible characteristics of the communications of even the more believable communicating personalities were difficult to view as other than the conscious or unconscious fabrications of Mrs. Piper's trance mind. "The intelligence communicating directly with the sitter through Mrs. Piper's organism," Mrs. Sidgwick states flatly, "is Mrs. Piper."[12]

---

[12]Sidgwick: A contribution to the study of the psychology of Mrs. Piper's trance phenomena. *Proceedings of the Society for Psychical Research. 28:* 5, 1915.

"To sum up very briefly my own conclusions about Mrs. Piper's trance, I think it is probably a state of self-induced hypnosis in which her hypnotic self personates different characters either consciously and deliberately, or unconsciously and believing herself to be the person she represents, and sometimes probably in a state of consciousness intermediate between the two."[13]

Controls and communicators of other famous mediums have also turned out to be fictitious personations apparently produced by the medium's subconscious mind under trance conditions.[14] For example, one of Mrs. Cooper's communicators, a "John Ferguson," appeared in Doctor S. G. Soal's sittings with Mrs. Cooper week after week and displayed a complete and integrated personality, in spite of the fact that Ferguson turned out never to have existed. Another Cooper communicator, a "James Miles," produced an impressive assemblage of true information about the former circumstances of one James Miles, but eventually it was learned that all the information about Miles had been published earlier in the *London Daily Express*. Indeed, every piece of information about Miles published in the paper had appeared in the Cooper communications. The case thus demonstrated not only the ability of a medium unconsciously to fabricate communicators, but also the spectacular memory of which a medium might be capable.[15]

Now, these fictitious communicators and controls appear typically in a dramatized form. That is, they present themselves as genuine individuals: they speak in their own idiosyncratic phraseology; they are consistent in their intonation, mannerisms, and forms of address; they display, in short, their own unique traits of personality. That fictitious communicators should seem so genuine is not, however, particularly surprising. The characters in the average dream display consistent, integrated, and unique personalities; and the dramatization of fictitious communicators by a medium would seem to be a case of the medium's dreaming out

---

[13]*Ibid.*, p. 330. Reprinted by permission of the Society for Psychical Research.

[14]See, e.g. S. G. Soal, A report on some communications received through Mrs. Blanche Cooper. *Proceedings of the Society for Psychical Research*, 35: 471–594, 1926.

[15]The word-reaction tests administered in 1935 by Whately Carington suggest (albeit inconclusively) that "Feda," too, was only a "secondary personality" made out of material repressed in Mrs. Leonard's subconscious mind. See Carington's The quantitative study of trance personalities. *Proceedings of the Society for Psychical Research*, 42: 173–240, 1934; 43: 319–361, 1935; 44: 139–222, 1937; and 45: 223–251, 1938–39.

loud, as it were. One is led to suppose that, when the medium dramatically portrays a fictitious communicator, she is merely acting out verbally the character she in effect dreams herself to be.

The two most famous examples of fictitious communicators created and dramatized at the subconscious levels of the medium's mind are met with in the Gordon Davis case, brought to light in the article by S. G. Soal noted above, and the so-called Réallier case.[16] In these two classic cases the mediums involved produced a wealth of assertions, which were later verified, about the former circumstances of the persons after whom the cases are named. The persons were at the time presumed to be dead; but Gordon Davis and Réallier turned out to be much alive (and very healthy) at the time of the communications. The "Gordon Davis" spirit communicated in a voice and manner so resembling the real Davis that the sitter, Doctor Soal, who had been a friend of Gordon Davis, found the likeness extraordinary.

In a similar but less well-known case, the French investigator Eugene Osty encountered a medium who correctly described the past life of a living person of whom Osty was thinking.[17] Nils Jacobson reports too a similar episode in which a group of British journalists attended several seances in which the mediums described the stories and circumstances of "deceased" relatives of the journalists. The "relatives," however, had been invented by the journalists to expose the mediums.[18]

This review of fictitious communicators supports two conclusions.

Evidentiary Value of Dramatization

The fact that the personalities of nonexistent individuals and still-living persons can be portrayed by a medium with convincing histrionics supports the conclusion of Doctor S. G. Soal that the mere dramatizing of a communicator has no value as proof of survival after death, and that "it is by the quality of the information they communicate and by that alone that we must test the

---

[16]See Hart: *The Enigma of Survival.* London, Rider, 1959, p. 135.

[17]See Flew: *A New Approach to Psychical Research*. London, C. A. Watts and Co., 1953, p. 64.

[18]See Nils O. Jacobson: *Life Without Death?* (Sheila La Farge, trans). Dell (n.p.), 1974, pp. 145–146.

claims of so-called 'spirits.' "[19]

That a person's manner, attitudes, and idiosyncrasies are as unique to him as his fingerprints is indisputable, but it is always a matter of opinion and difficult to assess objectively whether or not a portrayal of a person's mannerisms and other attributes is accurate and fully captures the person's character.

Further, as Mrs. Sidgwick has pointed out, it is easy to misjudge the resemblance of the supposed communicator and the deceased individual because the basis for comparison is often only the medium's voice or behavior within very atypical circumstances, or, worse, only her written script.

In addition, prior to the development of video-recording techniques, the sitter's estimation of the quality of the personification always depended on his recollection of both the personification and of the deceased. Recollection, we all know, changes and often weakens with the passage of time. During the seance the sitter may appraise the personification of the deceased as faithful and later regard it as defective, or appraise it initially as lacking and then later come to remember it as faithful.

Doctor F. Van Eeden, for example, reported on apparent communications he received from a deceased friend through the medium, Mrs. Thompson. At the time he received the communications it seemed to him that he was seeing a veritable manifestation of the friend himself. The language, the gestures, and even the facial expressions, were exactly like those of his friend. Later, though, Van Eeden changed his opinion and concluded that he had in fact dealt only with Mrs. Thompson, "who had acted the ghost."[20]

It is, accordingly, fair to agree with Doctor Soal that it is by the quality of information provided by mediums, and by that test alone, that we must evaluate any claim that the information was communicated through the medium by a surviving mind or spirit after physical death. Since the faithfulness of a personation of a deceased individual is entirely a matter of subjective opinion as filtered through memory, it is unjustifiable for a witness, and even more so for a nonwitness, to ground a belief in the afterdeath survival of a person on the accuracy of a dramatic portrayal of him by a medium.

---

[19]Quoted in Hart, *op. cit.*, p. 133.

[20]F. Van Eeden: Account of sittings with Mrs. Thompson. *Proceedings of the Society for Psychical Research,* 17: 81–84, 1901.

The Survivalist Explanation of Mediumistic Communications

That there are fictitious communicators like those reviewed above certainly weakens, if not refutes, any claim that a survivalist explanation alone can account for the most celebrated mediumistic cases.[21] In the Gordon Davis case, detailed and accurate information about someone who was alive was communicated with the mannerisms of that person. That case therefore does not differ from those other cases in which the supposed spirits of persons who are dead communicate through the medium. If the Gordon Davis case does not require and cannot have any survivalist explanation, why should the other cases?

Summary

Neither Mrs. Piper, Mrs. Leonard, nor other mediums in the late nineteenth century and early in this century were subjected to modern rigorous methods now employed to prevent mediums from acquiring information from living persons by sensory or extrasensory means. Nor was the information contained within their communications evaluated by modern techniques to preclude acceptance by investigators of "elastic" facts that might apply to many persons.

That it is necessary to employ rigorous safeguards both in observing mediumistic phenomena and in evaluating the communications of mediums is made plain by the existence of fictitious communicators, as well as by experiments with elastic messages. The fact that these safeguards were not employed in the investigations of the mediumships of Mrs. Piper and Mrs. Leonard is, I think, an important weakness in the mediumships as evidence of survival. This weakness is not relieved by the accurate and effective dramatic portrayals given by Mrs. Piper and Mrs. Leonard.

---

[21]George Zorab has pointed out (The survival hypothesis: an unsupported speculation? *Journal of the American Society for Psychical Research*, 50: 248-253, 1956), that interpretations other than the spiritistic or survivalist have been placed on mediumistic information in times past. For example, mediums before 1700 were reported to have done essentially what modern mediums have done, but were thought to have been controlled by demons and not departed spirits. The choice of explanatory hypothesis, Zorab suggests, is a matter of current fashion and is not dictated by the facts themselves.

CHAPTER 14

CROSS-CORRESPONDING COMMUNICATIONS

The "cross-correspondences" have won fame as impressive mediumistic evidence of survival after bodily death, though there are those, including a few who are very sympathetic to the possibility of survival, who have not viewed this phenomenon as so impressive.

What are the cross-correspondences?

Suppose that after death one should find himself still in existence, with the capacity to communicate via mediums to the physical world, and that he should wish to establish the reality of his survival to persons still living. It might occur to him to compose a message and then communicate it in bits and snatches through different mediums, so that only when the various components of the message, as these had been transmitted via all the mediums, were assembled, would the complete message emerge.

One would not want the message simply to be overlooked, or part of it not to be noticed or to be difficult to find, so he would append to the final transmission a description of what he had done and the names of the various mediums involved, as well as the dates of the various transmissions. No doubt he would make certain that when all the transmissions were assembled the complete message contained information that made it clear to those who had known him that he still existed.

One would make certain, too, that skeptics could not easily regard the communication as chance luck on the part of the mediums, or as the result of collusion among them, or as a case of their gleaning the information contained in the communication from still-living friends. Thus one would devise his message as not only appropriate but as unique to himself; it would contain the kind of personal and idiosyncratic information that would make most difficult any doubt that his surviving being was the communicating source.

It would not be easy for this survivor to select a message that would convince the especially dubious, but if the message were carefully selected and transmission to the mediums were good, then still-living friends, and perhaps most skeptics too, might possibly be convinced of the survivor's continued existence.

A plan essentially like this was attributed to the spirits of F. W. H. Myers (deceased in 1901) and of other deceased scholars who while living had been interested in survival research. Alice Johnson, Research Officer of the Society for Psychical Research, attributed the plan to the spirit of Myers on the basis of her study of the scripts of mediums in London, New York, and India after Myers' death.[1] The material in the scripts of one of the mediums had no special meaning, but, when it was placed alongside the material in the scripts of another of the mediums, it evidenced a coherent plan like that just described and displayed a content hinting at the authorship of Myers.

That Myers was communicating by this plan was put to the test of an experiment in 1906–1907 in which J. G. Piddington informed Myers' spirit in Latin, through Mrs. Piper, that Myers' still-living colleagues were aware of Myers' cross-correspondence plan. "Myers" (i.e. Myers' spirit or discarnate personality) was then requested by Piddington in Latin to transmit through two mediums messages between which there was no apparent connection and then to communicate via a third medium a clue that would reveal a hidden connection between the first two messages.

In the opinion of some, Piddington's Latin statement was acknowledged by "Myers," and the terms of his request were fulfilled in those communications known today as the Hope, Star, and Browning communications.[2]

The Hope, Star, and Browning communications, which I shall presently discuss, were by no means the extent of the so-called cross-correspondences. For more than a decade, hundreds of pages of transcripts thought to contain material suggestive of cross-

---

[1] The mediums were Mrs. Thompson, Mrs. Piper, "Mrs. Willett" (Mrs. Charles Coombe-Tennant), "Mrs. Holland," Mrs. Verrall, Miss Verrall, Mrs. Forbes, and others. When spirits communicate through the pen of the medium, the handwritten messages that result are called "scripts."

[2] See J. G. Piddington: A series of concordant automatisms. *Proceedings of the Society for Psychical Research*, 22: 19–416, 1908.

correspondence plans were accumulated. Indeed, some of the material has reportedly not even yet been published because of its highly personal nature.

An impressive series of cases among those published involved not just one but two supposed communicators, Doctor A. W. Verrall and Professor Henry Butcher, supposedly transmitting in intimate collaboration cross-correspondences of an exceedingly complex nature. I shall discuss these and others of the more important "cross-correspondences"[3] in this chapter.

Difficulties With the Cross-Correspondences as proof

Not all reviewers are agreed, as I noted at the outset, that the cross-correspondences constitute evidence of survival. Hereward Carrington, for example, commenting on one of the "impressive" cases involving the former Dr. A. W. Verrall, said:

> They [the scripts] represent...the piecing together of disjointed fragments of subconscious knowledge and subconscious memories; they have no systematic connection, and point to no "spirit" as their author. They are all fully explained upon purely psychological and naturalistic lines. And this criticism applies, it seems to me, not only to the Willett scripts in particular, but to almost the whole of the cross-correspondence... I believe, with Dr. Maxwell, that the evidence afforded by these cross-correspondences has been vastly over-rated; that chance has played a far greater part than is usually assumed; and that the evidence for survival which they furnish is distinctly inferior in all respects to the straightforward communications supplied in the Hodgson and Hyslop reports...[4]

Why this skepticism on the part of some commentators, even some who are sympathetic to the possibility of life after death? A certain amount of skepticism is no doubt justified by experiments, made by the Society for Psychical Research, in which, for example, "scripts" created by having people randomly open a book and write down the thought suggested by an arbitrarily selected passage were found to display some degree of correspondence to one another.[5]

---

[3]Those who wish to read the reports on the cross-correspondences themselves should consult the *Proceedings of the Society for Psychical Research*, especially between 1906 and 1919.

[4]H. Carrington: A discussion of the Willett scripts. *Proceedings of the Society for Psychical Research*, 27: 458–466, 1914. Reprinted by permission of the Society for Psychical Research.

[5]See F. Melian Stawell: The ear of Dionysius: a discussion of the evidence. *Proceedings of the Society for Psychical Research*, 29: 260–261, 1917.

Another reason for skepticism, which may have already occurred to the reader, is the improbability that a deceased individual would choose a proof of survival involving so many obstacles to success. His whole elaborate scheme might never be noticed. If noticed, skeptics would suspect that the information contained in the message had been obtained by the mediums through means other than contact with his departed spirit. The deceased individual would be aware of all the difficulties of achieving believable communication of a simple message through even a single medium. Why would he complicate his task further?

On the other hand, he well might reason that, if despite the obstacles he did get through with cross-corresponding communications, then those obstacles would enhance the believability of his message as coming from him.

Nonetheless, on the whole it would be far simpler and much less risky, and decidedly more effective, for one to leave a sealed message before he died and then, after his death, to communicate its contents. Or, one could set a combination lock and, after death, communicate the combination. True, he might fear that skeptics would attribute his communication to the clairvoyance of the medium and so not recognize it to be from him.[6] Nevertheless, the simplicity of the sealed letter or lock-combination techniques would be more attractive to someone contemplating a proof of his survival than would be an elaborate and risky plan of corresponding communications.[7]

But the principal reason for doubting the value of cross-correspondence as proof of survival is that there is such a marked contrast between the correspondences that actually appeared in what the mediums said and wrote and the correspondences that might be expected to appear if the plan had been executed fully, as contemplated above. The deficiencies of the supposed cross-correspondences in this regard are cause for continual apology

---

[6]Though if attempts by mediums *before* one's death to learn the contents of the sealed message or the numerals in the lock-combination met with failure, then success in such attempts made after one's death could not easily be attributed to clairvoyance or "super ESP." See A. Gauld: Discarnate survival. In Benjamin B. Wolman (Ed.): *Handbook of Parapsychology*, New York, Van Nostrand Reinhold Co., 1977, p. 621.

[7]Sealed-message and combination-lock tests of survival have been tried, but to my knowledge no communicator has ever been able to state the contents of an envelope that was sealed before the deceased's death or a lock-combination established prior to his death.

and excuses on the part of defenders of the cross-correspondences as proof of survival.

What emerged from the supposedly corresponding scripts were not complete messages, but rather, typically, allusions by two or more mediums at about the same time to the same topic or word; e.g. two mediums might both make some reference at about the same time to death; or might both use the word "star." Often, too, the allusions were somewhat indirect and disguised, and virtually had to be read into the material. There is never the clear message one would wish to communicate if he were attempting to prove his own survival by the cross-correspondence technique.

Further, the messages that emerged were not nearly as appropriate as they might have been in order to convince the living of one's continued existence. So, for example, in the celebrated Ear of Dionysius case, mentioned above and treated below, we do not find the purported communicators dictating the kind of personal, confidential, and idiosyncratic information about themselves (or their former circumstances) that would really serve to establish their oneness with the former Doctor Verrall and Professor Butcher. We do not get information, say, about the whereabouts of the keys to Doctor Verrall's lockbox, or about unique but obscure identifying marks, peculiar scratches and whatnot, on some of Professor Butcher's possessions, or about the details of Doctor Verrall's last manuscripts or the contents of some of Professor Butcher's private poetry. Rather, we find the supposed communicators conveying in the typical puzzle format of the cross-correspondences esoteric scholarly material of the sort that would have been of interest to the former Verrall and Butcher, but which would also have been of interest to other scholars in their disciplines.

Material like that from the Ear of Dionysius may of course suggest that Verrall and Butcher were the sources of the "communications" but it manifestly does not establish that fact. To borrow an analogy from Ducasse, it is as if I attempted to establish my identity via telephone to a long-lost friend, who mistakenly was sure that I had been killed, by talking about some esoteric subject in philosophy rather than by communicating the kind of idiosyncratic and personal information that would really tend to establish my identity.

Further reason for skepticism as to reported cross-correspondences as proof of survival arises from the occasional gross, and sometimes preposterous, mistakes and displays of ignorance on the part of the supposed communicator, which are completely at odds with the intelligence, education and experience of the deceased.[8]

Notwithstanding these various deficiencies in the cross-correspondences as proof of survival, it would be unjustifiable to overlook that many of the correspondences in the various messages are truly remarkable.

For example, in the scripts of the mediums, Mrs. Piper, Mrs. A. W. Verrall (the wife of Doctor A. W. Verrall), and Miss Verrall (Mrs. Verrall's daughter), which were made independently of one another, there appeared at about the same time repeated use of the words "laurel" and "wreath," and other references to laurel. Moreover, "Myers" (the possible spirit of F. W. H. Myers) at this time supposedly communicated through Mrs. Piper the statement, "I gave Mrs. Verrall laurel wreath."[9]

A better illustration of the strengths and weaknesses of a cross-correspondence as proof of survival comes from the Hope, Star, and Browning case, mentioned earlier in this chapter. This case too involves the mediums, Mrs. Piper, Mrs. Verrall, and Miss Verrall, each supposedly acting independently of one another.

Hope, Star, and Browning

J. C. Piddington, who, as I mentioned above, wished to test the theory that the spirit of F. W. H. Myers was communicating proof of his survival through a cross-correspondence method, dictated through Mrs. Piper (in sessions lasting from December 17, 1906 to January 2, 1907) instructions in Latin to what he hoped was the surviving personality of Myers. Piddington's instructions were in effect that "Myers" should communicate via two mediums messages between which there would seem to be no relationship and then communicate via a third medium an additional message that

---

[8]See Gardner Murphy: Triumphs and defects in the study of mediumship. *Journal of the American Society for Psychical Research, 51:* 125–135, 1957.

[9]For the details of this case, as well as the Hope, Star, and Browning case reported below, see J. G. Piddington: A series of concordant automatisms. *Proceedings of the Society for Psychical Research, 22:* 19–416, 1908.

would serve to connect or relate the first two messages to one another.

Within a month after January 2, 1907, the date when Piddington had completed his instructions to "Myers," there appeared in two scripts of *Mrs. Verrall* (not Mrs. Piper, the medium through whom Piddington had dictated his instructions to "Myers") an allusion to hope, a usage of the word, "star," and an allusion to Browning's poem, "Abt Vogler." The scripts were dated January 23 and January 28.

Then, six days later on February 3, there appeared in a script of *Miss* Verrall, usage of the word, "star," and a hint as to another Browning poem.

Next, eight days later on February 11, the hypothetical Myers-personality, seemingly communicating through Mrs. Piper, stated that "Hope, Star, and Browning" had been referred to in a communication through Mrs. Verrall.

So the deceased Myers appeared to be communicating through a third medium, i.e. Mrs. Piper, a statement serving to connect the meaningless references in the scripts of the other two mediums, Mrs. Verrall and Miss Verrall. The Myers-spirit seems to have done just what Piddington instructed it to do.

Further, six days later on February 17, Miss Verrall's script again contained references to a Browning poem, and a drawing of a star, followed by the words, "That was the sign she will understand when she sees it."

Finally and astoundingly, and seeming to clinch beyond doubt that the Myers-personality was the source of the communications, "Myers," through Mrs. Piper, indicated in sittings between February 27 and April 24 that he had been thinking of Browning's "Abt Vogler," and that "Hope, Star, and Browning" was his reply to the Latin instructions of Piddington. These instructions to "Myers" indeed appeared to have been fulfilled.[10]

There are certain flaws as to the evidentiary worth of this case. First, no usage of the word, "hope," or allusion to hope apparently is to be found in the scripts of Miss Verrall. The common refer-

---

[10]There are further seemingly corresponding allusions and references in other scripts of the Verralls at the time of the Hope, Star, and Browning case, but I have dealt with what are deemed to be the most significant ones.

ences in the material produced by Mrs. Verrall and Miss Verrall are limited to "Browning" and "star."

No doubt, under the circumstances, common allusions to Browning and his poetry in the scripts of all three mediums are intriguing, but they do not necessarily suggest the agency of a discarnate Myers. The Verralls were apparently both aware of the nature and purpose of Piddington's experiment. Apparently, too, Mrs. Verrall, and through her Miss Verrall, were kept informed of the latest developments therein; and Mrs. Verrall was even present at some of the sittings with Mrs. Piper at which Piddington tried to communicate with "Myers." Furthermore, Mrs. Verrall was familiar with "Abt Vogler," and would have understood its appropriateness as a communication from "Myers." Quite possibly the same could be said of Miss Verrall. Moreover, on the day after the experiment was begun, Piddington had attempted to transmit through Mrs. Piper to Mrs. Verrall words from a Browning poem, thus bringing Browning poetry to the attention of Mrs. Piper or her trance mind.

It is not surprising under any circumstances to find in the scripts of a mother and daughter at least some common references and information. Under these particular circumstances, in which the total isolation of each medium from the others was not attempted, and in which Browning or his poetry might well have been somewhere in the minds of all three mediums anyway, it is quite possible that the common allusion to Browning in the scripts of the mediums was *not* due to the efforts of the departed spirit of F. W. H. Myers.

As to common references to "star," it is impossible to ascertain their significance as proof of Myers' discarnate existence unless we are given information, which I have not located in the reports of the case, as to the frequency of the word in the complete and assembled scripts of the Verralls. One or two common references to the word could be merely by chance; certainly, the word is not unusual. The word does not seem to be emphasized in any script prior to the February 17 script of Miss Verrall.

However, in the script of February 17, the reference to a star is very striking: a star-like drawing appears, followed by the phrase, "That was the sign she will understand when she sees it." The word, "star," is also used in this February 17 script.

Nonetheless, the significance of this emphasis on "star" in this script of Miss Verrall is impaired by the fact that, prior to the sitting at which the script was produced, Mrs. Verrall had "by way of encouragement" given Miss Verrall a "general description" of the correspondences which had to that date been observed by Piddington. In her description Mrs. Verrall substituted imaginary words for the original words which had by that date acquired significance in the eyes of Piddington. For "star" Mrs. Verrall substituted, "Planet Mars." Now, given that Miss Verrall had been told that some sort of cross-correspondence had been found on a word similar to "Planet Mars," it would perhaps have been more surprising if some sort of prominent reference to a planet-like thing had *not* appeared in Miss Verrall's very next script. If one were going to draw a picture of a planet, then the result could very well look very much like a drawing of a star.

The February 17 script of Miss Verrall is also viewed as especially important for two additional reasons: (1) It links up with Miss Verrall's own script of February 3 (in both scripts there appears the word, "star," and in both there is something of a reference to Browning's "Pied Piper of Hamelin"). But, clearly, a correspondence between two scripts of the same medium is not *per se* noteworthy. (2) The February 17 script also contains certain common references with an unsigned script produced by Mrs. Verrall on the first night of the experiment, but these references have nothing to do with the later references to "hope" and "star"; and, though the two scripts contain in common an allusion to Browning's poetry, for the reasons suggested above, this correspondence is not necessarily significant.

To conclude, even though the correspondences of reference and allusion in the various Hope, Star, and Browning scripts are fascinating, by themselves they are inconclusive as evidence of survival. Their main significance as evidence of the existence of a discarnate Myers derives from the fact that "Myers" reportedly communicated through one of the mediums (Mrs. Piper) that "hope," "star," and "Browning" were of significance in the experiment.[11] But critical readers of the case may feel unconvinced.

---

[11]"Myers" also asserted certain other words to be significant that were not significant and made claims about his accomplishments through mediums that turned out to be false.

There was in general too much possibility of an unintentional flow or exchange of information among the persons involved; too much that could be merely accidental in common references and allusions; and too much knowledge on the part of everyone, both of Myers and of the purpose and progress of the experiment.

The Ear of Dionysius

A good synopsis of this celebrated case has been given by Miss F. Melian Stawell:

> In two scripts of Mrs. Willett's, herself no classical scholar, there appeared a number of classical allusions, some of them recondite, and all said to be connected with the "Ear of Dionysius" (a whispering-gallery constructed by the tyrant and opening on the stone-quarries of Syracuse which were used as a prison). Further, the allusions were given in such a way that their connection was a regular puzzle, even to trained scholars, e.g. the "One Ear" (of Dionysius) was, the script indicated, to be connected with the "One Eye," evidently the one eye of the Cyclops Polyphemus. But how? At last, in a later sitting, the clue was suddenly revealed by the half-word "Philox," indicating the name of Philoxenus, a Greek poet, closely associated with Dionysius, whom he satirised as Polyphemus. The story of Philoxenus, according to one version, a somewhat peculiar one, made all the allusions and connections perfectly clear. The communicator purported to be Dr. Verrall, aided by his friend Prof. Butcher, and the style in which the references were given strongly resembled his. Finally, after all the scripts were written, it was discovered that the story of Philoxenus in the appropriate version happened to be told with some detail in a book, Smyth's *Greek Melic Poets*, that Dr. Verrall used and had in his library.[12]

This case seems at first very promising as proof of personal survival. However, it suffers in this regard from the fact that the scholarly information contained in the scripts of the mediums was known by various living persons who, moreover, were aware of the fact that Doctor Verrall and Professor Butcher also had knowledge of the information.

Miss Stawell has argued, most persuasively, I think, that even though Mrs. Willett was not a classical scholar she had a fair amount of knowledge that would help her build up the script, and that it is not only possible but very likely that Mrs. Verrall, who

---

[12] F. Melian Stawell, *op. cit.*, p. 262. Reprinted by permission of the Society for Psychical Research.

held the sittings with Mrs. Willett, had full knowledge of the various classical references required. Miss Stawell concluded that in this case there is

> certainly what might fairly be called an elaborate *association of ideas*, ... but I have shown, I think, that this association might have been in Mrs. Verrall's subconscious mind. Of design in *communication* the evidence is much less clear. Much is made of the fact that the allusions are given in a scholar-like form, that they are veiled and fragmentary, and that the clue seems purposely withheld. But the scholar-like form would be natural to Mrs. Verrall, and we know that telepathic messages do often come through in a veiled and fragmentary form ... I suggest therefore that the effect of purposive design is accidental....[13]

So even the better corresponding mediumistic scripts are imperfect as evidence of survival after death. They are far from what a survivor would want, and from what one still living would want to occur after his death, to prove his survival to the skeptic.

Alternative Explanations

There are, of course, possible rationalizations to excuse weaknesses in the cross-correspondence cases as evidence of survival: mediums may be at best imperfect and inadequate communication-instruments for survivors; it may be difficult to devise a message of the sort that would convince a skeptic; and spirits may have other barriers to overcome to reach the living across the gap between the sensory and the nonsensory worlds. Such rationalizations are not any proof in themselves, of course. A fact is not proved by stating the difficulties that stand in the way of its proof.

Moreover, if the cross-correspondence phenomena are to be viewed as confirming or supporting the hypothesis that there is life after death, then that hypothesis must be more than merely consonant with those phenomena; it must provide the best explanation of them.

There may well be other explanations of the cross-correspondence cases that are no less satisfactory than the survivalist explanation. For example, could the cross-corresponding communications and the information contained in them have resulted from telepathic contact between the mediums and still-living

---

[13]*Ibid.*, p. 267. Reprinted by permission of the Society for Psychical Research.

acquaintances of the deceased persons? As A. G. N. Flew has pointed out,[14] the groping and disjointed nature of many of the key correspondences bears a striking similarity to the character of transcripts of telepathy experiments in which a receiver strives to grasp the idea the sender has attempted to transmit. In the telepathy experiments, also, disguised allusions resembling those attributed to the Myers personality sometimes occur. One such telepathy experiment was conducted, interestingly enough, by Doctor and Mrs. Verrall, two of the key figures of the cross-correspondences. Doctor Verrall attempted to inject three Greek words (translated as "one-horse dawn") into his wife's mediumistic scripts; reportedly, a continuing effort resulted over the next few months in "just such a series of groping references as would have been scored as a cross-correspondence if they had been occurring in the products of different automatists."[15]

Against the explanation of the cross-correspondences as the result of telepathy among living persons, W. H. Salter argued that such an explanation is defective because it in effect requires us to invent " 'ad hoc' a species of telepathy for which there is otherwise [i.e. otherwise than in the cross-correspondence cases themselves] practically no evidence."[16]

However, apart from the fact, noted above, that the grasping and groping character of cross-correspondences is replicated by the character of transcripts of certain telepathy experiments, the exponent of the telepathy-explanation of the cross-corresponding communications can turn Salter's argument around and use it against the survivalist explanation of the cross-correspondences. The survivalist explanation, he can say, is defective because it requires us to postulate something, namely, the existence of the spirits of the deceased, for which there is otherwise practically no evidence.

I have not myself found any decisive reasons for choosing between survivalist and telepathy-explanations of the cross-

---

[14] Antony Flew: *A New Approach to Psychical Research*. London, Watts and Co., 1953, p. 65.

[15] *Ibid.*, p. 66. It is ironic indeed that the cross-correspondences were at one time viewed as intended by the deceased Myers specifically to eliminate explanations of medium-produced material as due to telepathy among living persons.

[16] W. H. Salter, in a review of C. S. B. Roberts' essay, The truth about spiritualism. *Journal of the Society for Psychical Research*, 27: 331, 1932.

correspondence cases. If there in fact is no compelling reason for choosing between these explanations, then, it seems to me, the cases cannot be construed as *evidence* of survival *or* of telepathy.

Conclusion

Among those whose views are more or less favorable to the possibility of personal existence after death, opinion is divided as to the worth of the cross-correspondences as proof of survival. Sir Oliver Lodge, Lord Balfour, and others have been highly impressed by the phenomena as proof.[17] Others, such as Richet and Dodds, have been considerably less impressed.[18] Dodds indeed was not satisfied that the various supposedly corresponding materials even gave evidence of purpose or design, and believed that, in any case, "more difficult intellectual feats than the construction of these puzzles have before now been performed subconsciously."[19]

These reservations are justified. Even if the cross-correspondences display the coherence and integration which suggest that they were the product of an independent mind, there is nothing in the cases to establish that that mind was not a living person's.

---

[17] See, e.g. Sir Oliver Lodge: Evidence of classical scholarship and of cross-correspondence in some new automatic writings. *Proceedings of the Society for Psychical Research,* 25: 113–175, 1911; Gerald Williams, Earl of Balfour: Some Recent scripts affording evidence of personal survival. *Proceedings of the Society for for Psychical Research,* 29: 197–243; 260–286, 1918.

[18] See E. R. Dodds: Why I do not believe in survival. *Proceedings of the Society for Psychical Research,* 42: 147–172, 1934; and C. Richet, *Thirty Years of Psychical Research* (S. de Brath, trans.). New York, Macmillan, 1923.

[19] Dodds, *ibid.*

CHAPTER 15

DROP-IN COMMUNICATORS: RUNOLFUR RUNOLFSSON

An intriguing type of mediumistic evidence of afterdeath survival is that of the so-called "drop-in communicator" of information about a deceased person who is unknown either to the medium or to the medium's sitters. If a medium discloses information supposedly from or about a person who is deceased and if the person and the information were unknown previously to the medium, sitters, or anyone present at the disclosure, then it can safely be said that the medium did not obtain the information through sensory means, and did not obtain it through extrasensory means from those present.

Obviously, what must be ruled out before information from a drop-in communicator may be justifiably considered evidence of an afterlife is the possibility that the medium, sitters, or any others present had prior acquaintance with facts about the deceased communicator. Equally obvious is that this possibility is always difficult to rule out.

While several reports of drop-in communicators have been published since the late nineteenth century, I shall consider only the more credible of these. I begin with the case of Runolfur Runolfsson, as recently investigated by Erlendur Haraldsson and Ian Stevenson.[1]

"Runolfur Runolfsson" manifested himself during several sittings in the late 1930s, with the Icelandic medium, Hafsteinn Bjornsson. His first appearances were (reportedly) marked by unusual behavior, an unwillingness to give his name, and his

---

[1] A communicator of the "drop-in" type in Iceland: the case of Runolfur Runolfsson. *Journal of the American Society for Psychical Research*, 69: 33–59, 1975.

strange demand "for his leg." Eventually, there came a sitting in which he revealed his name, and claimed that while drunk he had been swept out to sea in 1879, near Sandgerdi, in the Sudurnes peninsula of Iceland. He also said that when his body was finally washed back to shore it had been dismembered by dogs, and that his thighbone was missing when his remains were subsequently buried. The thighbone, he claimed, was now in the home of one of the sitters, who lived in Sandgerdi, an individual who had joined the sittings only after "Runolfur Runolfsson" had manifested himself. Proof of his narrative could be found, he said, in the church records of Utskalar (a farm near the tip of the Sudurnes peninsula, about four miles from Sandgerdi).

Subsequent investigation by sitters into church records of Utskalar from around 1879 revealed that a Runolfur Runolfsson was indeed believed to have been swept out to sea in 1879 and that dismembered remains presumed to be his had later been washed ashore and buried in Utskalar. Though the church records did not mention that a thighbone was missing from the remains, a thighbone was eventually discovered in the walls of the home of the sitter who lived in Sandgerdi.

The case is deemed to constitute strong evidence of communication from a deceased spirit primarily because the information reportedly communicated by "Runki" (as the communicator came to be called by the sitters) about Runolfur Runolfsson and the circumstances of his death was supposedly not all contained within any single written source. This fact presumably reduced the chances that the communicated information was derived by the medium from written sources either through normal means or ESP. Only some of the correct information said to have been communicated by "Runki" was in the church records; other details reportedly related by "Runki" were confirmed through a book, *Annals of Sudurnes*, written by the clergyman who kept the church records at Utskalar. The fact that a thighbone was buried in the wall was not recorded anywhere.

Notwithstanding these interesting features of the case, critical readers will detect weaknesses in it as proof of a drop-in communicator.

Though the whereabouts of the thighbone probably was not

recorded, it is possible that all the other information about Runolfsson and the circumstances surrounding his death which "Runki" communicated *was* contained within a *single* written record, namely, the church records of Utskalar. For, in the first place, precisely what information was communicated by "Runki" is unknown, because no records were kept of "Runki's" communications at the sittings in which they occurred, and the notes made afterwards by the sitters were not kept.[2]

In the second place, it is not known exactly how much information about Runolfur was originally contained within the church records as some of their relevant pages are missing.[3] Apparently the only significant information communicated by "Runki" (apart from the whereabouts of the thighbone) that was contained in the *Annals of Sudurnes* but not in the church records was the fact that Runolfur had been drinking at the time of the accident. Could reference to Runolfur's intoxicated state have been made in the missing pages of the church records?

Moreover, at the time of the reported communications from "Runki," and probably some time before that, the church records of Utskalar had been housed in the National Archives in Reykjavik, which were open to the public, and thus the church records were accessible to the medium, Hafsteinn. Indeed, the Archives guest book shows that the medium had visited the Archives in late fall of 1939, which, however, may have been after the sitting in which "Runki" revealed the details of Runolfur's death.

But Hafsteinn's visit to the Archives may also have been before this sitting, though the guest book does not show it. For one thing, the exact date of the sitting was never recorded, and was only recalled, apparently in 1972, by former sitters as having been "in the late winter or spring of 1939."[4] For another thing, Hafsteinn at first told Haraldsson that he had *never* been to the Archives, and then "remembered" that he had, when informed that his signature had been found in the Archives guest book for the date November 24, 1939. He still maintained, though, that he had never visited the Archives prior to that date.

---

[2]*Ibid.*, p. 39, n. 11.

[3]*Ibid.*, p. 46, n. 20.

[4]*Ibid.*, p. 39, n. 11.

Haraldsson and Stevenson are willing to credit Hafsteinn with "an honest error of memory of an event that happened thirty-two years before our inquiries in 1971–1972."[5] But if Hafsteinn made one honest error of memory in claiming never to have been to the Archives, he could have made another when he claimed that he had not visited the Archives prior to the sitting in which "Runki" communicated his identity and the details of Runolfur's death.[6]

It is true that Hafsteinn's signature did not appear in the Archives guest book on any occasion earlier than November 24, 1939, but, Haraldsson and Stevenson discovered that people are so infrequently asked to sign the Archives' guest book that "it appears best to place more reliance on individual memories than on the signatures in the guest book in deciding whether a particular person had visited the Archives on any given date."[7] And so the thesis that Hafsteinn had not visited the Archives previously rests on very infirm ground, namely on Hafsteinn's fallible memory.

That Hafsteinn may have visited the Archives prior to the communications from "Runki" obviously is of great significance. Mediums have been known to supply themselves with information that might later turn out to be useful. Also, mediums in trance sometimes have remarkable powers of recall. Stevenson himself in another context claims to have witnessed "communications" from mediums that were almost exact reproductions of newspaper death notices.[8] Too, according to Haraldsson and Stevenson, Hafsteinn himself "has sometimes been suspected" of furnishing himself with information that could become useful later.[9]

One may presume, of course, that the fact that the house of one of Hafsteinn's sitters had a human thighbone hidden in it was not a matter of available public record. Could "Runki" have known of the existence and whereabouts of this bone without actually hav-

---

[5]*Ibid.*, p. 47.

[6]Hafsteinn, on some other, unrelated occasion, denied having been somewhere he evidently had in fact been. An informant attributed this to another "lapse of memory" on Hafsteinn's part. *Ibid.*, p. 47, n. 21.

[7]*Ibid.*, p. 48.

[8]See Stevenson: Some comments on automatic writing. *Journal of the American Society for Psychical Research,* 72: 315–332, 1978.

[9]Stevenson, *op. cit.*, p. 47, n. 21.

ing been the former Runolfur Runolfsson?[10]

Now, the house in which the thighbone was found had before the discovery been rumored to be "haunted," and the fact that there was a thighbone, and, incidentally, two skulls, hidden within the house was, at the time of the sittings with "Runki," known by several people in the area.[11] Indeed, some people even knew that the femur was hidden between the inner and outer walls of the house, and the carpenter who placed the bone between the walls was at the time of the sittings still around to point out its exact location.[12]

Further, Hafsteinn, prior to the "Runki communications," had lived for about two years only six miles away from this area; so, it is certainly not inconceivable that he overheard some mention of the haunted house and its contents. Could the conscious or subconscious mind of the medium, Hafsteinn, have drawn any connection between a report of the drowned Runolfur Runolfsson's dismembered remains lying on the shore and rumors of unidentified bones hidden in a house in the same area? It certainly is conceivable that such a linking of these two items might subconsciously have been made. Indeed, Haraldsson and Stevenson themselves point out that "it is natural to link any remains that are found on the beach with the few persons known to have died in accidents off the coast of that area."[13]

On consideration, therefore, I believe that there is room for real doubt that the "Runki communications" issued from a departed spirit. There is a genuine possibility that the medium (a) may have seen a certain report about a drowned man and become

---

[10]Skeptics might, of course, wonder how, even if "Runki" were the former Runolfur Runolfsson, this fact would enable "Runki" to know the whereabouts of his thighbone. Do the departed know all as to what happens to their remains?

[11]It seems an amazing coincidence that Runolfur Runolfsson's thighbone would end up together in the very same house with two skulls, at least one of which obviously was not the skull of Runolfur. One would certainly think that whatever fate befell the owners of the skulls probably also befell the owner of the thighbone, and vice versa. Thus, since Runolfur was evidently unaccompanied when he drowned, either his thighbone amazingly came together under one roof with someone else's skull, or the thighbone itself was really not his to begin with. (As Runolfur's remains have not been disinterred, the bone has not been positively identified as his.)

[12]It evidently would be very unusual, but not totally bizarre, to dispose of a human bone in this strange way in Iceland. Stevenson, *op. cit.*, p. 40, n. 13.

[13]*Ibid.*, p. 55.

aware of a local rumor about a haunted house and (b) then consciously or subconsciously have drawn some sort of connection between the two.

CHAPTER 16

GAULD'S "DROP-INS"

As widely known as the case of Runolfur Runolfsson is Alan Gauld's 1971 study: A series of "drop in" communicators.[1] Gauld's report is based on the records kept by one "L. G.," a retired British government officer and member of the Society for Psychical Research. From 1937 to 1964 L. G., together with his wife and certain acquaintances, held some 550 seances in Cambridge, England, at which, from time to time, primarily in 1942 and 1943, deceased individuals assertedly unknown to those in attendance communicated to them through an ouija board. Gauld, upon investigating L. G.'s reports and various public records, was able to verify some of the statements made about themselves by some ten of the unknown communicators.

The series of cases studied by Gauld is impressive to some people because of this verification and also because participants in the seances for the most part made no effort, themselves, to authenticate the statements of the unknown communicators. Had not Gauld some twenty years later investigated the L. G. notes, probably no one, including the participants in the seances, would ever have become aware that statements made by several of the unknown communicators were indeed true of the individuals these communicators claimed to be.

These facts dispel trickery and fraud, but is there any other plausible nonsurvivalist explanation for the "communication" of information that was authenticated twenty years later by Gauld?

Gauld thinks that telepathy is as implausible an explanation as is fraud, and thinks it unlikely too that the operator of the ouija board produced the information through cryptomnesia, *viz.*, that the operator unintentionally reproduced on the ouija board information that he or she had once seen in a newspaper obituary or

---

[1]*Proceedings of the Society for Psychical Research.* 55: 273–340, 1971.

121

the like and that was stored, forgotten, in his or her subconscious.

However, I think that the possibility of cryptomnesia as an explanation cannot be eliminated. As noted in the previous chapter, mediums (some operating with ouija boards) have been known to reproduce, almost verbatim, information contained in obituaries, with absolutely no recollection of having read the obituaries, even when it is certain that they have done so. Consequently, whenever a single source is discovered that contains all the information expressed in a particular communication, it is unjustifiable to suppose that the information came, not from that source, but from a departed spirit. For it is almost impossible to establish with any reasonable certainty that a medium did not have access to that source. Even if the information was contained in an obscure publication with a small circulation in an entirely different city from that in which the medium lives, the medium may have visited the other city. She, or some acquaintance, may have received merchandise in which the publication was used as packing material. The publication may have found its way into a dentist's waiting room or the home of a relative.

Five of the ten cases investigated by Mr. Gauld seem to me easily explainable as cryptomnesia by the operator of the ouija board or are so lacking in any facts suggestive of communication from the dead that no explanation is needed:

1. All of the information which came through the ouija board about one "Edward Druce" "was contained in a periodical known to have been readily accessible to one or more of the operators."[2]

2. As to a communicator known as "Max Cheyne": his name was merely spelled out on the board and a reference was made to the Royal Air Force, but this information evidently appeared on the *Times* "Roll of Honor," the official war casualty list.[3]

3. Just a few days before "Josephine Street" communicated information about herself through the ouija board, a death notice containing all of this information appeared in a local newspaper. Further correct information about Josephine Street came out at later sittings, but these were held after *Mr.* Street had joined the circle of sitters, and, as Gauld says, it is "quite impossible to say

---

[2]*Ibid.*, p. 329.

[3]*Ibid.*, pp. 318–319.

what information Mr. Street may have let drop at previous sittings."[4]

4. Gauld himself dismisses the case of "Walter Leggat."[5]

5. Finally, it is not clear that a decent real-life "match" for a communicator calling herself "Kathleen Clark" was ever found.[6]

To summarize the pertinent details of the remaining five of the ten cases, in which no single source of all of the communicated information was found by Gauld:

1. With one exception, the correct details spelled out on the ouija board about a communicator who identified herself as "Nora Hentall" were all contained in a single newspaper death notice of one Eleanor Hentall. The exception was that "Nora Hentall" used the word *clubhouse* in her communication. According to Gauld, the husband of Eleanor Hentall was a "club manager," a fact not mentioned in the death notice.[7]

2. Most of the information produced on the ouija board by a communicator named "Harry Stockbridge" was contained in local paper obituaries of an individual by that name.[8] However, the following facts were mentioned by the communicator, but did not appear in any known obituaries: (a) Whereas in the local papers it was stated that Stockbridge had been a member of the Northumberland Fusiliers, the communicator stated, correctly, that Stockbridge had been a member of the *Tyneside Scottish Battalion* of the Northumberland Fusiliers. (b) Whereas the local papers reported, *incorrectly*, that Stockbridge had been a lieutenant, the communicator reported, *correctly*, that Stockbridge had been a "second loot." (c) Whereas no physical description of Stockbridge appeared in the newspapers, the communicator accurately described Stockbridge as tall, dark, thin, and with large brown eyes. However, this description is too unspecific to be regarded as particularly significant. The details provided by the communicator under (a) and (b) above are, it seems to me, exactly the kinds of details that are likely to appear in obituaries.

Incidentally, Gauld notes that whereas Stockbridge's correct

---

[4] *Ibid.*, p. 318.

[5] *Ibid.*, p. 316.

[6] *Ibid.*, pp. 319–320.

[7] *Ibid.*, pp. 320–321.

[8] *Ibid.*, pp. 322–327.

rank and date of death were "communicated" via the ouija board, one of the printed records of Stockbridge's death erred with respect to Stockbridge's death-date, and another erred with respect to his rank. Gauld reasons that this makes it unlikely that the information about Stockbridge that came through the ouija board had been stored in the subconscious mind of one of the operators of the board. The operator, he writes, would have to have subconsciously "collated the two [published death notices] in such a way as to reject the erroneous death-date given in the one and the erroneous rank given in the other."[9] Gauld's reasoning rests on the unstated and unestablished premise that there was no third obituary read by the ouija board operator that was correct in both details.

3. A communicator calling himself "Duncan Stevens" reported several true pieces of information about a deceased pilot officer of the Royal Air Force who had that name. Almost all of the correct information was, however, contained (or could conceivably have been inferred from) a "missing-in-action" notice published in a religious weekly three weeks after Stevens' plane crashed. The correct information not contained in the "missing" notice was that Stevens came down over water and was killed, that his plane was a Blenheim, that he was known by his second rather than his Christian name, that he had been a curate of the "Parish Church" in "Frinton," and that his mother would not welcome being approached by members of the L. G. circle.[10] (Possibly most mothers of deceased sons would not welcome such an approach.)

Regarding this information, it would not have been unusual for a reader of the "missing-in-action" notice to have suspected that Stevens had been killed, and was possibly killed over water. (Stevens had been sent to attack ships off the Norwegian coast, though this fact was not mentioned in the "missing" notice.)

Could the remaining significant details have been contained in some as-yet-undiscovered newspaper article? Apparently, Stevens' mission when killed was of a secret nature. Nonetheless, Stevens' sister believes that an account of Stevens' death may have appeared in some newspaper, because she recalled that her mother had

---
[9]*Ibid.*, p. 328.
[10]*Ibid.*, pp. 295–301.

received a letter of condolence the sister thought might have been inspired by a newspaper report.[11]

4. A "Robert Fletcher" communicated true information about a deceased apprentice navigator by that name.[12] With but a few exceptions, all the correct information was discovered to have been published in a newspaper, in this case a newspaper which circulated in an area in which the principal operator of the ouija board, Mrs. G., had earlier lived. The significant information which wasn't contained in the newspaper report is limited to mention of Fletcher's age and approximate date of birth, items which might have been mentioned in a more complete obituary than the one Gauld discovered.

5. The last case, that of one "Gustav Adolph Biedermann,"[13] again presents ouija-board-produced information about a deceased individual, which for the most part appeared in published obituaries. The principal correct information which did not appear in any as-yet-discovered obituaries was that Biedermann's first name was "Gustav," that he had "rationalist views," and that he was connected with the "Rationalist Press."

That the information came from the spirit of Biedermann is unlikely. Biedermann was not an unknown person. He had once been shot in the back by his wife, and the event and subsequent trial were covered by several English newspapers. Further, Biedermann had contributed to the letters column of the *Times*, and had published a study of psychoanalysis. Other information about Biedermann had at various times appeared in newspapers, and obituaries had been printed in the *Times* and *Daily Telegraph*. Since Biedermann was hardly unknown (though he was by no means famous), one or more of the participants in the seances may subconsciously have accumulated information about him over the years. It would be pointless to speculate about the sort of information that could or could not have been acquired in this way.

In none of these last five drop-in cases were the disclosed details found in any single published source. However, these details were by and large the kind that typically appear in obituaries or were of insufficient specificity to be of great interest. True, in

---
[11]*Ibid.*, p. 300.

[12]*Ibid.*, pp. 302–306.

[13]*Ibid.*, pp. 306–315.

many instances, the obituaries found were in obscure publications or in newspapers that it might seem unlikely that the principal ouija board operator, Mrs. G, would have encountered, but it is very nearly impossible to know what the possibilities really were of Mrs. G having seen these sources of information.

To conclude in regard to the Gauld report, not every piece of correct information revealed in the communications of the "drop-ins" was found in pre-existing printed sources. But these pieces of information are few, and they usually exhibit an obituary-like quality. The possibility, or even probability, that obituaries or other pre-existing printed matter did not provide the information has not been eliminated.

CHAPTER 17

APPARITIONS

What may this mean,
That thou, dead corpse, again in complete steel
Revisits thus the glimpses of the moon,
Making night hideous; and we fools of nature
So horridly to shake our disposition
With thoughts beyond the reaches of our souls?
—Shakespeare, Hamlet[1]

Apparitions both of the dead and of the living have assertedly been seen on many occasions. Numerous reports of them, many with affidavits attesting to the authenticity of the sightings, have been filed with the Society for Psychical Research from its founding in 1882 until the present day, and many have been published in its *Journal* and elsewhere.[2] Because of the vast number of reports of apparitions, some survival researchers regard them as second in importance only to the best medium-produced material as proof of survival; indeed some regard them as the most important evidence in this respect.

Professor Hornell Hart, who studied reports of apparitions

---

[1] Jack Randall Crawford (Ed.). New Haven, Yale University Press, 1917, p. 25 (Act I, Scene IV).

[2] All of the following may be consulted for reports of apparitions: (1) E. Gurney, F. W. H. Myers, and F. Podmore: *Phantasms of the Living.* London, Trubner, 1886, 2 vols; (2) F. W. H. Myers: *Human Personality and Its Survival of Bodily Death.* London, Longmans, Green, 1903, 2 vols; (3) F. Podmore: *Apparitions and Thought-Transference.* London, Walter Scott, 1894; and (4) *Telepathic Hallucinations: The New View of Ghosts.* London, Milner, n.d.; (5) Mrs. Henry Sidgwick: Phantasms of the living. *Proceedings of the Society for Psychical Research, 33:* 23–429, 1923; (6) W. F. Prince: *Noted Witnesses for Psychic Occurrences.* Boston, Boston Society for Psychic Research, 1928; (7) W. H. Salter: *Ghosts and Apparitions.* London, Bell, 1938; (8) E. Bennett: *Apparitions and Haunted Houses.* London, Faber and Faber, 1939; (9) L. A. Dale: A series of spontaneous cases in the tradition of *Phantasms of the Living. Journal of the American Society for Psychical Research, 45:* 85–101, 1951; (10) C. N. M. Tyrell: *Apparitions.* (2nd ed. rev.) London, Duckworth, 1953; (11) A. Mackenzie: *Apparitions and Ghosts.* London, Arthur Barker, 1971; (12) C. E. Green and C. McCreery: *Apparitions.* London, Hamish Hamilton, 1975.

closely, collected from the literature over 250 cases of apparitions that, he thought, when considered together strongly support the belief in survival.[3] Professor Hart felt "driven" to conclude that an apparition seen of a *living* person, Jones, let us say, is in many instances not a mere hallucination on the part of the individual who sees it, but rather a carrier of Jones' consciousness, an "etheric body" that temporarily leaves Jones' physical body and, guided by Jones' intentions and purposes, actually "travels" or "projects" in some mode to the place where it is sighted.

These apparitions of living persons, Hart noticed, are the same in character and appearance as the apparitions of the dead. Therefore, he reasoned, the apparitions of the dead are likewise vehicles through which the dead make conscious contact with the living.

Other survival researchers do not agree with Hart's conclusions. His investigations were limited to published reports of so-called spontaneous cases, i.e. cases in which reportedly an apparition is unexpectedly or "spontaneously" witnessed. Consequently, his studies are marred by certain typical weaknesses of reports of spontaneous cases of supernatural or paraphysical happenings. These typical weaknesses have been catalogued by D. J. West and Antony Flew.[4]

A principal reason why seemingly supernatural spontaneous happenings cannot safely be taken as evidence of much of anything is that the spectators usually are neither trained nor ready to make capable and accurate observations, to make clear, complete, and unambiguous records of the observed phenomena, or to retain reliable memories of what they saw. Nor, usually, are they aware of the various nonparanormal explanations of these phenomena nor capable of quickly thinking of these explanations. The published material in these "spontaneous" cases, no matter how cogently it is analyzed, is ultimately based on the reports of untrained specta-

---

[3] See H. Hart: Six theories about apparitions. *Proceedings of the Society for Psychical Research,* 50: 153–239, 1956; *Toward a New Philosophical Basis for Parapsychological Phenomena.* Parapsychological Monographs, no. 6. New York, Parapsychology Foundation, 1965; *The Enigma of Survival.* London, Rider and Co., 1959; Scientific survival research. *International Journal of Philosophy,* 9: 43–52, 1967; ESP projection: spontaneous cases and the experimental method. *Proceedings of the Society for Psychical Research,* 48: 121–146, 1954.

[4] D. J. West: The investigation of spontaneous cases. *Proceedings of the Society for Psychical Research,* 48: 264–300, 1948; *Psychical Research Today.* London, Duckworth, 1954; and Antony Flew: *A New Approach to Psychical Research.* London, Watts, 1953.

tors who are not merely unskilled as witnesses but who are also frequently involved emotionally in the observed phenomena. Certainly, a person's emotional needs may warp and transfigure his perceptions. Thus, it is not surprising that there are examples of "fully authenticated" spontaneous "paranormal happenings" that have later turned out to be perfectly normal events.[5]

As the Research Officer for the Society for Psychical Research, West on one occasion had Miss Hilda Harding go through the spontaneous "Cases" published in the *Journal* of the society to estimate their value. Miss Harding, who claimed to have had psychic dreams and impressions herself, examined the cases in fifteen volumes of the *Journal*, from the 1884 issue to the current, and concluded that they had little, if any, value as evidence of any paranormal effects unless one were prepared to admit that "all that life has taught us of the strange results ensuing from lack of mental balance, honest error, illusion, expectancy, suggestion, and so forth, apart altogether from mischievous lying," could be offset by the "mere word of the percipient."[6]

Hart, however, placed considerable weight on twenty-five reports of apparitions in which the people whose apparitions were thought to have been seen claimed to have intended to "travel" or "project" themselves, or to have been conscious of being projected, to the place of the sighting. However, Louisa Rhine, in her study of the eight hundred-plus cases of "psychic-hallucinations" on file at the parapsychology laboratory in Durham, North Carolina, discovered that in none of the over four hundred cases of reported sightings of apparitions, supposedly of living persons, were those persons intending or aware of any projection.[7] So Rhine concluded that a supposed apparition is merely a product of the percipient's mind, and not an emanation in any way of the person whose apparition was thought to be seen.

Hart took exception to Rhine's findings on the ground that her cases had not been "verified" or even investigated. In Hart's cases, by contrast, the percipient allegedly described his sighting to some

---

[5]See either of the works cited in the preceeding footnote for a discussion of these cases.

[6]West, *op. cit.* (The investigation of spontaneous cases), pp. 292-293.

[7]See Louisa Rhine: Hallucinatory psi experiences, I, II, and III. *Journal of Parapsychology*, 20: 233-256, 1956; 21: 13-46, 1957; and 21: 186-226, 1957. See also her later study with I. Stevenson in *Journal of Parapsychology1, 34:* 143-163, 1970.

third party before the percipient learned of the intentions or experiences of the "projected" person, i.e. the person who was thought to have been sighted as an apparition. Hart's criticism of Rhine is most peculiar. What kind of "verification" *should* be given of the fact that the person whose apparition was seen said that he was neither intending to project himself nor aware of having done so? Would we think of requiring verification of a person's statement that he was not aware of a UFO or that he had not intended to make himself invisible?

Moreover, Hart's cases still rest ultimately on the reports of untrained spectators: this is not changed by the fact that the reports were given to a third party.

Hart also criticized Rhine's theory that apparitions are within the mind of the one seeing them, on the grounds that cases of sightings of the same apparition by more than one spectator could not be explained by Rhine's theory. Mirages, though having no existence outside the minds of those who see them, are perceived by more than one person, and cases in which several people have concurrently shared the the same hallucination, though not very common, have been well authenticated.[8]

Hart's theory of projection can also be criticized because it is difficult to explain why apparitions are supposedly sighted as fully clothed and sometimes as accompanied by pets. Is it possible that "apparitional tissue" might assume the form of clothing or a pet so that a percipient might more easily recognize the apparition? In general, efforts to explain the clothing of apparitions strain credulity.

According to Alan Gauld, the great majority of modern parapsychologists now regard apparitions as hallucinations, and thus agree with Rhine.[9] Obviously, what I have written discloses my own more favorable reaction to Rhine than to Hart in regard to their conflicting views of apparitions.

Nevertheless, it must be emphasized that very recently there has been evidence from controlled laboratory experiments relative to the possibility of travel or projection from one's body of one's consciousness. I shall treat this evidence, which obviously has a bearing on whether apparitions may be something more or other than hallucinations, in Part IV.

---

[8]West, *op. cit.*, pp. 295–298.

[9]Alan Gauld: Discarnate survival. In Benjamin Wolman (Ed.): *Handbook of Parapsychology.* New York, Van Nostrand Reinhold Co., 1977, p. 601.

CHAPTER 18

PROOF OR CORROBORATION?

That the continents drift cannot reasonably be believed by anyone simply because the east coast of South America and the west coast of Africa look like they were once joined. Yet the fit of these coastlines, when considered in conjunction with much more compelling evidence of continental drift, such as the distribution of certain fossils and confirmation of sea-floor spreading, does add further weight to that evidence.

In my view, the "survival-data" from the early period, in and of themselves, clearly do not constitute proof of an afterlife. The mediumships of Mrs. Piper and Mrs. Leonard, while investigated by capable observers, were not subject to the rigorous modern methods of investigation and appraisal that discount "elastic" communications and preclude acquisition by the medium of information from living persons. By no means all commentators on the cross-correspondences agree that these intriguing communications display a coherence suggestive of intelligent authorship; and even if this coherence were obvious and indisputable, the possibility that the authoring intelligence was that of living persons was never eliminated. The medium, sitters, and others present when information was communicated by a drop-in spirit could too easily have had prior acquaintance with that information. As for the sightings of apparitions, they could conceivably have been the products of the percipients' minds; the early evidence that they were not is too slender to compel belief.

Nevertheless, the weaknesses of the early survival-data are not of a character that would deprive the data of *corroborative* value. If these data coincide with any information from the late period, which is more compelling of belief in personal survival, then the early data would help confirm the later information, just as the fit of the coastlines corroborates the evidence of continental drift provided by other, more convincing types of geological evidence.

Final and accurate appraisal of the evidentiary value of the early data regarding survival must therefore await examination of the evidence from the late period.

PART IV

THE LATE EVIDENCE

CHAPTER 19

VISIONS AT THE BRINK OF DEATH

In 1959–1960, Doctor Karlis Osis surveyed 640 American physicians and nurses concerning the experiences of their patients who were close to death.[1] His work marks the beginning of the late period of survival research, a period characterized by diversification of studies and by great use of scientific methodology, including exacting systematic research. In treating the evidence from this period, I begin with the investigations of Doctor Osis.

The Osis-Haraldsson Studies

Doctor Osis's 1959–1960 survey suggested that patients who were very near death ("deathbed" patients) frequently had "survival-related" hallucinations that consisted of visions of deceased relatives or of religious figures. The purpose of the apparition seen was frequently deemed by the patient to be to take him to "another world."

Comparison of Doctor Osis's survey with studies of hallucinations in the general population indicated that these survival-related hallucinations occurred two to three times more frequently among the dying patients of Doctor Osis's study than they occurred in the general population.[2] Other, less systematic investigations of the experiences of persons at the brink of death have provided further indication that those persons may tend to have survival-related visions.[3]

---

[1] K. Osis: *Deathbed Observations by Physicians and Nurses.* New York, Parapsychology Foundation, 1961.

[2] According to Dr. Osis, 80 percent of the hallucinations of the deathbed patients were survival-related, i.e. were visions of departed relatives or of religious figures. In the Report on the census of hallucinations (H. Sidgwick and Committee, *Proceedings of the Society for Psychical Research, 10:* 25–422, 1894), it was recorded that 33 percent of the sample had hallucinations of the survival-type. Only 22 percent of the sample in a study made later by D. J. West were reported as having such hallucinations. See: A mass-observation questionnaire on hallucinations. *Journal of the Society for Psychical Research, 34:* 187–196, 1948.

[3] For further reports on the experiences, including hallucinations, of persons nearing death, see W. F. Barrett: *Death-Bed Visions.* London, Methuen, 1926; A. Ford: *The Life Beyond Death.*

In order to replicate Doctor Osis's original study, and in order to gather more information relevant to the question of life after death, Doctor Osis and Doctor Erlendur Haraldsson conducted two more surveys of physicians and nurses.[4] One survey was conducted between 1961 and 1964 among 1004 physicians and nurses in the northeastern United States, and the other was conducted in 1972-1973 among 704 physicians and nurses in northern India. Osis and Haraldsson wished specifically to consider the survival-related visions of near-death patients in relation to two "hypotheses": the "survival hypothesis" that physical death is not the end of life but a transition to another plane, and the "destruction hypothesis" that death destroys and ends personality and life.

If the destruction hypothesis is correct, then the survival-related visions of the dying patients, Osis and Haraldsson reasoned, must be purely subjective phenomena, hallucinations resulting from psychological or physiological causes. If the survival hypothesis is correct, then survival-visions are not really hallucinations at all, but rather glimpses of an objective, nonphysical reality in which the dead now exist.[5] Osis and Haraldsson therefore researched the data from the three surveys for significant correlations between the visions and selected other factors, including medical conditions, cultural influences, stress, desire for an afterlife, and fear of death. They found that the survival-visions of the near-death

New York, Putnam, 1971; B. Graham: *Angels: God's Secret Agents*. New York, Guideposts Associates, 1976; A. Heim: Remarks on fatal falls. *Yearbook of the Swiss Alpine Club, 27:* 327-337 (trans. by R. Noyes and R. Kletti in *Omega, 3:* 45-52, 1972); N. O. Jacobson: *Life Without Death?* Delacorte Press (n.p.), 1974; E. Kübler-Ross: (1) *On Death and Dying*. New York, Macmillan Company, 1971; (2) *Death: The Final Stage of Growth*. New Jersey, Prentice-Hall, 1975; C. W. Leadbeater: *The Astral Plane*. India, Theosophical Publishing House, 1973; C. Marshall: *A Man Called Peter*. New York, Avon, 1971; R. A. Moody: *Life After Life*. Covington, GA, Mockingbird, 1975; Noyes and Kletti: (1) Depersonalization in the face of life-threatening danger: a description. *Psychiatry, 39:* 19-27, 1976; (2) Depersonalization in the face of life-threatening danger: an interpretation. *Omega, 7:* 103-114, 1976; C. Panati: Is there life after death? *Family Circle, 89:* 78, 84, 90, 1976; J. B. Phillips: *Your God Is Too Small*. New York, Macmillan, 1971; R. H. Thouless: *From Anecdote to Experiment in Psychical Research*. London, Routledge and Kegan Paul, 1972; K. L. Woodward: (1) There is life after death. *McCall's, 103:* 134-139, 1976; (2) Life after death. *Newsweek, 41:* July 12, 1976.

[4]For the report of these two more recent surveys, see: Deathbed observations by physicians and nurses: a cross-cultural survey. *The Journal of the American Society for Psychical Research, 71:* 237-259, 1977. See also, Osis and Haraldsson: *At the Hour of Death*. New York, Avon, 1977.

[5]The "glimpses" would have to be nonsensory perceptions, I assume. It is, of course, difficult to comprehend how the nearness of physical death might serve to enhance or promote nonsensory perception.

patients were "relatively independent" of these other factors, and viewed this finding as "in conformity with the survival hypothesis."[6]

Medical and Psychological Factors

Medical Factors

Were the survival-related visions possibly the result of hallucinogenic medical factors? Osis and Haraldsson found that only one third of the patients who experienced the visions were subject to certain medical conditions or factors known to produce or to be associated with hallucinations, including high body temperature, alcoholism, mental illness, various injuries and diseases known to be associated with hallucinations, and consciousness-affecting medications such as morphine. Further, this one third of the vision-seeing patients who *were* subject to hallucinogenic medical factors, did *not* have more than their fair share of the survival-related visions:.there was no significant correlation between subjection to a hallucinogenic medical factor and the frequency of survival-related visions. Osis and Haraldsson concluded that the medical variables with which they were concerned were "relatively unrelated" to the survival-related visions.[7]

Stress

Hallucinations tend to occur in situations of severe stress, according to studies cited by Osis and Haraldsson. Could it be, they ask, that the deathbed visions were hallucinations "due to stress rather than to extrasensory awareness of 'visitors' from another mode of existence?"[8]

To answer their question, they correlated the patients' moods (as reported by their physicians or nurses) on the day before the survival-related visions, not only with the reported "purposes" of the apparitional figures that appeared in the visions and with

---

[6]Deathbed observations by physicians and nurses: a cross-cultural survey, *op. cit.*, p. 237.

[7]*Ibid.*, p. 250. Osis and Haraldsson also compiled evidence to the effect that dying patients who are subject to hallucinogenic medical factors are *not* more likely to have survival-related visions than are non-dying patients who are subject to such factors. But this finding would seem compatible with either the destruction or survival hypothesis.

[8]*Ibid.*, p. 250.

"what these apparitions represented," but also with the patients' emotional reactions to the visionary experience. They assumed that negative moods (e.g. anxiety, depression) would be indicative of more stress than would be positive moods, and that moods designated by the physician or nurse as "normal" or "average" would indicate the least amount of stress.

However, Osis and Haraldsson could find "no significant interactions" either between the patients' moods and "what the apparition represented" or between the moods and the patients' emotional reactions to the apparition. The reported *purpose* of the apparition also was not "significantly related to mood in either the American or the Indian sample taken separately," but, when the samples were considered collectively, patients with so-called normal moods were found to be somewhat more prone to experience apparitions with a peaceful, "take-away" purpose.

On the basis of these findings, Osis and Haraldsson concluded that it is not likely that the incidence of survival-related visions was affected by the stress felt by the patient.[9]

Desires, Expectations, Fears

Might survival-related deathbed visions have been caused by the desire for, or expectation of, encounters after death with deceased loved ones? This explanation of the survival-visions readily suggests itself. Osis and Haraldsson, however, reject it. They found that rarely did hallucinating dying patients, who had expressed a desire to be visited before death by *living* relatives, have visions of those relatives.[10]

Finally, with regard to whether the survival-related visions might have been engendered by the patients to help them "cope with their fear of dying," Osis and Haraldsson found that neither the reported intentions nor the reported identities of the apparitions seen in the deathbed visions were significantly correlated with the patient's expectations of living or fears of dying.[11]

---

[9]*Ibid.*, p. 252.

[10]*Ibid.*, p. 252.

[11]*Ibid.*, p. 252.

Survival or Destruction?

Do these various findings support the survival and undermine the destruction hypothesis?

Osis and Haraldsson found, I noted above, that the survival-related deathbed visions were relatively independent of the various medical factors which they surveyed. However, whether this finding supports the survival-hypothesis is another matter. Even if survival-visions are not the result of such medical factors as Osis and Haraldsson considered, i.e. alcoholism, high body temperature, mental illness, hallucinogenic medications, or kidney diseases or other hallucination-causing maladies, they might still have a physiological explanation. A survival-related vision may well be the result of the physiological decay and dissolution of an organism in its last extremity, even if it is not the result of other known causes of hallucinations.

Further, Doctor James F. McHarg has pointed out that Osis and Haraldsson apparently did not take into account one very important *known* medical possibility, namely, that the survival-related visions were the result of paroxysmal temporal lobe disturbances precipitated by transitory cerebral anoxia.[12] Having visions of people and other beings is, Doctor McHarg has observed, a typical feature of paroxysmal temporal lobe attacks, and a predisposition to these attacks, he has noted, is now believed to be quite high in the general population. In the majority of people who have this predisposition, the temporal lobe disturbances are likely to occur only if there is present an additional influence, such as, cerebral anoxia. An additional influence may manifest itself in the process of dying, and thus account for at least some of the survival-visions of the patients. Though temporal lobe seizures resulting from cerebral anoxia are, it seems, often associated with certain other experiences that the patients included in the Osis and Haraldsson studies were *not* reported to have had,[13] this type of disorder should have been taken into account by Osis and Haraldsson in their consideration of medical factors.

I am doubtful too about the findings of Osis and Haraldsson as

---

[12]James F. McHarg: Review of *At the Hour of Death. Journal of the Society for Psychical Research*, 49: 885–887, 1978.

[13]See next chapter.

to the lack of relationship between the survival-related visions and patient stress. That which Osis and Haraldsson took as the indicant of stress was the patient's mood, as reported by his physician or nurse, on the day before he experienced a survival-related vision. I think it altogether possible that the patient's vision was in some manner directly related to the stress resulting from bodily decay and the processes of dying, even though no connection was found between the vision and the patient's earlier mood, as it was reported by a physician or nurse. The physician or nurse may not have observed the patient's mood accurately, let alone have remembered it correctly. Even more importantly, it is most uncertain that the physiological stress on a patient can reliably be inferred from secondhand reports about his earlier moods.

I also doubt that Osis and Haraldsson's finding, that hallucinating patients who had earlier expressed a desire to be visited by living relatives did not have visions of those relatives, settles whether some of the survival-related visions might have been caused or shaped by the desire for an after-death meeting with deceased loved ones. A person who, terminally ill or not, is deprived of contact with a living relative, may well *not* have hallucinations of the relative, but the desire for life and hope for survival, I think, may be more fervent and overwhelming in a dying patient than the desire to be visited by a living relative. Just as the desire for water, to use an example given by Osis and Haraldsson, may cause a person dying of thirst to see a stream where there is none, so may the thirst for life of one who is losing it cause him to have visions of a hereafter.

In regard to whether the survival-related visions were caused by the patients' fears, it may be recalled that Osis and Haraldsson found that neither the reported intentions nor the reported identities of the apparitions seen in the survival-visions stood in significant correlation with the patients' expectations of living or fears of dying.

It is possible, though, notwithstanding this lack of correlation between fear of dying and "content" of vision, that the visions were produced by the patients' fears. We find the same lack of correlation in normal life between our fears and the contents of our dreams. At times, strong fears produce distressing and unpleasant dreams. At other times, these same fears trigger "escape"-type dreams with more soothing contents. Similarly, the visions of a dying patient may be influenced or shaped by his fears and worries in different ways at different times so that no discernible pattern emerges. On one occasion his fear of dying may lead to one kind of vision, and, on another occasion, to a different kind of vision. The effect of the fear of dying may vary too from patient to patient.

So, here again I do not find the data of Osis and Haraldsson discordant with "normal" explanations of the survival-related visions, the normal explanation in this instance being that some visions may have resulted from the hope for survival or the dread of death.

Cultural Differences

Osis and Haraldsson were very concerned with whether deathbed visions reflected cultural differences. They reasoned that if the visions tended to be the same for all patients, whether Indian or American, or if there were only "modest differences" in the main features of the visions, then this would support the survival hypothesis that the visions were "perceptions" (albeit of an extrasensory sort) of a nonphysical reality beyond the physical world.[14]

This reasoning is, I think, suspect. It is not axiomatic that if something is seen as the same by everyone then it must have objective reality. The "water" in a mirage looks substantially the same to observers from all cultures, even though it has no reality "outside the minds" of the observers. Similarly, lack of all but "modest" differences among the survival-related visions may not prove that what is "seen" is outside the minds of the dying patients.

Furthermore, whether or not the culturally aligned differences in the visions are "modest" is, I think, a matter of opinion. The opinion of Osis and Haraldsson is that the differences are modest enough to support the survivalist explanation of the visions as perceptions of a nonphysical plane.[15]

Many readers of their report will view the culturally aligned differences among the visions as not "modest" at all, but as quite pronounced. Dying Americans tended to see deceased relatives and dying Indians to see religious figures. Less than 1 percent of the Americans, but over 30 percent of the Indians, reported that

---

[14]Deathbed observations. *Op. cit.*, p. 256.

[15]*Ibid.*

the apparition was taking them away against their wishes. The gender of the "perceived" apparition was "largely determined by culturally conditioned preferences."[16]

Though it is a matter of opinion whether or not these differences should be called "modest," my own opinion is that they should not, and that they indicate a subjective origin of the survival-related deathbed visions.[17]

Osis and Haraldsson did find that the *frequency* of the survival-related visions does not seem to vary from culture to culture. This finding is, I think, quite consonant with both destruction and survival hypotheses.

Belief in Afterlife

There remain to be taken into account two more factors considered by Doctors Osis and Haraldsson. Belief in an afterlife, Osis and Haraldsson found, had no significant influence on the *frequency* of survival-related visions of the dying. Their data suggest to me that other aspects of the visions may have been influenced by this belief.

First, their data indicate that the dying patient who believes in an afterlife is more likely than other dying patients to have a vision of a figure whose purpose is assumed by the patients to be to "take him away."[18]

Secondly, whereas in the Osis-Haraldsson surveys 92 percent of the American dying patients who had survival-related visions believed in an afterlife, according to a 1960 Gallup poll, only 74 percent of Americans believed in an afterlife.[19] Thus, the believers among the patients included in the Osis-Haraldsson surveys may constitute a disproportionately large percentage of those who had survival-related visions.

Clarity of Consciousness

Finally, Osis and Haraldsson designed their surveys to ascertain the relationship of the clarity of consciousness of the dying patients to

---
[16]*Ibid.*
[17]However, it is not inconceivable that visitors from nonphysical realms might appear to the dying patient in a form dictated by the patient's culture so that the patient will be at ease.
[18]Deathbed observations. *Op. cit.*, p. 254.
[19]This poll was taken at about the same time that Doctors Osis and Haraldsson made their second survey of American physicians and nurses. George Gallup: *The Gallup Poll*. New York, Random House, 1972, Vol. III, p. 1663.

the survival-related visions. The various levels of clarity they defined as "clear," "mildly" or "severely impaired," or "fluctuating." Conditions that impede clarity of consciousness, they assumed, would serve to impede extrasensory communication with the dead and, thus, survival-visions as well, if the visions represented extrasensory contact with the dead. They reasoned that, if the survival-hypothesis were correct, then there would be a correlation between reduced clarity of consciousness and reduced incidence of survival-visions.[20]

Was there such a correlation? Osis and Haraldsson believe that there was, but I think that the data are ambiguous. On the one hand, 17 percent of the dying patients who had survival-related visions were in a severely impaired state of consciousness, 29 percent were in a mildly impaired state, 11 percent had fluctuating clarity, and almost half (43%) were in a clear state. These statistics suggest that the less impaired was the dying patient's consciousness, the more likely was he to have a survival-related vision.

On the other hand, there is another way of looking at these statistics. If it were true that reduced clarity of consciousness inhibits having survival-related visions, then one might expect most of the dying patients who had survival-related visions to have clear or unimpaired consciousness. Yet not even half (43%) of the patients who had survival-related visions enjoyed clear consciousness, and this fact suggests that reduced clarity of consciousness may *not* necessarily inhibit having survival-related visions.

Furthermore, I am not persuaded that, even if there were a clear correlation between reduced clarity of consciousness and reduced incidence of survival-related visions, this correlation could not be explained on a completely nonsurvivalist basis.

A hallucination is itself a conscious state. To hallucinate, a patient must have a brain and nervous system capable of carrying out certain basic integrative mental functions. Factors impairing clarity of consciousness, e.g. deterioration of the brain and thus the mind, probably impair mental and neural functions, including those required for hallucination, and so well may diminish the frequency of hallucination. So less clarity of consciousness may correlate with less frequency of survival-related visions *not* because the former hinders ability to "perceive" visiting spirits of the dead, but because it is caused by factors that impair functions that are physiologically essential to hallucination.

[20]Deathbed observations. *Op. cit.*, p. 255.

Thus, for example, one wonders just how "severely impaired" the consciousness was of those patients of whom only 17 percent had had visions. We are told that their states of consciousness were so severely impaired that little or no communication with them was possible. If their clarity of consciousness was that impaired, then perhaps the reason so few of them had visions was not because they were unable to "perceive" departed spirits but because they were beyond the ability to hallucinate.

So I think that, first, the data of Osis and Haraldsson do not elucidate the nature of the relationship between the clarity of consciousness of the dying patients and their survival-related visions, and that, second, in any case, nonsurvivalist explanations of the data are not plainly implausible.

Conclusion

Osis and Haraldsson compiled considerable information relative to the experiences of patients who are very near death. In my opinion, their investigations warrant three conclusions:

1. Persons upon nearing death may be more likely than are others to have visions of deceased loved ones and religious figures.

2. Most of these visions are probably not the result of high body temperature, alcoholism, consciousness-affecting medications, mental illness, or certain injuries and disease associated with hallucinations.

3. The survival-related visions are probably not affected by the mood of the patient, as reported by his physician or nurse, on the day prior to his vision.

The data of Osis and Haraldsson do *not* seem to me to indicate that survival-visions are not the result of stress, the fear of death, the desire for or belief in an afterlife, or unknown psychological or physiological causes. Furthermore, that the visions are subjective hallucinations is *not*, in my view, shown implausible either by 1, 2, or 3 above or any other of the findings of Doctors Osis and Haraldsson, including those that pertain to cross-cultural differences and to clarity of consciousness.

The Osis-Haraldsson data are compatible with the possibility that there is life after death, but, because nonsurvivalist explanations of the data are not clearly untenable, it would be unwarranted to count the data as *evidence* that there is life after death.

CHAPTER 20

OTHER STUDIES OF NEAR-DEATH EXPERIENCES

It is research such as Dr. Moody presents in his book that will enlighten many and will confirm what we have been taught for two thousand years—that there is life after death.
— Elizabeth Kübler-Ross, Foreword to
Life After Life[1]

Raymond Moody's *Life After Life*

The publisher of the best-seller, *Life After Life*, in which Raymond Moody examines the reported experiences of persons near death or revived from a state of declared clinical death, asserts matter-of-factly on the cover of the book that Doctor Moody's studies "reveal that there is life after death." Elizabeth Kübler-Ross has words to the same effect in her foreword to the book. By contrast, in the book itself Doctor Moody warns readers that his very informal study can scarcely be regarded as "scientific";[2] says that he refuses "to draw any conclusions" from his study;[3] and maintains only that "near death experiences represent a novel phenomenon for which we may have to devise new modes of explanation and interpretation."[4] The reader of the Moody book, too, should be more cautious than were the publisher and Doctor Kübler-Ross in the conclusions he draws from Moody's study.

In the first place, the selection in the book of cases of near-death experiences is small: Moody's findings are based on only some fifty cases of persons who either came very close to physical

---

[1] Raymond Moody: *Life After Life*. New York. Bantam Books. 1976–1978. p. xi.
[2] *Ibid.*, e.g. p. 181.
[3] *Ibid.*, p. 182.
[4] *Ibid.*, p. 177.

death or were resuscitated after having been adjudged clinically dead.

Secondly and more importantly, these cases were not selected on the basis of any statistical procedure which would ensure representative sampling of dying people. The cases involved people who chanced to relate their experiences after hearing Moody's lectures and people who were referred to him by their doctors because they had "reported unusual experiences."[5] So we have no assurances that the experiences reported to Moody are really very typical of the dying. Indeed, those cases referred to him by other physicians because of their unusual nature are obviously atypical.

Another reason why caution must be exercised in drawing conclusions from Moody's study, especially conclusions favorable to survivalist theories, is this. That which most strongly suggests the possibility that there is life after death, in Moody's book, is the description Moody gives of the "ideal" or "composite" experience of dying. This "ideal" or "composite" experience consists, we are told, of several elements or "features," including hearing (or seeming to hear) a loud buzzing or ringing noise upon being pronounced dead, feeling oneself to be transported swiftly through a long, dark tunnel, seeming to see one's body and its surroundings from a point of view beyond the body, having visions of deceased loved ones and other spirits, seeming to meet a "being of light" who helps one to evaluate his life, feeling forced against one's will to return to this life, and, finally, having overwhelming feelings of "joy, love, and peace."[6]

This "experience" is only a "model," Moody says, a "composite of the common elements found in very many stories." It is not "meant to be a representation of any one person's experience."[7] Not a single informant reported having every element of the composite, and not one of the several elements of the composite was experienced by every informant.[8]

As to how many people shared each of the various elements of the composite "experience," we are only told vaguely that "very many" have reported this element, or "numerous people" experi-

---

[5]*Ibid.*, p. 16.
[6]*Ibid.*, pp. 21–23.
[7]*Ibid.*, pp. 23–24.
[8]*Ibid.*

enced that, or in "many cases" such-and-such happened, and the like.

Therefore, although the composite "experience" may itself suggest that there is life beyond death, the individual elements are not necessarily equal to the composite in this respect, and the experience of no single person can be regarded as the same as the composite.

I think that it is clear that Moody never intended his book to be anything more than an informal account of the near-death experiences of a few people that came to his attention. Considering his intent, his small and unrepresentative sample, the gulf between his composite "experience" and the actual experience of any person, and the lack of specifics in regard to how many of his informants experienced which elements of the composite, caution is indeed warranted in drawing any conclusion from his book about the nature of "the" experience of dying or the likelihood of life after death.

Furthermore, Moody himself sets forth several plausible normal explanations of the various elements of the composite near-death experience. He refers, for one thing, to data, assembled by others, which suggest that subjects of sensory-deprivation and isolation experiments have experiences that "strongly resemble" those reported by his own informants; and he observes that "certain aspects of dying situations ... are much like the features found" in these sensory-deprivation and isolation experiments.[9]

But Moody is not satisfied that the results of isolation studies explain near-death experiences, his reason being that the various experiences which people are reported to have in conditions of isolation "cannot themselves be explained by any current theory."[10]

Nevertheless, while it may be that no one explanation of isolation-phenomena has been accepted by all psychologists, psychiatrists, and brain scientists, I have no doubt but the overwhelming majority would say that, whatever the real explanation may be, there is no reason to suppose that in an isolation experiment the subject experiences a contact with an afterdeath non-material plane.

---

[9]*Ibid.*, pp. 170 ff.
[10]*Ibid.*, p. 174.

Moody also notes that the "out-of-the-body" element of the composite near-death "experience" is similar to so-called autoscopic hallucinations (in which the subject sees himself as projected into his own visual field), and he notes, too, that still other elements (e.g. visions of inhabitants of other realms) are similar to hallucinations produced by drugs and cerebral anoxia.

Could the various features of the composite experience therefore have been brought into play by different factors, isolation in one instance, cerebral anoxia in another, hallucinogenic medications in another, and so forth?

Moody thinks not, principally for three reasons: (1) the descriptions given by his informants of their near-death experiences displayed uniformity and consistency; (2) the experiences that were reported were so vivid and "real" that his informants, whom Moody regarded as sane people, could not distinguish them from the perceptions of normal life; and (3) the reports of those who experienced the out-of-body element of the composite experience had "independent corroboration of a kind."[11]

Without more information than is available in *Life After Life* it is, however, difficult to gauge the extent of the uniformity among the descriptions of the experiences. Certainly the facts that no element of the composite experience was experienced by every informant and that no informant experienced every element of the composite experience mean that the experiences of the informants were not completely uniform. As to the reported vividness of the near-death experiences, it is well-known that certain hallucinations, and, indeed, even some dreams, are as vivid as normal perceptions. Therefore, neither the uniformity of the descriptions of near-death experiences nor the reported vividness of the experiences requires any paranormal explanation.

If, however, there truly is "independent corroboration" that those informants who had an out-of-the-body experience genuinely did "travel" outside their bodies, then those experiences would certainly require some sort of paranormal explanation. Unfortunately, "commitments to others" prevented Moody "from giving names and identifying details" and from saying anything

---

[11]*Ibid.*, p. 176.

else in regard to the independent corroboration.[12] Consequently the reader is unable to judge the extent or significance of this corroboration. Those who are familiar with the 1961 study of Doctor Osis, treated in the preceding chapter, may be especially reluctant to accept without further documentation Moody's reference to the alleged independent corroboration of out-of-body experiences. In that study Dr. Osis was unable to discover a single case of a person claiming to have out-of-body experiences who "actually brought back veridical information outside the range of simple inferences."[13]

In summary, *Life After Life* is, as Doctor Moody emphasizes, an informal and nonscientific work, and one must show the same restraint as does Moody in deriving from it any far-reaching conclusions about "the" experience of dying or the possibility of life after death. Nonetheless, to a certain extent it supports some of the findings of the Osis-Haraldsson studies, since some of the near-death experiences described by Moody's informants, like visions of deceased loved ones, correspond to the experiences of the near-death patients in the Osis-Haraldsson surveys. At the same time, other kinds of near-death experiences reported to Moody, such as encounters with "beings of light," do not.

Studies of Michael Sabom

That persons upon nearing death may experience some of the phenomena reported by Osis and Haraldsson and by Moody has been known, albeit not very widely, for many years.[14] Nonetheless, there has been but scant documentation within the professional medical literature of these phenomena.

Recently, however, Doctor Michael B. Sabom of the Veterans

---

[12]*Ibid.*

[13]K. Osis: *Deathbed Observations by Physicians and Nurses.* New York, Parapsychology Foundation, 1961, p. 77.

[14]In 1892, Albert Heim reported the results of interviews with survivors of mountain-climbing and other near-fatal accidents: Remarks on fatal falls. *Yearbook of the Swiss Alpine Club, 27:* 327–337, 1892, translated by Noyes and Kletti in *Omega, 3:* 45–52, 1972. More recently, Noyes and Kletti reported on over one hundred more cases of near-death experiences: Depersonalization in the face of life-threatening danger: a description. *Psychiatry, 39:* 19–27, 1976; and: Depersonalization in the face of life-threatening danger: an interpretation. *Omega, 7:* 103–114, 1976.

Administration Medical Center in Decatur, Georgia, has interviewed and reported upon some one hundred victims of near-fatal crises (e.g. cardiac arrest) resulting in unconsciousness.[15] Although thirty-nine victims remembered nothing from their period of unconsciousness, Doctor Sabom found that sixty-one recalled having had experiences while they were unconscious. Sixteen of these remembered having had an "autoscopic" experience of seeming to view their bodies from a height of several feet; thirty-two remembered a "transcendent" experience similar to being conscious in a foreign region or dimension; and thirteen recalled having an experience that combined autoscopic and transcendent features.

The "transcendent" experience contained several elements, including typically the seeming passage of consciousness first into a "black void" or "tunnel" and then to a brightly lit region of "great beauty" where sometimes deceased relatives and friends, or occasionally a "brilliant white light," seemed to be present. Elements of the transcendent experience were thus similar to some of the experiences of the subjects of both the Osis and Haraldsson and the Moody studies. The main element of the "autoscopic" experience, *viz*, seeming to see one's body from somewhere above it, was, as noted above, experienced by some of Moody's informants.

Sabom could find no significant social, demographic, medical, or psychiatric differences between those sixty-one informants who recalled having experiences while unconscious and the rest of the informants, who did not.

Those who remembered having had one of these autoscopic, transcendent, or "combination" experiences while unconscious tended afterwards to be less afraid of death and more believing in an afterlife.

Sabom informs us that at present there is no generally accepted explanation of these near-death experiences and that none of the most likely medical explanations are as of now entirely satisfactory:

---

[15]Sabom's complete research has, as of this writing, not yet been published, but his preliminary findings may be found in: (1) The experience of near death. *Death Education, 1:* 195–203, 1977; (2) Near-death experiences. *Journal of the Florida Medical Association, 64:* 648–650, 1977; and in (3) Physicians evaluate the near-death experience. *Theta, 6:* 1–6, 1978. These articles were co-authored with S. A. Kreutziger.

1. While a temporal lobe disturbance resulting from brain hypoxia may cause visual illusions, this type of disorder also produces illusions of people as distorted, feelings of despair, suicidal urges, and vestibular and olfactory sensations. None of the patients of Sabom's study (nor any of those in the Osis and Moody studies) reported having had any of these experiences.

2. While drugs can cause convincing distortions of reality, the widely divergent types of hallucinations produced by drugs stand in contrast to the relative consistency and uniformity of the near-death visions. Further, patients who have experienced both drug-induced hallucinations and the near-death phenomena regard the two as clearly different. Raymond Moody, it will be recalled, found a similar consistency and uniformity in the descriptions given by his informants of their near-death experiences.

3. Finally, although autoscopic hallucinations, in which one seems to see one's double, have been reported and described in the psychiatric literature, in the typical autoscopic hallucination one's double is seen only as a transparent face or bust, and the hallucination is often accompanied by a feeling of sadness. Thus the "autoscopic" experiences reported by Sabom's victims of near-fatal crises are somewhat different from autoscopic experiences generally as treated in psychiatric literature.

Of course, from the fact that there is no generally accepted medical explanation of these near-death experiences it does not necessarily follow that the true explanation is that there is an afterlife. One reason that suggests itself to me why presently there is no fully satisfactory or generally accepted medical explanation is that very few physicians (according to Sabom) are even aware of the occurrence of these near-death experiences, and consequently medical theorizing about them is only in its infancy. Furthermore, according to Sabom, most health-care professionals who are aware of these experiences deem them hallucinatory and give them no further thought.

Conclusion

As has been seen, studies of the visions and other experiences had by some persons upon nearing death are found in the parapsychology literature (Osis and Haraldsson), medical literature

(Sabom), and the popular press (Moody). These studies, considered together, indicate that the experiences of many persons on the brink of death can plausibly be interpreted as "perceptions" of a hereafter as seen from its threshold.

I do think, however, that these experiences, as reported, cannot yet be viewed as strongly indicative of life after death. The fact that (according to Doctor Sabom and Doctor Moody) there is at present no wholly satisfactory medical explanation of these near-death experiences does not automatically mean that a normal explanation of the experiences is unlikely to be forthcoming. Scientific investigation and medical theorizing about the experiences are only beginning. Until there is some reason to think that normal explanations of the experiences *cannot* be given, I think that we must agree with Doctor Ian Stevenson, who is regarded by many as America's foremost survival researcher: "The published reports of close encounters with death," Doctor Stevenson has written, "have not yet contributed anything to the objective evidence of the survival of the human personality after death."[16]

---

[16]See: Research into the evidence of man's survival after death: a historical and critical survey with a summary of recent developments. *The Journal of Nervous and Mental Disease*1, *165:* 161, 1977.

CHAPTER 21

OUT OF BODY PHENOMENA

"OBE" is the acronym for "out-of-the-body experience." An OBE consists in seeming to perceive the world from a position other than that occupied by one's body. In an OBE, one often seems to view one's own physical body as if from the perspective of another person situated above or to the side of oneself. The vivid impressions of detachment from self that have been described by patients undergoing light general anesthesia and by the victims of head injuries or of near fatal drownings and falls qualify as OBEs, as do the experiences, mentioned in the chapters above, of some patients who are nearing death, who report having seen their own bodies as if from several feet up.[1]

As just made clear, not all OBEs are had by dying or injured persons. Indeed, some people have reported having these experiences since adolescence or early childhood, and the experiences can, reportedly, take a variety of forms. In the most ornate form, one experiences his consciousness as escaping from his body, which then is seen as a lifeless shell. The escaping consciousness will seem to be enveloped by a mist or ball of light or ethereal body. The ethereal body, mist, or light ball sometimes appears to be attached to the physical body by a silvery or white cord. It may seem to move spatially, sometimes through walls or closed doors.[2]

The question which is important for this study is whether all OBEs are a kind of autoscopic, i.e. self-seeing hallucination, or whether some of them are actual departures of one's conscious

---

[1] Freud has pointed out tht since we cannot really imagine our own death we are acustomed to envisioning it from the point of view of a spectator. Perhaps at the time of our death, for psychological protection, our mind excludes the reality of annihilation by witnessing our own death as that of another. Some psychiatrists have accepted this hypothesis, apparently. See Russell Noyes, Jr.: The experience of dying. *Psychiatry, 35:* 178, 1972.

[2] See D. Scott Rogo: Aspects of out-of-the-body experiences. *Journal of the Society for Psychical Research, 48:* 329–335, 1976; and Robert Crookall: *The Study and Practice of Astral Projection.* London, The Aquarian Press, 1961.

being from one's physical body.[3] For if one's consciousness can truly leave his body before death, then it may be possible for his consciousness to survive death.

Accounts of OBEs appear in almost endless number in spiritualistic magazines and the popular paperback trade, but more reputable studies of these phenomena are also reported in the parapsychology literature, and discussions of autoscopic hallucinations may be found in professional medical literature. The possibility that these experiences may in some instances actually be departures of one's mind or consciousness from one's body is, of course, not even contemplated in the professional medical literature, and the lack of corroboration and documentation of the tales in the popular and spiritualistic press make them an unlikely source of creditable information. The principal examination of OBEs in the parapsychological literature may be found in the work of Hart, Crookall, Smith, Monroe, Tart, Green and McCreery, and of a team of researchers headed by Robert L. Morriss.[4]

Robert Monroe's book is distinctive and interesting in that the author gives instructions on how to produce your own OBE. Monroe also discusses the history of his own OBEs, which began with intentional repeated inhalations of the fumes of contact cement and Trilene and progressed to experiments with self-hypnosis; the latter experiments seem to have triggered his first OBE.

---

[3] The paradigmatic autoscopic hallucination, as described in medical texts, consists in seeing an image of one's face or upper body projected within one's own visual field; sometimes this mirror image will become quite animated and will seem to talk to or mock oneself. This experience qualifies as an OBE, of course, though many OBEs are unlike it in important respects, as is evident from the text above.

[4] (1) R. Crookall: *The Study and Practice of Astral Projection*. London, The Aquarian Press, 1961; *The Supreme Adventure*. London, James Clark and Co., 1961; *More Astral Projections*. London, The Aquarian Press, 1964. (2) H. Hart: Six theories about apparitions. *Proceedings of the Society for Psychical Research*, 50: 153–239, 1956; *The Enigma of Survival*. London, Rider, 1959; and with E. B. Hart: Visions and apparitions collectively and reciprocally perceived. *Proceedings of the Society for Psychical Research*, 41: 205–249, 1933. (3) C. E. Green: Ecsomatic experiences and related phenomena. *Journal of the Society for Psychical Research*, 44: 111–131, 1967; *Out-of-the-Body Experiences*. Oxford, Institute of Psychophysiological Research, 1968; and, with C. McCreery: *Apparitions*. London, Hamish Hamilton, 1975. (4) R. A. Monroe: *Journeys Out of the Body*. Garden City, N.Y., Doubleday, 1971. (5) R. L. Morriss et al.: Studies of communication during out-of-body experiences. *Journal of the American Society for Psychical Research*, 72: 1–21, 1978. (6) S. Smith: *The Enigma of Out-of-Body Travel*. New York, Garrett Publications, 1965. (7) C. T. Tart: A psychophysiological study of out-of-the-body experiences in a selected subject. *Journal of the American Society for Psychical Research*, 62: 3–27, 1968.

Were Monroe's OBEs simply medically recognized mental phenomena that are explicable without any reference to nonphysical or paranormal happenings? It is known that a person can develop skill in concentrating his attention on an idea or image or on an object so that the normal multivarious flow of mental imagery and association funnels down to a single unchanging thought, and at that point dissociative mental phenomena, notably hallucinations, may be experienced. When reading Monroe's book, one suspects that the technique he describes for having an OBE amounts to an autohypnotic or concentration-focusing device, especially since tests conducted on Monroe at the Topeka Veterans Administration Hospital Research Department indicated that during an OBE Monroe was able to focus his consciousness so that his brain energy was in a very narrow frequency band.[5]

Even so, it is not *a priori* impossible that the OBE produced by this technique is an actual departure of Monroe's consciousness from his body. It certainly is interesting that when Monroe was having an OBE at the Topeka Veterans Administration Hospital, the psychiatrist who is Chief of Research and one other physician both observed a "heat-wave-like distortion of Monroe's upper body" and other anomalous physiological symptoms (including a "most unusual" galvanic skin response measurement).[6] No doubt something physiologically strange goes on when Monroe has an OBE.

On the other hand, tests done on Monroe by Doctor Charles Tart, both in and outside the laboratory, seem not to indicate that during an OBE Monroe (or his mind or consciousness) really is able to depart from his body.[7] Also, there are medical data that indicate that Monroe suffers from an arteriosclerotic narrowing of the blood vessels to his brain: this condition could create cerebral anoxia, i.e. an abnormally low amount of oxygen in the brain, which is a known cause of hallucinations.[8]

Reports of experiences similar to those claimed by Monroe appear in great number in the studies (cited above) of Robert

---

[5]Robert Monroe: *Journeys Out of the Body*. New York, Anchor, 1977, p. 280.

[6]*Ibid.*, p. 279.

[7]*Ibid.*, pp. 10–18. In these tests, Monroe was asked to describe "targets" he would not have been able to see (or otherwise sense) at the time he was having an OBE.

[8]*Ibid.*, p. 275.

Crookall, Suzy Smith, and C. E. Green. In my view, these studies are of doubtful value as proof of departures of consciousness from the physical body. While some of the cases reported in these studies have been published by the Society for Psychical Research, in general, they lack critical verification and are often reported even third-hand. Some have been taken from spiritualistic periodicals or are of the "so-and-so-told-me type," without indication of source or dates.

Whether or not there really is out-of-body travel of the human consciousness or mind is, I believe, subject in principle to experimental confirmation. The cases reported in these studies, though suggesting the need for such experimental study, do not themselves constitute that confirmation.

Studies of apparitions by Hornell Hart, discussed above in Chapter 17, involve more adequately documented cases of apparent out-of-body travellers who are seen by others as apparitions. As there stated, other psychical researchers consider these reported sightings of apparitions as probably the hallucinations of the viewer.

The similarity among and wide geographical and historical distribution of the reports of OBEs and the fact that many of these reports come from children are sometimes proffered as evidence of the reality of travel of consciousness beyond the body. OBEs may, despite these facts, still be subjective hallucinations resulting from underlying physiological causes.[9]

Clearly, what are required, in order to resolve whether OBEs are ever objectively real departures of the mind from its normal physical moorings or are always subjective hallucinations resulting from underlying physiological causes, are tests done under controlled conditions. Some subjects are able to have OBEs in the laboratory. If, while having OBEs, closely monitored subjects effected changes at removed locations with memory of having

---

[9] That OBEs, regardless of their reportedly wide geographical distribution, are in principle explainable physiologically and require no nonphysical interpretation is perhaps suggested by the fact that so-called psychical hallucinations, including those of seeming to be elsewhere from where one in fact is, have been produced by the electrical stimulation of the depth structures of the temporal lobe. See, e.g. Weingarten, Cherlow, and Holmgren: The relationship of hallucinations to the depth structures of the temporal lobe. *Acta Neurochirurgica, Supplement 24:* 199–216, 1977. As noted in Chapter 19, the propensity to temporal lobe disturbances is thought by some to be widespread in the general population.

done so, or came to possess, while in an OBE, specific and detailed information about remote targets, then this would certainly indicate that the experiences were not hallucinatory. Obviously refinements would be necessary to distinguish out-of-body travel from clairvoyance and telepathy.

Unfortunately, experimental testing for the reality of out-of-body travel is only in its infancy. As far as I am aware, there is not yet available unassailable experimental confirmation that the human mind or consciousness can depart from its living body and travel elsewhere.

The most extensive study of OBEs in this country to date has been that sponsored by the American Society for Psychical Research, and reported in the January, 1978 issue of the *Journal* of the Society. Although some aspects of the experiment were suggestive of out-of-body travel, "the overall results" of tests designed to determine whether a subject could describe remote targets "seen" while in an OBE, according to the report, "were at chance."[10]

Another experiment, by Professor Charles Tart of the University of California at Davis, done with a subject with reportedly high ability for OBEs, was slightly more promising as evidence of out-of-body travel. On one occasion the subject, presumably informed by out-of-body vision, reportedly called correctly a five-digit number thought to be hidden from her view. However, Doctor Tart discovered that there were ways in which the subject might have determined the number surreptitiously, so the experiment is not conclusive.[11]

It is sometimes speculated too that if one's consciousness departs one's body, then one's body might suffer a subtle loss of weight. However, according to the editor of the *Journal of the Society for Psychical Research*, a long, careful, and elaborate series of experiments designed to test this hypothesis was carried out in the 1960s

---

[10] Robert Morriss, Stuart Harary, Joseph Janis, John Hartwell, and W. G. Roll: Studies of communications during out-of-body experiences. *Journal of the American Society for Psychical Research*, 72: 1, 1978.

[11] C. Tart: A psychophysiological study of out-of-the-body experiences in a selected subject. *Journal of the American Society for Psychical Research*, 62: 3–27, 1968. For further experimental work see J. Palmer and C. Vassar: ESP and out-of-the-body experiences: an exploratory study. *Journal of the American Society for Psychical Research*, 68: 257–280, 1974; and J. Palmer and R. Lieberman: The influence of psychological set on ESP and out-of-body experiences. *Journal of the American Society for Psychical Research*, 69: 193–213, 1975.

among a great number of sensitive subjects, but yielded no significant positive results.[12]

I think, though, that there can be no doubt that people have OBEs. I have myself had feelings of separation or detachment from myself that I think qualify as OBEs. They have come to me in times of stress, forgetfulness, and musing about things generally, and also, unexplainably, in times of attentiveness to my immediate activities or thinking.

However, on the basis of the evidence now available, it has not been established that the mind or consciousness of a human being is at any time literally able to depart or travel from the physical substance of its body. Accordingly, no inference of human survival beyond physical death can at this time be drawn from the occurrence of OBEs.

---

[12]See the editor's reply to a letter in the *Journal of the Society for Psychical Research*, 50: 39, 1979.

CHAPTER 22

THE ELECTRONIC VOICE PHENOMENON

In the early 1970s certain survival researchers became excited by the possibility that there might be at hand widely available concrete proof of afterdeath survival. The proof lay in tape-recorded messages from discarnate survivors, messages that could actually be recorded by anyone owning a tape recorder.

Interest in this "electronic voice phenomenon" began with the publication in 1964 of a book entitled *Rösterna fran Rymden* (Voices from Space), written by Friedrich Jurgenson. Jurgenson had accidentally discovered that faint voices, additional to the matter he had intentionally recorded and entirely inexplicable to him, seemingly could be heard when tape recordings which he had made in normal ways were played back. He gradually became convinced that the voices were not those of living beings. His book attracted the attention of Doctor Konstantin Raudive, a Latvian, who listened to Jurgenson's tapes and, impressed, attempted independently to replicate Jurgenson's discovery.

Raudive, whose name came to be virtually synonymous with the electric voice phenomenon, collected over 72,000 "ghost" messages on tape, out of which he "identified" some 25,000 as coming from deceased friends and relatives, as well as from famous writers and statesmen, including Tolstoy, Jung, Churchill, Stalin, and Hitler. Raudive found that the voice-phrases usually had a "polyglot" composition of several languages, and thought that they exhibited a distinctive rhythm. Other persons too have been able to hear the ghost messages on Raudive's tapes and have been able to produce similar tapes themselves. Raudive reported the results of his research in *Breakthrough: An Amazing Experiment in Electronic Communication with the Dead.*[1]

It is not difficult to produce "Raudive" tapes. I myself have

---

[1] New York, Taplinger, 1971.

done it. One has merely to connect an audio tape recorder to an open microphone or to a radio, and, while the recorder is operating, direct questions to deceased persons. When the tape is played back, one can, with some practice, learn to distinguish certain voiced "extras" from normal radio transmissions and the background of amplifier and atmospheric noises. These voiced extras are mostly fragmentary utterances that occasionally bear a kind of obscure relevance to the questions that have been posed. Sometimes too, the ghost voices will seem to address listeners by their own names.

Acquiring the ability to hear and discriminate the ghost voices on tapes requires patience; it might take some up to three months, according to Raudive.[2] The difficulty is that the "messages" are very faint and fragmented. The utterances are primarily mere snatches of speech and are usually unintelligible, inappropriate, or nonsensical. A reading of *Breakthrough* will give one the flavor of these fragmented extras that, with practice, can be heard on tape playback.

Nonetheless, since the ghost voices are sometimes heard to speak the names of those present when the recordings are made and to utter relevant phrases, the early reports of the phenomenon created considerable excitement. The publicity used to promote *Breakthrough* contributed to the excitement by emphasizing the solid scientific footing of Doctor Raudive's research and the support he received from technicians and electronics experts.

However, excitement about Raudive voices has much abated in recent years due to the investigations of D. J. Ellis, who in the early 1970s received the Perrott-Warrick Studentship for Psychical Research (Trinity College, Cambridge) to study the phenomenon. Ellis began his investigation fully ready to accept the voiced extras as paranormal, but gradually came to conclude that they were not. There is no reason, he wrote in 1974, to postulate anything but natural causes to explain the electronic voice phenomenon. The ghost voices, he concluded, were in all probability merely "indistinct fragments of radio transmissions, mechanical noises and unnoticed remarks, aided by imaginative guesswork and wishful

---

[2]Though others, myself included, have detected voiced extras after only a few playbacks of appropriately-made tapes.

thinking."³

Several discoveries contributed to Mr. Ellis's gradually coming to his critical conclusion. One was that, in spite of enthusiastic claims in the promotion of *Breakthrough* that the phenomenon had been rigorously and extensively tested by technicians and scientists and that alternative natural explanations of the voices had been eliminated, careful experimentation had been very much absent. The various recording techniques involving radios all permitted normal radio transmissions, from fragments of commercial broadcasts to short-wave signals, to be received and recorded indiscriminately. The techniques utilizing open microphones, in addition to allowing the recording of radio signals, permitted as well the taping of unconscious utterances on the part of the listeners and of other naturally occurring sounds.

Although strict precautions would have been required to eliminate the recording of these various additional natural sounds, Ellis could find no evidence that such precautions had ever been taken. Indeed, it was Raudive's presumed ability to hear the difference between a "voice" and extraneous normal sounds that constituted the principal method for dealing with normal effects. In other words, investigators just simply assumed that Raudive could tell the difference between a ghostly voice and, e.g. a radio transmission.[4]

Furthermore, Ellis soon learned that there was little warrant for confidence in Raudive's ability to distinguish the ghostly from the non-ghostly. Not only were what turned out to be commercial radio announcements in some instances "identified" by Raudive as "voices," but also, far from "being the first to spot the radio origin [of these 'voices'], Dr. Raudive continues to insist that they are paranormal effects."[5] Similarly, a comment made (in English) by Doctor Andrija Puharich during an experiment using the "microphone" method was, on playback, identified as a "voice" by Raudive (and even fitted with Latvian words).[6]

---

[3]D. J. Ellis: *The Mediumship of the Tape Recorder.* (Fernwood, Nightingales, West Chiltington, Pulborough, West Sussex: by the author), 1978, p. 145. (Available from the Society for Psychical Research.)

[4]*Ibid.*, p. 136.

[5]*Ibid.*, p. 137.

[6]*Ibid.*, p. 57.

Ellis was disappointed, too, with his own series of tests made in Germany with Doctor Raudive in 1971. In spite of the fact that the tests were without strict controls, the results were so meager, so generally lacking in even ostensible paranormal effects, that they were not thought by Ellis to justify further, more refined, tests. Indeed, perhaps the most important lesson of these tests was that Raudive had a disturbing tendency to hear "voices" in almost any recorded noise not immediately identifiable, as, for example, the noise of footsteps, doors opening and shutting, chairs creaking, and mechanical-equipment sounds.[7]

Ellis became dubious as well about the claim in *Breakthrough* that a large percentage of the voices had been independently heard and verified. He discovered, for one thing, that Raudive did not think it important that there be independent verification of his interpretations. Even more significantly, Ellis soon discovered that "verification" to Raudive essentially meant either agreeing with him or not hearing "correctly." In Raudive's listening tests, the listener was first given Doctor Raudive's interpretation of a given taped sample, which presumably contained a "voice," and the sample was then played several times. The listener was then in effect given the choice of agreeing with Doctor Raudive's interpretation or of being classified as hard of hearing; he was given no opportunity to make his own interpretation.[8]

Thus, Ellis eventually became aware that the existence of not even one paranormal voice had ever really been established. Doctor Raudive and others claimed, nonetheless, that the "voices" heard were not fragments of radio transmission or other naturally occurring sounds because the voices seemed to address by name those who interrogated them and, to some extent, to respond to questions with appropriate comments. However, Ellis concluded that it is impossible to determine sufficiently accurately what the voices say so as to verify this claim, because the interpretation of the voices is almost wholly subjective:

A voice thought by one listener to be in English will be thought by another to be in German, and in general the language heard, including the "polyglot" language heard by Raudive, will corre-

---

[7]*Ibid.*, p. 68.
[8]*Ibid.*, p. 138.

spond to the linguistic knowledge of the listener. Doctor Raudive will hear a voice remark, "Te Mark Clu, mej dream, my dear, yes." Another listener will interpret the same voice as having said, "Mark you, make thee mightier yet." A fragment evidently from a Radio Luxembourg broadcast, "Hello, this is Kid Jensan," was interpreted by Raudive as a voice saying, "Glaube du, Cedin" (Believe you, Cedin), and a fragment that students familiar with the Radio Luxembourg program identified as "reminding you about Dimensions" was interpreted by Raudive as "Romani Nimowald Zamuchils" (Romani Nimowald is exhausted to death). It is strange, too, that some of the famous deceased persons expressed themselves to Raudive in languages they had not known when alive.[9]

That the interpretation of the voices is a subjective process was suggested also by Raudive's tendency to hear voices in naturally occurring sounds and also by what Ellis calls the Uncertainty Principle: the more interesting and evidential a "Raudive" voice is, the harder it is to hear it.

Ellis refers, in addition, to one experiment in which a group of people were played a tape that contained only "white noise" (background radio static). The subjects were told that the tape was a poor quality copy of a talk on a certain topic. When asked to write down as much of the "talk" as they could hear, many of the subjects produced a number of phrases and even sentences on the suggested topic. The experiment, if authentic, would, as Ellis says, be rather the ultimate in subjective interpretation.[10]

Eventually, Ellis surmised that the long period of training ostensibly required to detect and hear the ghost voices is in reality a period in which the listener learns to spot fleeting sounds that are below the level of accurate recognition and develops a facility for producing confident "interpretations" of the sounds by means of guesswork. Such interpretations manifestly should not, he thought and I agree, be proffered as confirmation of paranormal causes.

Furthermore, contrary to the impression created by the publicity attending the publication of *Breakthrough*, cases in which the voices provide information that is not known by the listener at the

---

[9]*Ibid.*, pp. 20, 61, 96, and 137.
[10]*Ibid.*, p. 140.

time he hears it, which is then later verified, are extremely rare. Ellis thought that there was only one such message worthy of mention, and describes a plausible nonparanormal explanation of the message.[11]

So, in the end, Ellis, who as he says "had believed in that magic voice," found it unreasonable to postulate a paranormal phenomenon whose effects were so "closely similar to those derived from a naturally-accountable process of error and wishful thinking."[12] His final, critical, conclusion:

> So far there have been no really conclusive experiments to demonstrate the validity of the phenomenon; so far no "genuinely paranormal" voice has been distinguished from any other voice—although of course a number of "spurious" voices have been eliminated; the whole idea of the voice phenomenon has been built up on a combination of misinterpretation, voices which may have a natural origin, experiments subject to error, and wishful thinking. To extrapolate from here to a genuine [paranormal] phenomenon... is still wishful thinking.[13]

Others, most notably perhaps R. K. Sheargold, have not agreed entirely with Ellis's very skeptical conclusions.[14] Sheargold was critical of Ellis because the latter, instead of making and listening to his own "Raudive-tapes," was primarily concerned with investigating the experimentation of Doctor Raudive. Ellis, however, had become aware through his own research of the difficulties involved in attempting to exclude all normal sources of the voiced messages, and so, quite reasonably, looked at the efforts of others, primarily Doctor Raudive, to see whether anyone had ever taken steps to ensure that the voices did not "arrive by natural means."[15] Ellis was quite right in thinking it largely pointless (except to satisfy curiosity) to spend time making and listening to one's own tapes if no one had shown it likely that the voices one was listening to were truly of paranormal provenance. The most comprehensive and careful study by far of Raudive's "amazing experiment" is that of D. J. Ellis.

---

[11]*Ibid.*, p. 145.

[12]*Ibid.*, p. 143.

[13]*Ibid.*, p. 143. Reprinted by permission of David Ellis.

[14]See, e.g. The "Raudive Voices." *The Journal of the Society for Psychical Research, 48:* 250–252, 1975, or *Hints on Receiving the Voice Phenomenon*, Maidenhead: by the author, 1973.

[15]Ellis, *op. cit.*, p. 129.

CHAPTER 23

THE REINCARNATION CASES

One of the most famous cases of possible reincarnation was that of Virginia Tigue, who was known to millions as "Bridey Murphy," a purported nineteenth century Irish maid of whom Virginia Tigue was thought by some to be the reincarnation. In the early 1950s Tigue, during six sessions with a hypnotist, Morey Bernstein, was hypnotically "regressed" to her "earlier life" as Bridey Murphy, and revealed many details about that "life" and about nineteenth century Ireland. Several of the details were subsequently verified by newspaper reporters and other investigators and Bernstein and others thought that Tigue could not have become aware of these details in any normal manner.[1] Since the story of Bridey Murphy has been told so often, I shall not retell it here. For those who desire to know more about the case, a complete summary has been presented by Ducasse, who, though believing in life after death and treating the case with sympathy, concludes ultimately that the verified information revealed by Tigue does not constitute "particularly strong" evidence that she was the reincarnation of Bridey Murphy.[2]

My own opinion about the case is that at least some of the information revealed by Tigue appears to have been learned by her in her own childhood, and I have not been convinced that it could not all have been learned in this way. Indeed, the main difficulty with the case as proof of reincarnation is that Tigue was thirty when she related the details of the life of "Bridey." Tigue's own childhood was by this point so far removed in time that it is next to impossible to determine the extent to which the information she revealed about nineteenth century Ireland really came from the circumstances of her own childhood.

---

[1] M. Bernstein: *The Search for Bridey Murphy*. Garden City, N.Y., Doubleday, 1956.

[2] C. J. Ducasse: *A Critical Examination of the Belief in a Life After Death*. Springfield, Thomas, 1974, p. 299. Ducasse devotes all of Chapter XXV of his work to the case of Bridey Murphy.

This difficulty which so weakens the Bridey Murphy case is to some degree eliminated in cases in which the subject who relates information purportedly about a past life is himself a very young child whose sources of information about the past can be more easily ascertained and monitored, and who has had less exposure to such sources to begin with.

A number of cases suggestive of reincarnation in which the subject is a young child have been recently investigated in painstaking detail by Dr. Ian Stevenson.[3] It is these cases that today constitute the bulk of the empirical support for the theory of reincarnation.

Stevenson's "Cases of the Reincarnation Type"

Stevenson and his associates have gone to great trouble and expense in investigating these "cases of the reincarnation type," as Stevenson calls them. The detailed and objective nature of his reports as well as the systematic and scientific character of his investigative procedures have earned Stevenson praise, even from conventional scientists. The prestigious *Journal of Nervous and Mental Disease*, for instance, has recently published an article by Stevenson entitled "Research Into the Evidence of Man's Survival After Death."[4] The editor of the journal emphasizes that the publication of the article is not an endorsement of the theory of reincarnation, but makes it clear that Stevenson's methodology is to be approved, and the publication of the article implies that the journal regards Stevenson's material as deserving of the attention of other scientists.

I do not think that Stevenson maintains that the cases which he has investigated establish the existence of reincarnation. But I think that he views the facts of the cases as sometimes as explainable by reincarnation as by any other explanation and in a few instances as more easily so explainable.

Since I cannot here consider every case on which Stevenson

---

[3]*Twenty Cases Suggestive of Reincarnation*, 2nd rev. ed. Charlottesville, University Press of Virginia, 1974; *Cases of the Reincarnation Type. Vol. 1. Ten Cases in India.* Charlottesville, University Press of Virginia, 1975; *Cases of the Reincarnation Type. Vol. 2. Ten Cases in Sri Lanka.* Charlottesville, University Press of Virginia, 1977; *Cases of the Reincarnation Type. Vol. 3 Fifteen Cases in Thailand, Lebanon, and Turkey.* Charlottesville, University Press of Virginia, 1978.

[4]*165:* 152–170, 1977.

has reported I shall focus on a single, representative case which is thought to lend itself very easily to interpretation in terms of reincarnation.

The case I shall examine is that of Sujith Lakmal Jayaratne.[5] This case has been said by reviewers of Stevenson's material to be one of his best cases; and Stevenson himself reports that the case is "one of the strongest known to me" (as evidence of reincarnation, presumably).[6]

"Sujith": Background

As is typical in Stevenson's "cases of the reincarnation type," the subject in the Sujith case is a young child who is thought to know far more than he should about someone who lived before. As also is typical in these cases it is not through hypnosis that the child reveals his apparent knowledge of the past, but through normal communication.

In this particular case, the child, Sujith, lived in a town called Mt. Lavinia, which is a suburb of Colombo, in Sri Lanka (formerly Ceylon). When the child, who was born in 1969, was one-and-a-half to two years old, he reportedly began making statements about persons who were, supposedly, unknown to his family. In addition, he purportedly said that he was from "Gorakana," which is a small village about seven miles to the south of Mt. Lavinia. Sujith's family assumed that Sujith was talking about a prior life, since a belief in reincarnation is quite common in Sri Lanka. But they reportedly did not know anyone from Gorakana and so did not know whether any of his utterances corresponded to individuals from Gorakana.

When Sujith was about two and one-half, his *grandmother*[7] took him to her brother, a local Sinhalese monk, whose *younger colleague* interviewed Sujith in an attempt to see if there was any truth in his reincarnation-suggestive statements. The younger monk recorded in writing as coming from Sujith several pieces of information

---

[5]*Cases of the Reincarnation Type, Vol. 2. Ten Cases in Sri Lanka.* Charlottesville, University Press of Virginia, 1977. pp. 235–280.

[6]*Ibid.*, p. 277.

[7]I shall designate the key characters of the case by italicizing my first references to them; they should be remembered.

related to Gorakana and to a possible prior life of the child (I shall detail the information later).

Since some of what Sujith said in his interview was in reference to someone named *Kusuma*, the monk went to Gorakana, seven miles away, to locate someone by this name. He did so and this person, a girl, was able to connect some of Sujith's statements with her own family. The girl, no doubt curious about the child who was in possession of information about her family, subsequently visited Sujith in Mt. Lavinia on her own initiative and reportedly was recognized and named by him. Other of Kusuma's relatives followed her, and were also said to have been recognized by the child. Then the child was himself taken to Gorakama where he reportedly recognized still other persons and made additional statements about relatives of Kusuma. The younger monk was present at some of these tests of recognition and recorded in writing what Sujith said and did. At some point, though the report does not make it clear just when, everyone evidently concluded that Sujith was the reincarnation of the uncle of Kusuma, a trafficker in illegal alcohol who was struck and killed by a truck in 1969. The uncle's name was Sammy Fernando, or as his friends would say, "Gorakana Sammy."[8]

After Sujith's visit to Gorakana, one of Stevenson's investigator-interpreters, an inhabitant of Sri Lanka, arrived in Mt. Lavinia, as did Stevenson himself a few months later. By this time Sujith was over three years old.

What Sujith Said and Did

The information Sujith communicated in his interview with the younger monk when Sujith first was taken to him was, as I noted above, recorded in writing at the time of the interview. The monk also recorded in writing the behavior and statements made by Sujith at the subsequent tests of Sujith's powers of recognition, at which the monk was present. The other details concerning what

---

[8]According to Dr. Stevenson's report, Sujith claimed that his name was "Sammy," and referred to himself as "Gorakana Sammy." One is likely to get the impression from reading the report that Sujith referred to himself by this name from the very start. But a closer reading of the report shows that Sujith's identification of himself as "Sammy" is not listed by Stevenson among those items which turned up in the younger monk's interviews with Sujith.

Sujith said and did came from the unrecorded recollections of other people, who reported what they recalled to Stevenson and his interpreter.

The information Sujith conveyed in the interview with the younger monk was that he was from Gorakana; that he lived in the "Gorakawatte" section of Gorakana; that he traveled by bus and by train; that he had attended the "dilapidated school" and had had a teacher named "Francis"; that he had given money to a local temple (Stevenson's account is unclear as to whether or not Sujith identified the temple by name) in which there were two monks, one of whom was named "Amitha"; that he (Sujith) had bathed in cool water; had lived in a white-washed house, the lavatory to which was "beside the boundary"; and that he was the son of a one-eyed man called "Jamis." The final piece of information was that "someone" had fallen down and become lame.

. What Sujith was remembered by others to have said and done, as recorded by Stevenson and his interpreter, falls into three categories: (1) Sujith reportedly gave utterance to details concerning the activities and surroundings of Gorakana Sammy and his friends and relatives; (2) he purportedly recognized or identified certain people, places and things associated with Sammy; and (3) he was said to have displayed behavior reminiscent of Sammy.

Sujith's Utterances

According to Stevenson, the members of Sujith's and Sammy's families remembered that Sujith had given the following information: that Kusuma lived in Gorakana and was Sujith's younger sister's daughter and had long, thick hair; that his wife was called "Maggie," and his daughter was called "Nandanie"; that he lived in a house with a tiled roof, bathed in cool water, and bathed in the well; that there was a king coconut tree near the well and that both the well and the tree were behind the house; that he could approach the house along a jungle footpath, smoked Four Aces cigarettes, ate bread and fish curry for breakfast, had worked for the railways, had climbed Adam's Peak, had transported arrack in a boat and continued to do so even though the boat once sank; that he quarreled one day after drinking with Maggie, who left the house and went down the road; and that he went to a boutique for cigarettes and a lorry ran over him when he was crossing the road.

All of this which Sujith reportedly communicated as though it were true of himself was, according to Stevenson, true of Gorakana Sammy and his circumstances.

Sujith's "Recognitions"

According to Stevenson, Sujith was reported to have recognized two sisters of Sammy and two of Sammy's nieces (one of whom was, of course, Kusuma); Sammy's wife, mother, and father; Sammy's nephew, brother-in-law, and illegitimate son; and a "distant relative" and second cousin of Sammy.

Sujith was also reported to Stevenson to have recognized Sammy's drum, chair, ring, belt, and brass knuckles, and a dance shelter at the home of Sammy's parents, as well as changes in the road, fences, and a tree near Sammy's property.

Sujith's Behavior

Stevenson himself witnessed behavior on the part of Sujith that he was informed was similar to Sammy's. Sujith made requests for arrack, wade, manioc, hot curries, cigarettes, and Terrylene shirts; he used indecent language and was fond of singing, afraid of lorries, generous to others, and lacked inhibitions. In addition, the child wore his sarong knotted below the navel as, reportedly, did Sammy; and, just as Sammy had a tendency to become physically violent when drunk, the child demonstrated a similar tendency to hit and kick other people when he was "frustrated." Too, the child was reported to Stevenson to have resisted "worshiping the monks in the usual way of Buddhists," and to have asked not to be taught the *pancha sila*, "the five key precepts" of Buddhism, one of which requires Buddhists not to drink intoxicants. (This behavior could be thought to correspond to Sammy's indifference to outer forms of religion.) Finally, the child demonstrated a remarkable aptitude for imitating the behavior of drunks. Reportedly, Sammy had invariably been drunk.

The Significance of Sujith's "Recognitions"

Was Sujith able to "recognize" what and whom he reportedly

did because he was the reincarnation of Sammy Fernando?

The persons Sujith was said to have recognized were all relatives of Sammy Fernando. In virtually every case, the "tests" of recognition were conducted with several members of the Fernando family present and were not witnessed by anyone who was not a member of the family. It is therefore impossible to determine the extent to which the recognitions were the result of cues given to the child by the people present. Sammy's family would probably have been fascinated by the thought that Sammy himself might be embodied in the small child before them, and might well have inadvertently coached, prompted, or given hints to the child, or have regarded ambiguous and inconclusive utterances as signs of recognition. That there would have been such inconclusive utterances there can be no doubt. Children of Sujith's age possess only the rudiments of speech and grammar, and, frequently, their utterances require interpretation by others. Stevenson indeed cautions that Sujith frequently resorted to non-verbal sounds to convey his meaning, and notes that the tendency of listeners and translators to make inferences about key words which were missing from Sujith's utterances occasionally led to confusion.

Two tests of Sujith's recognition of persons were, however, witnessed by individuals who were not themselves relatives of Sammy Fernando, but it is difficult to attach much significance to these tests, either. In one "test," Sujith was said to have recognized Sammy Fernando's wife in the presence of *Sujith's* (not Sammy's) family, but Sujith recognized the wife only after she had identified herself to Sujith's family in his presence, and according to Stevenson Sujith probably heard the woman identify herself. In the other test, Sujith reportedly recognized Sammy Fernando's nephew in the presence of the monk (who had interviewed the child), but the nephew had been with the child for some undetermined amount of time before the monk arrived.[9]

Sujith was also said to have identified, in the presence of the monk, the ring, belt, and brass knuckles of Sammy and to have said that these items were his. However, many children of Sujith's age will display signs of ownership or possession of virtually any

---

[9]Interestingly enough, Sujith did not recognize Kusuma the *first* time he saw her, but, instead, the second time, on the following day. In the meantime, according to Stevenson, his family "most probably" informed themselves about her identity.

unusual or attractive item which is handed to them, especially when they are rewarded for doing so with the smiles and other signs of approval, which may well have accompanied Sujith's assertions. Further, Sujith's reported indications of ownership and other signs of recognition of objects and changes in the landscape may well have been inferences drawn from those present from what was in fact ambiguous behavior. For example, Sujith's recognition of Sammy Fernando's chair was gleaned from the fact that he "did not say anything, but went and sat on it with his legs tucked up somewhat in the manner of a man who was drinking or drunk,"[10] whatever that might be.

Too, not even the monk could have been certain that the child had not seen the items before. Were the portable items, for example, carried by Sammy's relatives to Mt. Lavinia when the relatives went there to test the powers of recognition of the child? The possibility that the child had on some earlier occasion been confronted with the objects which he "identified" in the presence of the monk has not been ruled out. For these various reasons, one must be very dubious about the value of the child's "recognitions" as evidence of reincarnation.

The Significance of Sujith's Behavior

Several considerations lessen the significance of the observed similarities in behavior of Sujith and Sammy Fernando.

For one thing, if any of Sujith's behavioral patterns were pleasing to those around him, those patterns would tend to be displayed and repeated. According to Stevenson, Sujith's family "took some pleasure in having such an unusual child in their midst." The family "seemed more amused than annoyed by Sujith's requests for arrack, cigarettes, wade, and manioc." The family "probably enjoyed the many visitors who came to them after news of the case reached Gorakana and then, following the publication of accounts of it in the newspapers, a larger public.[11]

Under these conditions, I, for one, would be surprised if Sujith had *not* displayed a tendency towards behavior that accorded well

---

[10]Stevenson, *op. cit.*, (*Ten Cases in Sri Lanka*), p. 263.
[11]*Ibid.*, p. 276.

with the notion that he was Sammy Fernando reincarnated. His requests for certain kinds of food, drink, and clothes, his use of indelicate language, his boisterous singing, his preferences in style of dress, his generosity, and his imitation of the behavior of drunkards are precisely the sorts of things I would expect under the circumstances. Sujith's tendency to hit and kick other people, while not likely to have been encouraged by his family, is typical infantile conduct. The child's reported resistance to "worshiping the monks in the usual way of Buddhists" and reluctance to learn the five principal precepts of Buddhism (assuming that these reports were accurate and not wishful thinking) are consonant with the child seeking to behave like Sammy Fernando so as to please his elders.

Sujith was also reported to have been terrified by lorries, and Sammy Fernando had been killed by one. If Stevenson's vivid description of the lorries in the area and of the lethal velocity with which they travel the highway is accurate, it might be difficult to find a child who was not afraid of lorries.

Nonetheless, Sujith's mother reported that when Sujith was but eight months old he was even afraid of the word "lorry" (or its equivalent in Sri Lanka). Yet considering the lorry danger it is not unlikely that the mother would try to instill a fear of lorries in her child at a very early age. If her lessons were sufficiently severe or dramatic, and involved the word "lorry," the word might itself have unpleasant associations for the child.

The Significance of Sujith's Utterances

Many of Sujith's reported utterances about Sammy Fernando and Sammy's circumstances do not, by themselves, suggest much of anything. The information conveyed by Sujith to the effect that he lived in a house with a tiled roof, bathed in the well, went to a dilapidated school, had a king coconut tree nearby, ate bread and fish curry, and that his house was white-washed is not sufficiently specific or idiosyncratic to provide evidence of reincarnation.

Some of Sujith's utterances, namely those that made use of proper names (e.g. "Jamis") and involved references to specific places (e.g. Gorakana), are not so easily discounted. These utterances are indeed the bed-rock of the entire case, and the question of whether or not the case provides any worthwhile evidence of reincarnation really comes down to the question of whether or not the child's reported recitation of these specifics can plausibly be explained by hypotheses other than that of reincarnation. If not, his "recognitions" and "Sammy-like" behavior take on a new significance as supportive of reincarnation.

What must be determined, therefore, is this: is Sujith likely to have said about Sammy Fernando what he reportedly did without having actually been Sammy?

Sources of Information About Sammy Fernando

The colorful Sammy Fernando would have been a visible figure in his own town of Gorakana. A quick-tempered, hard-drinking local equivalent of a rum-runner, whose taste for expensive clothing and fine tobaccos was exceeded only by his generosity to the poor and needy, "Gorakana Sammy" was the sort of person whose name might well have been on the tongues of local townsfolk, with whom he evidently was popular. It was, for example, reported that contributions to his funeral were so extensive that the funeral cost his family nothing.

Gorakana is just seven miles away from Mt. Lavinia, the home town of Sujith, and Mt. Lavinia and Gorakana are connected by a heavily traveled highway. Several inhabitants of, and visitors to, Sujith's town were known to be connected with Gorakana and in some cases even with Sammy Fernando himself. Nonetheless, Sujith's mother and grandmother, who were the only members of Sujith's family, denied having heard of Sammy Fernando before the development of the case.

However, it is not difficult to imagine that from time to time they heard or overheard, quite possibly without remembering it, bits and snatches of gossip about "Gorakana Sammy." That some colorful local crime figure had just made a large contribution to his neighborhood temple might, for example, have been sufficiently unusual as to have been reported widely and heard by any number of individuals.[12]

---

[12] It will be recalled that one of the original pieces of information communicated by Sujith in the presence of the monk was that he had given money to a temple.

Moreover, one of Sammy Fernando's personal friends and drinking companions was even a neighbor of Sujith, and was indeed close enough to Sujith's family to be asked occasionally by the family for favors. This neighbor denied talking about Sammy Fernando with Sujith's family prior to the development of the case, but then the neighbor was a drinking man, and drinking men often do not have the best recollection of what they have and have not said. The possibility that information passed from this neighbor to Sujith's family, perhaps even in the presence of Sujith, cannot be ruled out and constitutes a serious flaw in the case as proof of reincarnation.

Nor would much information have to pass from neighbor to family for the entire case to develop. Had a name or two been mentioned in Sujith's presence in a snatch of breezy chatter about the picturesque Sammy, Sujith might well have repeated the names. The repetition of a few strange names by Sujith could then have been enough to capture the attention of an idle and fanciful grandmother and to have set her imagination into motion. Discussion with her brother about her "strange grandchild" and the subsequent interview of the child by the monk who was her brother's younger colleague would then follow, and by the time of the interview the child's unusual oral behavior could have been significantly reinforced.

It may be, of course, that in arousing the interest of his family Sujith did more than repeat a few names, but we really don't know this. The only account of what the child did and did not say, apart from that written down by the monk, comes almost entirely from the memory reports of the child's grandmother, and who can testify to the accuracy of her memory? Perhaps some of the child's utterances were in fact made later than she recalled them to have been made; perhaps others were not made at all. Perhaps remarks of a general nature were innocently rendered more specific by the grandmother through "hindsight"; i.e., were rendered more specific only after the reincarnation hypothesis had settled in her and others' minds and had taken shape around a particular individual, Sammy Fernando.[13] The only potentially reliable record of what

---

[13] It is certainly rather striking that, although the mother and grandmother claimed that Sujith called himself "Gorakana Sammy," he did not even use the name "Sammy" when he

the child really said is the record of the monk.

The Monk's Record

The first thing a critic will wonder about the monk's "interviews" of the child is whether the grandmother or mother of Sujith was present at these interviews. Sujith had only a primitive vocabulary and but a rudimentary command of grammar, and, as has been noted above, his utterances sometimes required interpretation. Did the grandmother help interpret the child's utterances at the interview with the monk in accordance with her own views of what they meant? Did she perhaps unconsciously (or consciously) prompt him to repeat the unusual names, "Jamis," for instance? Was the monk sufficiently objective, let alone trained as a scientific interrogator, even to be aware of subtle or unconscious cuings from the grandmother? And, if he were aware, would he have made an issue of them in view of the fact that the grandmother, as I pointed out above, was the sister of an older colleague?

As to the "information" about Sammy Fernando revealed by the child in these interviews, the most impressive items were those that involved proper names: "Jamis," "Kusuma," "Francis" (Sammy's former teacher), and "Amitha" (a monk at a temple in Gorakana). Reference to a "Kusuma" and a one-eyed "Jamis" in the chatter of a child does not seem particularly surprising in view of the child's contact with a drinking companion of a relative of these two persons. Nor, for that matter, does reference to an "Amitha" and a "Francis." We don't know how close the connection was between Sujith's neighbor and "Amitha" or "Francis." For example, Francis might have been the neighbor's teacher as well as Sammy Fernando's, and perhaps in some conversation with Sujith's family something was said that made it appropriate for the neighbor to make a reference to a former teacher.

On the other hand, that Sujith claimed that Kusuma had prepared string hoppers for him, and that he was the *son* of "Jamis" may strike even a skeptic as extraordinary. Yet it is not

---

was interviewed by the monk. One cannot help but wonder if after the reincarnation-speculation gathered momentum the child's grandmother or mother didn't simply imagine that the child had earlier called himself "Gorakana Sammy." Something he had said earlier may have sounded somewhat like that.

difficult to conceive of plausible explanations of these utterances either. For instance, although Sujith no longer had a father, or perhaps indeed *because* he no longer had a father, reference by the neighbor to someone's father might very well have caught the child's attention, especially if the reference were conjoined with mention of a one-eyed person. And unfortunately there is only Kusuma's word that she prepared string hoppers for Sammy. It is not out of the question that Kusuma, motivated by excitement at the possibility of being in the presence of a genuine reincarnation, stretched the truth on this point.

Conclusion

The evidence contained in Stevenson's report thus supports a clear alternative to reincarnation as an explanation of Sujith's utterances and other behavior. The child might possibly have merely repeated a few names and phrases he had heard, directly or indirectly, from a neighbor, and this might have been sufficient to excite a possibly bored or idle grandmother who did not recall having heard the same names and phrases herself. The interview with the monk, in which the child, with or without help from another member of his family, gave voice to bits of information about his neighbor's friend, led to the monk's trip to Gorakana, where the monk encountered the niece of the neighbor's friend. The niece, naturally startled that a child she had never heard of had knowledge of her family, visited the child. The child did not recognize her, but the child's family informed themselves of her identity, and on revisiting the child the niece found his power of recognition greatly improved. The niece, impressed, told her relatives about the fascinating child, and they too visited the child. Thus began a snowballing accumulation of further "evidence," of innocent gestures and inarticulate babbles being taken as possible signs of recognition; of possible signs of recognition then being remembered and described to others as iron-clad recognitions; then finally of the "history" of the case being revised unconsciously to conform to what at that point had come to be regarded as certainties. Throughout all of this the child was learning that certain verbal and nonverbal behavior brought attention, acceptance, and other rewards.

Of course, the case of Sujith may not have developed in this natural way, but the main and crucial point is that it *could* have developed this way; so it is not reasonable to believe in reincarnation on the basis of the case.

A final feature of the case, not yet discussed but worthy of brief mention, is that Sammy Fernando died only a little more than six months before Sujith was born. Sujith's mother was said to have given birth to Sujith after only a seven month pregnancy, but even so (and the fact that the mother did give premature birth is nowhere documented by Stevenson), the embryonic child was thus at least about one month old before Sammy Fernando died. At this stage in its development it would already have a primitive heart, its own system of blood vessels, and a rudimentary nervous system and brain, and would be manufacturing its own blood quite independently from the blood supply of its mother. So we know beyond question that at one point Sujith definitely was *not* Sammy Fernando, and thus, on the assumption that he later *became* Sammy Fernando, we are left with the question of what became of the individual who earlier was not Sammy Fernando. Was he too reincarnated?

Stevenson does not make much of the fact that Sammy Fernando had died only six months before Sujith was born, and observes that reincarnation challenges orthodox biology on details far more important and fundamental than this.[14] If Stevenson is correct in this observation, then proof of reincarnation would require disproof of orthodox biology, and thus would require evidence even more vast than that which supports orthodox biology.

Stevenson's Other Cases

Stevenson remarks that the Sujith case is "one of the strongest known to me because of the recording in writing of sixteen items stated by Sujith before they were verified." However, Sujith's family had earlier been directly exposed to a potential source of the information contained in Sujith's statements. The latter fact obviously undercuts the significance of the former fact as evidence of reincarnation. The strengths of a case cannot overcome a fun-

---

[14]Stevenson, *op. cit.*, p. 279.

damental weakness.

This is true of all of Stevenson's cases. They are obviously not all exactly similar in their strengths and weaknesses as evidence of reincarnation, but in every case with which I am familiar the "strengths" are sapped or overcome by certain important weaknesses.

I have heard it suggested that it is only when the cases are considered collectively that they are most suggestive of reincarnation and their collected strengths offset their collected weaknesses. I am very dubious about this reasoning, as it assumes that the weaknesses of one case can be overcome by the strengths of some other case.

Can any generally applicable explanation be given of the assorted cases investigated by Stevenson? The best general explanation of most of the cases seems to me to be that of Doctor Eugene B. Brody in his review of the volume of Stevenson cases which includes that of Sujith.[15] There Brody observes that cultural and familial dynamics unconsciously influence the interpretation and indeed the very perception by parents of the communicative and exploratory behavior of their children. Brody thinks that the behavior of the children in the reincarnation-type cases is basically a deviant form of this essentially communicative and exploratory behavior, but it is perceived, organized, interpreted, and reported by the parents in terms of a model of reincarnation supplied to them (usually) by their culture. In most of Stevenson's cases, a deceased person, the details of whose life correspond to the statements of the unusual child, is *not* discovered, and these cases very easily lend themselves to Brody's explanation. Also, in those cases where there has been discovered some deceased person who corresponds to the child's statements, it might be that the previous person was unconsciously chosen by the child's family to fit the child's statements and behavior patterns.

---

[15]*Journal of the American Society for Psychical Research*, 73: 71–81, 1979.

CHAPTER 24

XENOGLOSSY

What is "xenoglossy" and how does it relate to reincarnation and to life after death? The word has been coined to describe the "gift of tongues"—the capability of talking in a foreign language previously unknown to the speaker. Suppose a medium during a trance or a person in a hypnotized state should utter words in a foreign language, which previously was unknown by him or her so far as we are informed. Could the explanation be that the person learned the language in a previous life? If this "xenoglossy" were responsive to questions, and not merely recitative, would not it be even more suggestive of a previous life in a vanished body, assuming no normal explanation of the phenomenon could be postulated?

"Jensen"

In 1955 and 1956, a Philadelphia physician, whose initials are K.E., conducted a series of hypnotic age-regression experiments on his wife, T.E. During these experiments T.E. was instructed, while in hypnotic trance, to relate information from successively earlier periods of her life. Three of the sessions ended when she was unable to recall anything earlier than a frightening experience of being forced into water and being then hit over the head. On the fourth occasion, the physician instructed T.E., under hypnosis, to go back ten years before the frightening experience with the water. She responded with the startling announcement, "I am a man."

She then gave her name as "Jensen Jacoby," and during this and seven additional sessions she presented the details of a life of a Scandinavian peasant farmer. Because her narrative contained foreign words thought to be Swedish, the physician invited persons able to speak Swedish and other Scandinavian languages to the last three of the eight sessions in which the "Jensen-personality" manifested itself through the hypnotized T.E. "Jensen" reportedly spoke almost entirely in Swedish and was questioned extensively in that language. As will be seen, there is reason to believe that T.E. may never have learned Swedish.

Reportedly, "Jensen" described his life as that of a farmer who raised cows, horses, goats, and chickens. He lived somewhere called "Morby Hagar," evidently a tiny village near the place of someone named "Hansen," a local prince or other dignitary whom "Jensen" revered. "Jensen" would take his produce by horse to a port he called "Havero." He and his wife, "Latvia," were childless though he was himself one of three children of "Hans" and "Lotte." Lotte was Norwegian.

"Jensen" had built a stone-house, perhaps on a portion of his parents' homestead. He drank goat's milk, brandy, and poppy-seed juice. He hunted bears, played games, and drank in the village tavern. He knew little of life beyond his own village, though he had heard of Russian and English sailors and was apparently afraid of them both. He seemed to have died from a blow to his head delivered in a fight in water.

This, in sum, is the case of "Jensen," which has attracted much attention as possible strong evidence of reincarnation. The case has been investigated by Doctor Stevenson.[1] The value of the case as possible evidence of reincarnation presumably does not lie in the fact that the hypnotized T.E. was able to relate information about a "prior existence." The description she gave of "Jensen's" life was not sufficiently detailed to permit a specific determination of his time and place, though most of the details suggested that "he" lived somewhere either in Scandinavia or New Sweden between 1500 and 1800. Due to the lack of specific and idiosyncratic information, investigators were unable to track down anyone to whom the hypnotized woman's description uniquely corresponded.

---

[1] Ian Stevenson: Xenoglossy: a review and report of a case. *Proceedings of the American Society for Psychical Research*, 31: 1–268, 1978. Although the age regression experiments with T.E. began some six years before 1961, which is the date I have set as marking the beginning of the "late period" of survival evidence, the investigation by Doctor Stevenson of the case was not completed until after that date. Further, the methods employed by Doctor Stevenson in investigating the case were very much in keeping with the more meticulous scientific methods of survival research characteristic of the late period. For this reason, I have included the case of "Jensen" as part of the late evidence of survival.

The value of the case as possible proof of reincarnation lies, rather, in T.E.'s supposed ability to converse in Swedish, if T.E. could not have acquired that ability in her own lifetime. Otherwise, the case would be worth little as evidence of a former life, since nobody could be found who corresponded to "Jensen," and no person or place could be found that corresponded to persons and places mentioned by him. The nonspecific allusions of T.E. to a previous life could too easily be her imaginative response to the hypnotist's demand for details of a previous life, and there would be no reason to contemplate an alternative explanation of "Jensen."

The ability to converse intelligently in a language that one has not learned through normal means is called by Stevenson *"responsive xenoglossy."* True cases of responsive xenoglossy are thought by many survival researchers strongly to support some form of personal survival after death, most likely reincarnation.

Presumably, however, one must distinguish between a true case of responsive xenoglossy and certain cases that superficially are very similar. There are, for instance, records of people who, usually in delirium or trance, have mouthed words and phrases in tongues that are unknown to them, apparently without understanding anything of what they have said. These *"recitative xenoglossies,"* in which the subject displays an ability to recite fragments of a foreign language but not to understand the language, may easily result from the subject's once having learned fragments of the language, or having seen passages written in the language, and then having forgotten about it.[2]

Cases also reportedly occur in which a person during illness or sleep or old age reverts suddenly to a language learned in childhood, and is indeed able to converse in it. While such an occurrence may surprise those who witness it, it of course does not constitute evidence of life after death. There are records too of persons who, during altered states of consciousness such as those produced by hypnosis, illness, or drugs, have spoken what sounds like a foreign language, even sometimes like some particular

---

[2]Of course, even mere recitation of foreign words without understanding, if the recitation cannot be explained as related to the subject's life after his birth, can be asserted to show the dim influence of a previous life, an influence that shines through brightly in responsive xenoglossy.

foreign language such as, say, Spanish, but which is in fact gibberish.[3] These cases likewise have no bearing on life after death.

Cases like these are distinguishable from instances of true, responsive xenoglossy, in which the subject not only recites the foreign language but is able to converse in it and thus to understand it, though never having been exposed to it in his or her present life. Nils Jacobson explains why he thinks that a case of true responsive xenoglossy would so strongly suggest reincarnation:

> It is completely unheard of for anyone to learn a language telepathically, clairvoyantly, or through retrocognition. Through ESP one can receive knowledge of matters and events in past, present, and future time. But no experiences are known which indicate that a person has ever acquired a skill through ESP—and the ability to speak a language is precisely such an acquired skill.[4]

Jacobson's point is thus that a true case of responsive xenoglossy, in which the subject did not acquire his ability to converse in the foreign language through normal means, cannot plausibly be explained by ESP, and thus must be received as a case of reincarnation (though possession would seem to be another alternative to reincarnation).

But Jacobson overlooks that proven cases of reincarnation are as "unheard of" as proven cases of language-learning through ESP. Thus he could as easily have made the reverse point: a true case of responsive xenoglossy, in which the subject did not acquire his ability to converse in the foreign language through normal means, cannot plausibly be explained by reincarnation, and thus must be received as a case of language-acquisition through ESP.

In any event, cases of responsive xenoglossies are, according to Stevenson, rare, "and well-documented cases even rarer."[5] In fact, Stevenson, who exhaustively examined the various reports of the phenomenon, believes that there are only three cases of xenoglossy

---

[3]For a full discussion of the various types of pseudo-responsive xenoglossies, the reader should consult Stevenson, *op. cit.*, pp. 1–5, 10–14.

[4]Nils O. Jacobson, *Life Without Death?* Delacorte Press (n.p.), 1971, p. 209. Reprinted by permission of Delacorte Press/Seymour Lawrence. "Retrocognition" is knowledge of the past through ESP.

[5]Stevenson, *op. cit.*, p. 1.

which have received anything close to thorough investigation and recording.[6] Only two of these cases does Stevenson regard as instances of responsive xenoglossy, and one of these two, the case of "Rosemary," is marred by certain weaknesses which I mention below. The remaining case is that of "Jensen."

The Investigation of the "Jensen" Case

A systematic investigation by Doctor Ian Stevenson of the case of "Jensen" took six years, and was intended to bring to light any normal explanation of T.E.'s Swedish. Of the eight sessions in which the "Jensen" personality manifested itself, the fourth through the seventh were tape-recorded, and detailed notes were taken at the eighth. Swedish-speaking interpreters interviewed "Jensen" in Swedish, and six other scholars were involved in various capacities in the examination of the case.

Both the physician, K.E., and his wife, T.E., were investigated in all ways thought likely to explain T.E.'s knowledge of Swedish. Their backgrounds were explored. Inquiry was made about T.E.'s opportunities to have learned Swedish or Swedish words and phrases. To ascertain T.E.'s ability to learn foreign languages in general, she was given the Modern Language Aptitude test. Effort was made to determine her psychological stability. Both T.E. and K.E. were given a word association test, the Minnesota Multiphasic Personality Inventory, and two polygraph tests for lie detection. Seven relatives were interviewed, as were as well seven other witnesses to various aspects of the case.

However, while Stevenson's investigation was thus careful and extensive, it was not flawless. Stevenson did not himself attend any of the sessions at which the subject, T.E., manifested the Jensen personality. So, unfortunately, we do not have his personal testimony as to what occurred and as to what the interpreters did, if anything, to safeguard against unintentionally supplying T.E. with hints as to grammar, pronunciation, vocabulary, phrasing, and intonation.

Stevenson's report contains a lengthy transcript of some, but not all, of the recorded material, and this transcript does not in

---

[6]*Ibid.*, p. 86.

itself suggest that the interpreters inadvertently communicated linguistic information to T.E. The annotations to the transcript indicate that such information *might* have been communicated, since on at least one occasion, according to the annotations, unrecorded Swedish was spoken in T.E.'s presence.

A deficiency in the *report* of the case, if not in its investigation, is that Stevenson does not provide any information about the interpreters' experience with hypnotized subjects. Even experts cannot always tell when a subject is feigning a hypnotic trance.[7]

"Jensen's" Knowledge of Swedish

In view of the great deal of interest Stevenson had in this case, not to mention the time and money he and others must have expended in its investigation, one might expect "Jensen" to have displayed a striking and indisputable ability to converse in Swedish. However, the transcript in Stevenson's report quickly reveals to the reader that whether or not "Jensen" displayed an ability to understand and to converse in Swedish is clearly a matter of opinion, which of course is precisely why Stevenson cites the opinions of the Swedish interpreters as to whether "Jensen" really understood the language.

My own opinion is that the ability of "Jensen" genuinely to understand and to converse in Swedish is *not* disclosed by the transcription. I think that it would be an unwarranted oversimpliplification to assert without qualification that he "knew" Swedish.

Almost none of "Jensen's" utterances were complete phrases, and those that were, as for example, "I am tired," are of the sort ordinarily learned as complete units. There is no doubt, assuming that the transcript is correct, that "Jensen" uttered several Swedish words in appropriate response to questions, as indeed a parrot might do. There is no doubt, that is, that "Jensen" possessed what Stevenson calls a recitative xenoglossy.

There is a real question as to whether "Jensen's" xenoglossy qualifies as responsive or truly conversational. His "conversation" was always one-sided (as one interpretor remarked), with "Jensen"

---

[7]This is illustrated by the disagreement of experts as to whether a suspect in the case of the "Los Angeles Hillside Strangler" was really hypnotized (see *Time*, January 14, 1980, p. 50).

doing nothing more than responding to the interpreters' questions. "Jensen's" responses were almost invariably single words or parts of words, often with incorrect endings and missing articles, and were frequently inappropriate to the questions asked, were often mispronounced, and were sometimes totally unintelligible. "Yes" and "no" were often the only responses given. The infrequency with which "Jensen" responded appropriately with a word that had not already been used by the interpreters is indicated by the surprise the interpreters expressed when he did so.

All in all, it is very difficult to avoid thinking that "Jensen" understood little Swedish, if any, and that he was merely a hypnotized subject doing his best to respond favorably to the desires and commands of the hypnotist and other interrogators. Most of the transcribed "conversation" was a "fishing trip," with "Jensen" searching for a word or sound that the interrogators would approve, and with them searching for any slender meaningfulness in his utterances. When "Jensen" finally hit upon something even vaguely appropriate to the question asked, the interpreters would evince pleasure and the appropriate utterance would be repeated over and over, until some clue in the interpreters' further questions — some cognate, some previously used phrase, some emphasized word — enabled him to stab again at an acceptable response. That "Jensen" was genuinely able to converse in Swedish is, in short, far from clearly evident.[8]

Nevertheless, "Jensen" did respond occasionally in ways that suggest that he understood what had been asked. In addition, by Stevenson's count, "Jensen" introduced into the various tape-

---

[8]What is required to demonstrate a genuine comprehension of language, as opposed to the ability merely to parrot or mimic verbal behavior, is a matter of current controversy among scientists. Chimpanzees that have been taught to "communicate" with humans in American Sign Language (a language-system for the deaf) have seemingly demonstrated mastery of a far larger vocabulary than that possessed by "Jensen," and have been credited with inventing phrases of their own to insult their trainers and to compose rhymes. Yet there is a growing belief on the part of experts that in spite of their display of language, which seems in general much more impressive than "Jensen's," the chimpanzees do not really have even a rudimentary comprehension of syntax (the essence of language-understanding). Significantly, one of the main reasons researchers have for concluding that, appearances to the contrary, the chimpanzees do not really understand the language they "speak" is that the animals, like "Jensen," by and large "talk" only in response to questions from humans; i.e. they, like "Jensen," only rarely make "spontaneous" utterances. See Herbert Terrace: *Nim.* New York, Knopf, 1979.

recorded sessions some sixty words that had not previously been used by his interviewers.[9] Stevenson excluded from the list utterances that were doubtful words, required correction by the interviewers, or had English cognates, e.g. "makrill" ("mackerel"). I think, though, that the exclusion might have been more rigorous.[10]

Still, the subject, T.E., claimed that she had never learned Swedish, and she passed two polygraph tests to this effect. Further, she insisted, even while under deep hypnosis, that she had never studied or learned any Scandinavian language, and she demonstrated poor language-learning ability on the Modern Language Aptitude Test. Moreover, she displayed no tendency toward abnormalities of feeling or behavior on the Minnesota Multiphasic Personality Inventory, and she showed no suspicious traits on the word association test. How could a person of whom all of this is true possibly have come to possess the knowledge of Swedish that T.E. did?

To answer this question, it must be determined how much previous education and experience would have been required for T.E. to acquire her capability in Swedish. Stevenson thinks that tutoring in Swedish would be required. This again is a matter of opinion. It would be one thing if some sixty vocabulary items were available to the immediate recall of T.E. and she were able to deploy them consciously and deliberately in the give and take of a true conversation. It would have been astounding if this had occurred without T.E.'s having been tutored. What did occur is an entirely different thing: i.e. having the remnants of that many items dragged from her in bits and pieces with the painstaking efforts of sympathetic speakers of the language while she was in hypnotic trance. In my view, the Swedish capability of T.E. was equivalent to that which most people would possess after spending a short time with a self-pronouncing phrase book. (Indeed, many, though not all, of "Jensen's" Swedish words were typical of those found in such a phrase book, e.g. "I am tired," "I don't understand you," "brandy," "wine," "animal.")

---

[9] As compared with the over four hundred vocabulary items some chimpanzees reportedly have within their command. *Time*, March 10, 1980. p. 50.

[10] E.g. "brannvin" ("brandy") was accepted. Because as a child T.E. was exposed to Yiddish, it would have been desirable to exclude words with German cognates such as "plass" ("Platz"), "frukt" ("frucht"), and "fru" ("frau").

While "Jensen's" pronunciation at times was excellent, in the opinion of Stevenson and other speakers of Swedish, at other times it was not. A number of his utterances were incomprehensible; at times they were pronounced with a "Norwegian accent" and at others displayed an "American quality." The transcript makes it clear that from time to time an interviewer would deliberately imitate "Jensen's" mispronunciation of a word in order to humor or encourage him. This limited success in pronunciation is precisely what would be expected if T.E. had at some forgotten time perused a self-pronouncing phrase book.

The point I wish to make here, however, is only that whether the Swedish capability of T.E. could have been attained without tutoring is a matter of opinion, and not a clear matter of settled fact. Even if T.E. never in her life had contact with a Swedish phrase book, there are other ways in which she may very well have learned or been exposed to Swedish, as I shall now suggest.

T.E.'s Possible Prior Acquaintance With Swedish

It obviously would be very difficult, if not impossible, to eliminate the possibility of T.E.'s having had some prior acquaintance with Swedish. Testimony of her husband and others that they never knew of her having had the opportunity to learn a foreign language, though conclusive as to what they knew, certainly is not conclusive that she never had the opportunity. Few Americans, and certainly not the wife of a general medical practitioner, are under continuous surveillance or have their whereabouts constantly monitored so that it could be known with certainty that they could never have been exposed to Swedish.[11]

The investigation of T.E., as reported, does not preclude the possibility that she had many contacts, some perhaps even intimate and thus purposely undisclosed by T.E., with persons who spoke Swedish or had Scandinavian ties. It is almost impossible, I think, to live in many places in this country without at times

---

[11]Because there were major gaps in the observation of T.E. by her intimates between 1943 and 1950, Stevenson concedes that we must rely on T.E.'s testimony to decide whether she learned Swedish during this period. Though he accepts as honest her statement that she did not learn Swedish during this period, I suggest in the following text that she may have been exposed to Swedish even though honestly not remembering the fact.

hearing Swedish spoken or imitated and without knowing that the language was Swedish or an imitation of it. This is especially true in many metropolitan communities as in Philadelphia, where, apparently, T.E. was raised.

If T.E. had had prior acquaintance with Swedish, would not the lie detector test have shown her denial of it to have been false? Moreover, wouldn't she have admitted having learned or been exposed to Swedish when the question was asked of her while she was in deep hypnotic trance?[12] Certain facts and strange happenings in her life bear significantly on the answer to these two questions.

After the "Jensen" experiments, T.E. became, interestingly enough, a "conventional" medium, complete with controls, communicators, and messages from "beyond." Once, after she had become a medium, a notebook was found in her purse, which contained material that resembled a message that she had earlier uttered while in a trance. On another occasion, a book that she had borrowed from a library was discovered to contain passages that were almost identical to another "message" she had given while in trance.

Stevenson was on hand when she was told about the existence of the material in her notebook and the passages in the library book. According to him, she became frightened and claimed to have no memory of having read the book or of having written the messages in her notebook, and when she was shown her handwriting she "concluded that she must have made these entries during an involuntary trance for which she was afterwards amnesic."[13]

Assuming that T.E. truly did not remember having read the book or having written the messages in her notebook, it is conceivable that the true explanation of the source of her mediumistic "messages" would not have been revealed in a lie detector test, if administered, or in an inquiry during hypnosis, if made.

---

[12]There is evidence, cited by Stevenson, that instructions given in previous hypnosis enable a person to conceal the truth even while in a later hypnotic trance. Stevenson, *op. cit.*, p. 68.

[13]*Ibid.*, p. 58. That T.E. was subject to involuntary trances or similar states in which she might unconsciously acquire information is further suggested by the fact that she was once seen to be sleep-walking; while doing so she was observed to leaf through a book as if reading it, to make writing motions with one of her hands, and all the while to be muttering the name of one of her "communicators."

That T.E. had the ability to read something, and then to repeat what she had read almost verbatim without any recollection of having read it, certainly must be viewed as of great significance as to the probative worth of the "Jensen" case. For whatever the explanation of this remarkable ability may be, it is distinctly possible that it could account for her display of Swedish. True, she was discovered to have this ability only *after* the "Jensen" experiments, but presumably she would have had the same ability during those experiments as well.

Stevenson considers the hypothesis that T.E. acquired familiarity with Swedish through some such phenomenon as "involuntary trances," and, surprisingly to me, rejects the hypothesis as "improbable" principally because it leaves unexplained what the "agency of induction" of such involuntary trances might be.[14] What is the "agency of induction" of reincarnation? If a good reason for rejecting the hypothesis of involuntary trances is that the hypothesis leaves important causative factors unexplained, then it is an equally good reason for rejecting the hypothesis of reincarnation.

Nor must we suppose, as Stevenson thinks we must if we subscribe to the "involuntary trance" theory, that to gain familiarity with Swedish T.E. would have had to wander around Philadelphia either as "Jensen" or as some third personality and thus would have attracted attention. When later, after T.E. had become a conventional medium, and was in the process of subconsciously gathering information from the library book, which she subsequently "communicated" in trance, did she go about either as the communicating personality or as some third party? She was in any case able to acquire this information without attracting attention. Stevenson himself notes that cases have been reported in which mediums acquire the contents of trance messages from public libraries.

It therefore seems very possible to me that the Swedish T.E. knew, those "stumps and roots" (to borrow Stevenson's expression) of words and phrases, could have been learned as effortlessly and as unobservedly as was the information in the library book. The book was, apparently, of a scientific nature and might therefore even have been technical. The fact that T.E. could subcon-

---

[14]*Ibid.*, p. 69.

siously absorb such material and then later reproduce it without remembering its source suggests to me that her subconscious mind could absorb even complex information easily and quickly.

In short, the possibility that the limited Swedish manifested by T.E. under hypnosis could have resulted from prior forgotten acquaintance with the language (in this life) has not, in my view, been satisfactorily eliminated by Doctor Stevenson's report.

Other Cases of Xenoglossy

As noted above, Stevenson considers the Jensen case one of the two instances of responsive xenoglossy that have approached being thoroughly investigated and recorded. The other case is that of "Rosemary," investigated and reported by F. H. Wood.[15] This celebrated case involved a subject who was said to have conversed responsively in the language of ancient Egypt. However, in the opinion of Doctor Stevenson, the xenoglossy in the case is marred as proof of reincarnation for the following reasons: (1) It is not known how the vowels of ancient Egyptian sounded, so the authenticity of "Rosemary's" pronunciation cannot be determined. (2) Wood was unable to convince any Egyptian scholar other than A. J. H. Hulme to take the case seriously, so it did not in fact receive a full investigation.[16]

---

[15]Wood: *After Thirty Centuries*. London, Rider, 1935; and: *This Egyptian Miracle*, 2nd ed. London, Watkins, 1955.

[16]Stevenson, *op. cit.*, p. 7. Some readers may wonder about the famous case of "Patience Worth," a self-proclaimed communicator from the seventeenth century who "dictated" to the medium, Mrs. Pearl Curran, a long epic poem, "The Story of Telka." Stevenson has concluded that the case is a "pseudo-xenoglossy." *Ibid.*, p. 14.

CHAPTER 25

REINCARNATION WORKSHOPS

A review of the evidence of reincarnation must take note of two recent books by psychologist Helen Wambach. In the earlier work, *Reliving Past Lives: The Evidence Under Hypnosis*,[1] Wambach presents the data she collected from questionnaires filled out by eleven hundred persons who participated in small hypnosis "workshops." Each workshop lasted eight hours and was divided into three sessions. In each session Wambach's subjects were hypnotized as a group and then each hypnotized subject was allowed to choose one of ten specified past time periods, from 2000 BC to the twentieth century, and then asked about his "life" during the period chosen. The subjects were queried about their gender in the previous life, and about their appearance, clothing, food, utensils, occupation, and other similar things. A posthypnotic suggestion given to each subject at the end of every session enabled the subject to remember, after awakening, the experiences that were brought to mind during hypnosis, and thus to complete a questionnaire about his "past life."

In the later of the two books, *Life Before Life*,[2] Wambach examines the reports of some 750 subjects who participated in other small group hypnosis workshops. In this instance, however, the subjects were not asked to concentrate on past lives but rather on their "return" to this life. They were queried on such matters as whether they had chosen to be born, whether they had chosen their sex, what their purpose was in choosing this life, whether persons known to them in this life were known to them in earlier lives, at what point their soul had entered their fetus, and what the experience of being born was like. Again, the subjects filled out questionnaires about these things immediately upon awakening.

---

[1] New York, Harper and Row, 1978.
[2] New York, Bantam Books, 1979.

Life Before Life

Some of what is written in the later book, *Life Before Life*, may well cause critics to question the author's techniques. For example, she tells her hypnotized subjects, as if their hypnotized minds would understand such instructions, to "reduce your brain-wave electric potentials down to five cycles per second."[3]

Critics will wonder also how deeply Wambach's subjects were hypnotized, if indeed they were hypnotized at all. It is not clear that Wambach's attempts to "hypnotize" so many people at once could lead many of them, if any at all, into deeper hypnotic stages. What Wambach would call "hypnotic" visions other psychologists might well call daydreams; and her group-hypnosis workshops may merely be what some refer to as daydream-exploration or "guided daydream" seminars.[4]

On the other hand, does it really matter if her subjects were merely daydreaming? Is there any reason why an earlier life could not be recalled as easily and as authentically in reveries as in deep hypnosis?[5]

In any case, the discussion in *Life Before Life* is centered around the

---

[3] Wambach, *op. cit.* (*Life Before Life*), p. 16.

[4] Evidently there are no sure physiological indicators of a hypnotic trance; that is, those who are said to be hypnotized cannot be distinguished from those who are not by any physiological indicant such as EEG, pulse rate, electrooculogram, etc. (See Benjamin Wolman [Ed.]: *International Encyclopedia of Psychiatry, Psychology, Psychoanalysis and Neurology*. New York, Van Nostrand Reinhold Co., 1977, p. 460; and T. X. Barber: *Hypnosis: A Scientific Approach*. New York, Van Nostrand Reinhold Co., 1969, p. 7.) T. X. Barber, indeed, doubts that there is a special or unique state of consciousness that might be called "the hypnotic state," and questions as well such assumptions as that the greater the "depth" of the "hypnotic state," the more readily are hypnotic phenomena elicited from the subject. Barber marshals much evidence that phenomena thought to be due to a subject's "being in a hypnotic state" are in fact due to his attitudes, his motivation to perform suggested tasks, and his expectations of being able to do so. (*Ibid.*, pp 221–225.)

[5] Barber cites studies that indicate that "age regression," as indicated by the subject's testimony that he is in another place at an earlier time, can be produced in the great majority of "nonhypnotized" control subjects merely by emphatically suggesting that they have been returned to a past time. He also cites studies that indicate that "hypnotically regressed" subjects were not significantly better in their powers of recall than were those nonhypnotized control subjects who were "regressed" by mere suggestion. He discovered as well that subjects who were "hypnotically regressed" to childhood failed to perform on intelligence or behavioral tests in a manner correct for a child of the specified age. Barber concluded that it is inappropriate to view "hypnotically induced" age-regression as a "faithful reproduction of the subject's past behavior." *Ibid.*, pp. 179–192.

subjects' "rebirth" in this world rather than around their past lives; so, the book does not really purport to offer much evidence of reincarnation. Of course, if one really did choose whether or not to be born, then, logically, he must have existed prior to his birth, but there is no reason that I can see for believing that Wambach's subjects actually made that choice.

What Wambach's study in *Life Before Life* really shows, I think, is that most human beings, if hypnotized and asked the following questions will give responses implying that they have lived before: as, "Did you choose to be born?" "Why did you choose to be born in the 20th Century?" "Did you choose your sex before you were born?" "When does your soul enter the fetus?" This fact is hardly surprising. The implication is already present in the questions. The questions are perfect examples of what logicians call "complex" questions, or what lawyers and others call leading questions that suggest the answer. *Any* grammatically appropriate response to such questions logically presupposes that the respondent existed prior to this life.

Does the fact that many of Wambach's subjects were able, under hypnosis, to describe the "birth-canal experience" suggest the reality of reincarnation? I think not. Even if it could be shown that the birth process is recorded in the human subconsciousness, it clearly would not necesarily follow that there is reincarnation.

For that matter, Wambach's studies do not indicate that people have subconscious memories of the process of birth. There is, as far as I can ascertain, no reason to suppose that her subjects were doing anything other than imagining what, if they had been fully conscious at the time, it would have been like to have experienced their own births. When I, without undergoing hypnosis, attempt to picture what it would have been like to experience my own birth, the picture I get is quite similar to the descriptions of the "birth canal experience" given by many of Wambach's subjects.

Nevertheless, Wambach thinks it significant that, while over 95 percent of her subjects were able under hypnosis to "recall" past lives, only about half of them were able to answer her questions about the nature of the birth experience. She writes: "If past-life recall is fantasy, and if the birth trip is fantasy, why wouldn't one be as easy to get as the other?"[6]

---

[6]Wambach, *op. cit.* (*Life Before Life*), p. 176.

The question is fair enough, but my own opinion is that some things are easier to imagine than others: many may find a past life easier to imagine than life in the womb. Perhaps this is why more of Doctor Wambach's subjects were able to "recall" past lives.

What her subjects actually did "recall" about their past lives is explained by Doctor Wambach in her earlier book, *Reliving Past Lives*.

Reliving Past Lives

In *Reliving Past Lives*, Wambach in effect asks her hypnotized subjects to report what they have experienced at a given time, e.g. 1700. They respond, I think, with information as to what they imagine might have been experienced if they had been alive at that time.

Wambach apparently thinks, in part because the reports of her subjects conform largely to historical reality, that her subjects may indeed actually have lived past lives.

However, almost all of the information about the past provided by her subjects was of a very nonspecific nature. A subject will say, for example, that in a previous life she wore a "sturdy, worn-thin dress" or ate "fruit" or "bread" and used a "wooden bowl," or will list "tending my man" or "writing" as her activity. It is, I think, hardly surprising that the imaginings of a group of middle-class Americans living in the last half of the twentieth century—a group of people who could scarcely be regarded as ignorant or illiterate—would conform to historical reality in details such as these. It is not, after all, as if late twentieth century Americans as a group are unexposed to history or have no conception as to what people in times past might have worn or eaten, etc. Movies and works of fiction set in the past conform largely to historical reality in these very broad categories. If Wambach's subjects really were hypnotized, then it is eminently reasonable to expect the bits and snatches of information about the past they had consciously and unconsciously acquired in their present lives to surface in their efforts to "recall" a life from the past.

Wambach's principal reason for believing that her subjects may actually have led past lives is as follows:

> I knew that in any given time period in the past, roughly half of the population was male and half female... I decided to check each time period and determine how many regressions were to male lives and how

many were to female lives. *If past-life recall was fantasy, I would expect to have more male lives:* Surveys show that the average citizen, given the opportunity, would prefer to live life as a male (italics supplied).[7]

Wambach then discovered that the past lives "recalled" by the members of her sample were *not* predominantly male. Rather, past lives "recalled" under hypnosis were about 50 percent male and 50 percent female.

Nonetheless, the overall results of Wambach's study are exactly what, according to Wambach in the passage quoted above, one would expect if "past-life recall was a fantasy." What one would expect, she says, is more regressions to male lives, and this is exactly what one gets, for there were more women than men to begin with in Wambach's sample. While the lives "recalled" under hypnosis were about 50/50 male to female, the women in Wambach's sample outnumbered men 72 percent to 28 percent.

However, there is one complication in regard to Wambach's statistics that *prima facie* seems to support her interpretation of her data. Wambach's total sample was divided into two groups. In the first group, which consisted of eight hundred subjects, 78 percent of the subjects were women. The lives "recalled" by this group were 50.3 percent male and 49.7 percent female, i.e. roughly 50/50 male to female. In the second group, which consisted of three hundred cases, only 55 percent of the subjects were women, but the lives "recalled" by this group again split close to 50/50: the lives "recalled" by this group were 50.9 percent male and 49.1 percent female.

Now, what does this prove? What is clear, of course, is that there was a marked difference between the two groups in the percentage of recalls of past male lives: the subjects in the first group were more likely to recall male lives than were the subjects in the second group. This difference between the two groups suggests only that the gender of the lives "recalled" is independent of the gender of the subjects.

This apparent independence of "recalled" gender from the actual gender of the subjects is *not* in turn indicative of reincarnation, since factors other than reincarnation could account for

---

[7]Wambach, *op. cit.* (*Reliving Past Lives*), p. 123. Reprinted by permission of Harper and Row. Wambach does not identify the surveys she mentions.

the independence. For example, it would seem far easier to imagine male lives from times past than female lives, because of the emphasis placed on males and their circumstances and activities in historical works, fiction, and movies. Thus, if the "recalls" of Wambach's subjects were mere fantasies, one would expect the gender "recalled" by the subjects to be independent of their actual gender.

Wambach, however, has further reasons for regarding her data as supporting the hypothesis of reincarnation. It will be remembered that her subjects chose three out of ten specified past times (e.g. "B.C. 500," "A.D. 400") for past-life "recall." Wambach found that the subjects were far more likely to choose to recall lives from a recent time than from a remote time. In fact, twice as many A.D. 1600 lives were recalled as A.D. 400, and twice as many A.D. 1850 lives were recalled as A.D. 1600. These increases correspond to the actual worldwide increase in population during this time span. Wambach regards this correspondence between the recall trends of her subjects and the worldwide population trends as "very suggestive" of reincarnation.[8] Her reasoning, apparently, is that if past-life recall were mere fantasy, then one would *not* find the increase in the world's population in more recent times mirrored in her data.

However, I would think that, if past-life recall were fantasy, there would be more "recalls" of lives from more recent times than of lives from more distant times, because more is known about recent times. Wambach admits that the possibility "cannot be ruled out" that her subjects experienced "more lives in recent time periods because they had more data available to them with which to construct fantasies."[9] If this possibility cannot be ruled out, then why should the data be regarded as suggesting reincarnation?

Wambach also speculates that she may have been "tapping" a "representative sample" of the world's population. Yet if she had been tapping a representative sample of the world's population, I would think that the population trends within a given geographic area, say Europe or North America, would be repeated by her

---

[8]*Ibid.*, p. 139.
[9]*Ibid.*, p. 138.

data. This does not happen. For example, in a period (1700 to 1850) in which the population of Europe dramatically increased, there was evidently a decline in the European lives "recalled" by her subjects.

Wambach also compiled various statistics on the social class and race of the persons whose lives were "recalled" by her subjects, and on such things as food and footwear from past "remembered" lives. The statistics are interesting in themselves, but I see no significance in them for the theory of reincarnation.

It is likewise of little significance that what many of the subjects "recalled" was not what Wambach suggested they look for. Wambach might ask the subjects if they were seeing a plate or a bowl, but many of them would see no such thing. She concludes: "They saw what they saw regardless of my instructions.... If past-life recall is fantasy, one would expect that all of them would have seen the plates or bowls I suggested."[10]

Again, I would not expect this, if past-life recall were fantasy. In guided-daydream workshops, in which subjects while daydreaming are given instructions or "guidance" by a psychologist, the subjects often "see what they see" regardless of the suggestions and instructions of the psychologist. One's fantasies ordinarily have some internal consistency. If one's fantasy takes him to the mountains, he will not ordinarily be able to see the sea.

I have concluded, therefore, that neither of Doctor Wambach's studies really offers much reason for believing in reincarnation. I suspect that data similar to hers would result if 1,100 nonhypnotized middle-class Americans were asked to choose one of ten specified past time periods and to write a brief story about some imaginary person from that period. Those so asked would, I think, show the same tendency to select the more recent periods. They would exhibit the same inclination to write about males. Their stories would probably display the same vagueness and lack of specificity with regard to historical facts. The stories, like the "recollections" of Wambach's subjects, would still conform to reality in the more general areas of food eaten, clothing worn, activities, and the like.

It is not absolutely impossible, of course, that a story about the past would reflect not only the historical knowledge of its author,

---

[10]*Ibid.*, p. 136.

but also his hidden memories of past lives; I personally see little reason to suppose this to be the case. It is also not absolutely impossible, as Bertrand Russell once remarked, that the world was created five minutes ago complete with fictitious memories and false records, but I see little reason to suppose that to be the case either.

Similarly, I see little reason to suppose that the "recollections" of Doctor Wambach's subjects are the product of hidden memories of past lives. If we truly have these memories, memories that come forth in "hypnosis," or in daydreams about the past or when writing historical novels or plays, etc., then there must have been some mechanism other than the present body and its brain and neural system for inscribing those memories on the hidden record. It does not seem to me to be at all necessary to postulate either the hidden memories or a mechanism to record those memories, since the "facts" remembered can be explained by imagination and historical knowledge with no resort to reincarnation.

Furthermore, even if some extra-normal explanation of the "recollections" of Doctor Wambach's subjects were called for, why should that explanation be reincarnation? Wambach thinks, evidently, that we can foresee the future through ESP.[11] If so, why not the past? If apparent knowledge of the future is regarded as evidence of ESP of the future, then why shouldn't apparent knowledge of the past be considered as evidence of ESP of the past, rather than of reincarnation?

---

[11] *Ibid.*, pp. 25–29.

CHAPTER 26

WHAT ARE THE PROBABILITIES?

"Then, Cebes, beyond question, the soul is immortal and imperishable, and our souls will truly exist in another world." Cebes replied, "I am convinced, Socrates."
— *Plato,* Phaedo[1]

Death is not an event in life. Death is not lived through.
— *Ludwig Wittgenstein,* Tractatus Logico-philosophicus[2]

Socrates concluded that we continue to exist after the death of our bodies, but his conclusion cannot be sustained by *a priori* reasoning. As I noted in Part II, there is no contradiction in supposing that a person might *not* survive his biological death.

Further, the opposite conclusion, that we do not continue to exist after biological death, also cannot be proved *a priori*. If a person is purely physical and is identical with the body he now has (or with a part of it), or if a person, though not identical with his present body, nonetheless must have his present body to exist, then the death of that body will end his existence forever, unless he is resurrected. However, as I endeavored to make clear in Part II, it is by no means certain that a person is a purely physical entity or requires either this body or any other for his continued existence. Life after death, even in a discarnate form, is not theoretically impossible.

If personal survival is, as I believe, neither *a priori* certain nor *a priori* impossible, the question is whether or not it is probable, and this question can be answered only on the basis of the evi-

---

[1] B. Jowett (trans.): *The Dialogues of Plato.* New York, Random House, 1937; Vol. I, p. 492.

[2] D. F. Pears and B. F. McGuinness (trans.). London, Routledge and Kegan Paul, 1961, p. 146. (sec. 6.4311)

dence that bears on the matter.

Do the phenomena that have been reported in the last one hundred years, that have been regarded by many as evidence of life after death, lend support to the conclusion of Socrates?

Certainly the phenomena are consistent with a survivalist interpretation. Indeed, at first glance they even invite a survivalist interpretation: if they did not, they would not have been mentioned in this book.

The phenomena also fall under an impressively broad range of categories. Mediumistic communications alone have occurred in a variety of forms: there have been straightforward communications from a "departed spirit" to a living friend or relative through a single medium; "cross-corresponding" communications by a single spirit through two or more mediums acting independently of one another; communications from two or more spirits communicating in concert through two or more mediums; communications from a spirit through a medium to the "proxy" of the living person; and communications from "drop-in" spirits who are reportedly known neither to the medium nor the sitters, but who convey information about their former living namesakes that is later discovered to be true. In addition to the mediumistic communications, there are the reported sightings of apparitions, visions of persons at the brink of death, out-of-body experiences, tape-recorded messages from the dead, xenoglossies, and remembrances of past lives.

It is possible that the very diversity of the phenomena that at first appearance point to the actuality of survival persuades some that there is a hereafter. Diversity by itself proves nothing. Magicians deliver an amazing diversity of "evidence" of supernatural power and black magic. If the "survival phenomena" are to count as true evidence of afterdeath survival, then, when they are examined carefully, they must prove to be extremely resistive to all but survivalist explanations.

Are the mediumships of Mrs. Leonard and Mrs. Piper extremely resistant to nonsurvivalist explanations? One cannot say unqualifiedly that they are, since, as I explained in Part III, the mediumships were not subjected to those modern methods of investigation and appraisal that discount "elastic messages" and preclude acquisition by the medium of information from living persons. Can the cross-correspondences or drop-in communications be explained plausibly only on the assumption that there is life after death? The possibility that living persons were the source of the information in these communications was never satisfactorily eliminated.

Do any of the other phenomena emphatically resist nonsurvivalist explanations? The Raudive voices could have been taped radio transmissions and other recorded natural sounds. The Swedish xenoglossy in the "Jensen" case may have resulted from the subject's contact with Swedish in this life. The sightings of apparitions could very well have the same "natural" explanations as do so-called spontaneous cases in general. OBEs have apparently not been established experimentally as genuine departures of the human consciousness from the physical body, and thus could be subjective fantasies. Imagination, not reincarnation, could be the explanation of Wambach's findings. Even the best of Stevenson's "reincarnation cases," while having been so painstakingly investigated, are subject to plausible nonsurvivalist explanations, as is illustrated by the case of Sujith.

True, according to Doctor Sabom and Doctor Moody, there is at present no fully adequate or generally accepted medical explanation of the survival-suggestive experiences of persons on the brink of death, but this fact certainly does not make a survivalist explanation of the experiences more likely than a nonsurvivalist. Survivalist explanations of the experiences could hardly be described as fully adequate or generally accepted either; and, as Dr. Sabom notes, most health care professionals do regard the experiences as hallucinatory.

So the trouble with the various phenomena I have considered in this book, as evidence of personal survival, is that none of them prove on close examination to be stubbornly resistant to all but survivalist explanations. If only some data had been uncovered which not merely are amenable to a survivalist explanation but also strongly defy explanation in any other terms, then the phenomena I have considered might reasonably be deemed to carry weight as *corroborative* evidence of survival. If, for example, purported spirits had ever succeeded in communicating lock-combinations set by persons prior to death or in revealing the contents of messages written and sealed by people before they died, then the phenomena considered in this book could be regarded as providing further confirmation of survival. By themselves these phenomena are, so to speak, evidentially incomplete. The various survival-phenomena have mere *potential corroborative value.*

However, to establish the probability of life after death, is it really necessary that there be at least one phenomenon that resolutely refuses to be explained except in survivalist terms? Do not the various survival-phenomena, though having mere potential corroborative value when considered independently from one another, collectively form a very compelling pattern of evidence of personal survival? Time and again I have heard it said that what produces conviction that there is life after death is the entire "sweep" of evidence. It is said: do not consider the phenomena individually, one by one; consider them collectively: it is the assembled data that convince.

I am not convinced. On the one hand are the millions upon millions of human beings who have died without having left any known indications of their continued existence after death. On the other is the comparative handful of cases of mediumistic messages, apparitional visits, taped voices, xenoglossies, and so forth that might be signs of the continued existence of people after physical death. In truth, the "sweep" of the evidence that bears on the matter is against survival.

Doctor Raudive reportedly collected seventy thousand tapings of what he deemed to be the voices of "departed spirits." He did not think that each voice was that of a different spirit, but let us suppose, nonetheless, that seventy thousand different spirits had possibly imprinted their voices on Raudive's tapes. Let us suppose further that Mrs. Piper and Mrs. Leonard each had received seventy thousand possible communications from different spirits; that Doctor Stevenson had investigated seventy thousand possible cases of reincarnation and had discovered seventy thousand different possible xenoglossies; and that the other survival-phenomena likewise were many thousands of times more numerous than they in fact were.

Even when those cases that might constitute signs of the continued existence of people after death are multiplied by several thousand, the number of such cases is still very small in comparison to the millions who have died during the past one hundred years in Europe and America. For example, nearly 40 million people have died in the United States alone in only the past twenty years.

Our sayings and practices themselves reflect the fact that encounters with "the dead" are the exception rather than the rule. "All men are mortal"; "dead men tell no tales." After a shipwreck or aircrash, as Flew has observed, we distinguish "exclusively and exhaustively between the Dead and the Survivors, with no third category of Both or Neither."[3]

Of course, there are possible explanations for the apparent relative scarcity of indications of the existence of "the dead." For example, if the dead are discarnate, perhaps they do not wish to communicate, or cannot. As I have explained in Part II, the "experience" of discarnates would have to be almost unimaginably different from ours. Who could say what the concerns and interests and abilities of disembodied survivors might be?

Perhaps the dead have endeavored to communicate with us, but we have not recognized their efforts for what they are. Maybe their communications have been recognized, and are really quite common, but have gone unreported. Perhaps they are merely unreported in our society. Perhaps the "evidence" discussed in this book is but the porridge at the top of the pot. Maybe future studies will show that "encounters" between living persons and what seem to be the spirits of the dead are the rule rather than the exception. Certainly the studies of Osis-Haraldsson, Moody, and Sabom suggest that experiences by persons nearing death, which hint at contact with the dead, are far more common than we once had reason to suppose.

Explanations of the apparent comparative scarcity of evidence of survival, no matter how plausible, do not themselves substitute for evidence, and the promise of forthcoming proof in future studies is not itself proof.

The conclusions I have come to on the basis of this study are these. Personal survival beyond bodily death is neither *a priori* impossible nor, ruling out divine revelation or miraculous disclosure, *a priori* certain. However, the relevant data suggest that, in all probability, after the death of my body I shall cease to communi-

---

[3]A. Flew: Is there a case for disembodied survival? In J. Wheatley and H. Edge (Eds.): *Philosophical Dimensions of Parapsychology*. Springfield, Thomas, 1976, p. 331.

cate any evidence of my continued existence. Most people, the vast majority of people, have not, as far as I am aware, given any evidence of their continued existence after death. Why should I believe that I shall be different from the majority in this regard?

The fact that in all probability I shall not, after my death, give any further indication of my existence does not *necessarily* mean that my death will terminate my life, but I think that, in general, it is rational not to believe in that for which there is no evidence. Since I regard it as very likely that there will be no evidence of my having survived my death, I can only think that it is very likely that my death will end my existence.

BIBLIOGRAPHY

1. Allison, L. W.: *Leonard and Soule Experiments*. Boston, Boston Society for Psychic Research, 1929.
2. Allison, L. W.: Proxy sittings with Mrs. Leonard. *Proceedings of the Society for Psychical Research*, 42:104–146, 1934.
3. Aquinas, Thomas: *Summa Theologica* (Trans. by the Fathers of the English Dominican Province). London, Burns, Oates, and Washbourne, 1912.
4. Bahi, R.: A new ethical question: head transplants. *Science Digest*, 81:76–78, 1977.
5. Balfour, G. W.: Some recent scripts affording evidence of personal survival. *Proceedings of the Society for Psychical Research*, 29:197–243, 260–286, 1918.
6. Balfour, G. W.: A study of the psychological aspects of Mrs. Willett's mediumship. *Proceedings of the Society for Psychical Research*, 43:43–318, 1935.
7. Barber, T. X.: *Hypnosis: A Scientific Approach*. New York, Van Nostrand Reinhold, 1969.
8. Barrett, W. F.: *Death-Bed Visions*. London, Methuen, 1926.
9. Bennett, E.: *Apparitions and Haunted Houses*. London, Faber and Faber, 1939.
10. Bernstein, M.: *The Search for Bridey Murphy*. Garden City, N.Y., Doubleday, 1956.
11. Broad, C. D.: *The Mind and Its Place in Nature*. New York, The Humanities Press, 1951.
12. Brody, E. B.: Review of *Cases of the Reincarnation Type. Vol. 2. Ten Cases in Sri Lanka*. *Journal of the American Society for Psychical Research*, 23:71–81, 1979.
13. Campbell, K.: *Body and Mind*. New York, Anchor Books, 1970.
14. Carington, W.: The quantitative study of trance personalities. *Proceedings of the Society for Psychical Research*, 42:173–240, 1934; 43:319–361, 1935; 44:139–222, 1937; and 45:223–251, 1938–39.
15. Carrington, H.: A discussion of the Willett scripts. *Proceedings of the Society for Psychical Research*, 27:458–466, 1914.
16. Cooke, R.: *Improving on Nature: The Brave New World of Genetic Engineering*. New York, The New York Times Book Company, 1977.
17. Crookall, R.: *The Supreme Adventure*. London, James Clark and Co., 1961.
18. Crookall, R.: *The Study and Practice of Astral Projection*. London, The Acquarian Press, 1961.
19. Crookall, R.: *More Astral Projections*. London, The Acquarian Press, 1964.
20. Dale, L. A.: A series of spontaneous cases in the tradition of Phantasms of the Living. *Journal of the American Society for Psychical Research*, 45:85–101, 1951.
21. Dodds, E. R.: Why I do not believe in survival. *Proceedings of the Society for Psychical Research*, 42:147–172, 1934.

22. Ducasse, C. J.: *A Critical Examination of the Belief in a Life After Death.* Springfield, Thomas, 1974.
23. Eccles, J.: Cerebral activity and consciousness. In Ayala, F. J., and Dobzhansky, T. (Eds.): *Studies in the Philosophy of Biology.* Berkeley, University of California Press, 1974, pp. 87–107.
24. Eccles, J.: The brain and free will. In Globus, G., Maxwell, G., and Savodnik, I. (Eds.): *Consciousness and the Brain: a Scientific and Philosophical Inquiry.* New York, Plenum Press, 1976, pp. 87–107.
25. Eccles, J., and Popper, K.: *The Self and Its Brain.* New York, Springer International, 1977.
26. Edwards, P., Alston, W., and Prior, A. N.: Bertrand Arthur William Russell. In Edwards, P. (Ed.): *The Encyclopedia of Philosophy.* New York, Macmillan, 1967, Vol. VII, pp. 235–258.
27. Ellis, D. J.: *The Mediumship of the Tape Recorder.* Fernwood, Nightingales, West Chiltington, Pulborough, West Sussex: by the author, 1978.
28. Flew, Antony: *A New Approach to Psychical Research.* London, C. A. Watts and Co., 1953.
29. Flew, Antony: Is there a case for disembodied survival? In Wheatley, J., and Edge, H. (Eds.): *Philosophical Dimensions of Parapsychology.* Springfield, Thomas, 1976, pp. 330–347.
30. Ford, A.: *The Life Beyond Death.* New York, Putnam, 1971.
31. Gallup, George: *The Gallup Poll.* New York, Random House, 1972, Vol. III, p. 1663.
32. Garrett, E. J.: *My Life as a Search for the Meaning of Mediumship.* London, Rider, 1939.
33. Garrett, E. J.: *Many Voices: The Autobiography of a Medium.* New York, Putnam, 1968.
34. Gauld, A.: A series of "drop in" communicators. *Proceedings of the Society for Psychical Research, 55*: 273–340, 1971.
35. Gauld, A.: Discarnate survival. In Wolman, Benjamin B. (Ed.): *Handbook of Parapsychology.* New York, Van Nostrand Reinhold Co., 1977, pp. 577–630.
36. Geach, Peter: *God and the Soul.* New York, Schocken Books, 1969.
37. Geels, D.: The resurrection of Christ. *New Catholic Encyclopedia.* New York, McGraw Hill, 1967, Vol. XII, pp. 402–419.
38. Globus, G. G., Maxwell, G., and Savodnik, I. (Eds.): *Consciousness and the Brain: a Scientific and Philosophical Inquiry.* New York, Plenum Press, 1976.
39. Graham, B.: *Angels: God's Secret Agents.* New York, Guideposts Associates, 1976.
40. Green, C. E.: Ecsomatic experience and related phenomena. *Journal of the Society for Psychical Research, 44*:111–131, 1967.
41. Green, C. E.: *Out-of-the-Body Experiences.* Oxford, Institute of Psychophysiological Research, 1968.
42. Green, C. E. and McCreery, C.: *Apparitions.* London, Hamish Hamilton, 1975.
43. Grosso, M.: The survival of personality in a mind-dependent world. *Journal of the American Society for Psychical Research, 73*:367–380, 1978.

44. Gurney, E., Myers, F. W. H., and Podmore, F.: *Phantasms of the Living.* London, Trubner, 1886.
45. Haldane, E. S., and Ross, G. R. T.: *The Philosophical Works of Descartes.* Cambridge, Cambridge University Press, 1968, 2 vols.
46. Hansel, C. E. M.: *ESP: A Scientific Evaluation.* New York, Charles Scribner's Sons, 1966.
47. Haraldsson, E. and Stevenson, I.: A communicator of the "drop in" type in Iceland: the case of Runolfur Runolfsson. *Journal of the American Society for Psychical Research,* 69:33–59, 1975.
48. Hart, H. and Hart, E. B.: Visions and apparitions collectively and reciprocally perceived. *Proceedings of the Society for Psychical Research, 41*:205–249, 1933.
49. Hart, H.: ESP projection: spontaneous cases and the experimental method. *Proceedings of the Society for Psychical Research, 48*: 121–146, 1954.
50. Hart, H.: Six theories about apparitions. *Proceedings of the Society for Psychical Research, 50*:153–239, 1956.
51. Hart, H.: *The Enigma of Survival: The Case For and Against an After Life.* London, Rider, 1959.
52. Hart, H.: *Toward a New Philosophical Basis for Parapsychological Phenomena.* Parapsychological Monographs, no. 6. New York, Parapsychology Foundation, 1965.
53. Hart, H.: Scientific survival research. *International Journal of Philosophy,* 9:43–52, 1967.
54. Heim, A.: Remarks on fatal falls. *Yearbook of the Swiss Alpine Club, 27*:327–337. Trans. by Noyes, R., and Kletti, R., in *Omega, 3*:45–52, 1972.
55. Hick, J. *Death and Eternal Life.* New York, Harper and Row, 1976.
56. Hobbes, T.: *Leviathan.* Oxford, Basil Blackwell, 1955.
57. Hodgson, R.: A further record of observations of certain phenomena of trance. *Proceedings of the Society for Psychical Research, 13* 1:284–582, 1898.
58. Hume, D.: A Treatise of Human Nature. (Selby-Bigge, L. A., Ed.) Oxford, the Clarendon Press, 1968.
59. Jacobson, Nils O.: *Life Without Death?* (La Farge, S., Trans.) Dell (n.p.), 1974.
60. Jowett, B.: *The Dialogues of Plato.* New York, Random House, 1937, 2 vols.
61. Kübler-Ross, E.: *On Death and Dying.* New York, Macmillan, 1971.
62. Kübler-Ross, E.: *Death: The Final Stage of Growth.* New Jersey, Prentice-Hall, 1975.
63. Leadbeater, C. W.: *The Astral Plane.* India, Theosophical Publishing House, 1973.
64. Le Shan, L.: The vanished man: a psychometry experiment with Mrs. Eileen J. Garrett. *Journal of the American Society for Psychical Research,* 62:46–61, 1968.
65. Lodge, O.: Evidence of classical scholarship and of cross-correspondence in some new automatic writings. *Proceedings of the Society for Psychical Research,* 25:113–175, 1911.
66. Lodge, O.: *Raymond of Life and Death, with Examples of Evidence for Survival of Memory and Affection after Death.* London, Methuen and Co., 1916.

67. Los Angeles hillside strangler, *Time*, Jan. 14, 1980, p. 50.
68. Lucretius: *de Rerum Natura* (Munro, H. A. J., Trans.) Cambridge, Deighton Bell, 1886.
69. Mackenzie, A.: *Apparitions and Ghosts*. London, Arthur Barker, 1971.
70. Marshall, C.: *A Man Called Peter*. New York, Avon, 1971.
71. McElwain, H. M.: Resurrection of the dead. *New Catholic Encyclopedia*. New York, McGraw Hill, 1967, Vol. XII, pp. 419–427.
72. McHarg, James F.: Review of *At the Hour of Death*. *Journal of the Society for Psychical Research*, 49:885–887, 1978.
73. Monroe, R. A.: *Journeys Out of the Body*. Garden City, N.Y., Doubleday, 1971.
74. Moody, R. A.: *Life After Life*. Covington, GA, Mockingbird, 1975.
75. Morriss, R. L., Harary, S. B., Janis, J., Hartwell, J., Roll, W. G.: Studies of communication during out-of-body experiences. *Journal of the American Society for Psychical Research*, 72:1–21, 1978.
76. Murphy, G.: Triumphs and defects in the study of mediumship. *Journal of the American Society for Psychical Research*, 51:125–135, 1957.
77. Myers, F. W. H.: *Human Personality and Its Survival of Bodily Death*. London, Longmans, Green, 1903, 2 vols.
78. Nagel, Thomas: Brain bisection and the unity of consciousness. In Perry, John (Ed.): *Personal Identity*. Berkeley, University of California Press, 1975, pp. 227–245.
79. Noyes, R.: The experience of dying. *Psychiatry*, 35:174–184, 1972.
80. Noyes, R. and Kletti, R.: Depersonalization in the face of life-threatening danger: an interpretation. *Omega*, 7:103–114, 1976.
81. Noyes, R. and Kletti, R.: Depersonalization in the face of life-threatening danger: a description. *Psychiatry*, 39:19–27, 1976.
82. Osis, K.: *Deathbed Observations by Physicians and Nurses*. New York, Parapsychology Foundation, 1961.
83. Osis, K. and Haraldsson, E.: *At the Hour of Death*. New York, Avon, 1977.
84. Osis, K. and Haraldsson, E.: Deathbed observations by physicians and nurses: a cross-cultural survey. *The Journal of the American Society for Psychical Research*, 71:237–259, 1977.
85. Palmer, J. and Lieberman, R.: The influence of psychological set on ESP and out-of-body experiences. *Journal of the American Society for Psychical Research*, 69:193–213, 1975.
86. Palmer, J. and Vassar, C.: ESP and out-of-the-body experiences: an exploratory study. *Journal of the American Society for Psychical Research*,. 68:257–280, 1974.
87. Panati, C.: Is there life after death? *Family Circle*, 89:78, 84, 90, 1976.
88. Parfit, D.: Personal identity. In Perry, J. (Ed.): *Personal Identity*. Berkeley, University of California Press, 1975, pp. 199–223.
89. Parfit, D.: Lewis, Perry, and what matters. In Rorty, A. (Ed.): *The Identities of Persons*. Berkeley, University of California Press, 1976, pp. 91–107.
90. Parsons, D.: On the need for caution in assessing mediumistic material. *Proceedings of the Society for Psychical Research*, 48:344–352, 1946–49.
91. Penelhum, T.: Personal Identity. In Edwards, P. (Ed.): *The Encyclopedia of*

Philosophy. New York, Macmillan, 1967, vol. VI, pp. 95–107.
92. Perry, J.: Can the self divide? *Journal of Philosophy,* 69:463–488, 1972.
93. Perry, J. (Ed.): *Personal Identity.* Berkeley, University of California Press, 1975.
94. Perry, J.: Personal identity, memory, and the problem of circularity. In Perry, J. (Ed.): *Personal Identity.* Berkeley, University of California Press, 1975, pp. 135–155.
95. Perry, J.: The importance of being identical. In Rorty, A. (Ed.): *The Identities of Persons.* Berkeley, University of California Press, 1976, pp. 67–90.
96. Phillips, J. B.: *Your God Is Too Small.* New York, Macmillan, 1971.
97. Piddington, J. G.: On the types of phenomena displayed in Mrs. Thompson's trance. *Proceedings of the Society for Psychical Research, 18:104–307, 1904.*
98. Piddington, J. G.: A series of concordant automatisms. *Proceedings of the Society for Psychical Research,* 22:19–416, 1908.
99. Podmore, F.: *Apparitions and Thought-Transference.* London, Walter Scott, 1894.
100. Podmore, F.: *The Newer Spiritualism.* London, Milner, 1909.
101. Podmore, F.: *Telepathic Hallucinations: The New View of Ghosts.* London, Milner, n.d.
102. Pratt, J. G., Rhine, J. B., Smith, B. M., Stuart, C. E., and Greenwood, J. A.: *Extrasensory Perception after Sixty Years.* Boston, Branden Press, 1966.
103. Price, H. H.: Survival and the idea of another world. *Proceedings of the Society for Psychical Research,* 60:1–25, 1953.
104. Prince, W. F.: *Noted Witnesses for Psychic Occurrences.* Boston, Boston Society for Psychic Research, 1928.
105. Radclyffe-Hall, M. and Trowbridge, U.: On a series of sittings with Mrs. Osborne Leonard. *Proceedings of the Society for Psychical Research,* 30:339–554, 1919.
106. Randi, The Amazing: *The Magic of Uri Geller.* New York, Ballantine, 1975.
107. Rao, K. R.: *Experimental Parapsychology: A Review and Interpretation.* Springfield, Thomas, 1966.
108. Raudive, K.: *Breakthrough: An Amazing Experiment in Electronic Communication with the Dead.* New York, Taplinger, 1971.
109. Reply to a letter concerning studies of weight loss during reported OBEs. By the editor, *Journal of the Society for Psychical Research,* 50:39, 1979.
110. Rhine, Louisa: Hallucinatory psi experiences, I, II, and III. *Journal of Parapsychology,* 20:233–256, 1956; 21:13–46, 1957; and 21:186–226, 1957.
111. Richet, C.: *Thirty Years of Psychical Research.* (de Brath, S., Trans.) New York, Macmillan, 1923.
112. Richmond, K.: Preliminary studies of the recorded Leonard material. *Proceedings of the Society for Psychical Research,* 44:17–52, 1936.
113. Rogo, D. Scott: Aspects of out-of-the-body experiences. *Journal of the Society for Psychical Research,* 48:329–335, 1976.
114. Rorvik, David: *In His Image.* New York, Lippincott, 1978.
115. Russell, B.: *Why I Am Not a Christian.* New York, Allen and Unwin, 1957.
116. Ryle, G.: *Concept of Mind.* New York, Barnes and Noble, 1949.

117. Sabom, M.: Near-death experiences. *Journal of the Florida Medical Association*, *64*:648–650, 1977.
118. Sabom, Michael: The experience of near death. *Death Education*, *1*: 195–203, 1977.
119. Sabom, M., and Kreutziger, S. A.: Physicians evaluate the near-death experience. *Theta*, *6*:1–6, 1978.
120. Salter, H. de G. (Mrs. W. H. Salter): A further report on sittings with Mrs. Leonard. *Proceedings of the Society for Psychical Research*, *32*:1–143, 1921.
121. Salter, H. de G. (Mrs. W. H. Salter): A report on some recent sittings with Mrs. Leonard. *Proceedings of the Society for Psychical Research*, *36*:187–332, 1926.
122. Salter, H. de G. (Mrs. W. H. Salter): Some incidents occurring at sittings with Mrs. Leonard which may throw light on their *modus operandi*. *Proceedings of the Society for Psychical Research*, *39*:306–332, 1930.
123. Salter, W. H.: Review of C. S. B. Roberts' essay, The truth about spiritualism. *Journal of the Society for Psychical Research*, *27*:331, 1932.
124. Salter, W. H.: *Ghosts and Apparitions*. London, Bell, 1938.
125. Savage, C. W.: An old ghost in a new body. In Globus, G., Maxwell, G., and Savodnik, I. (Eds.): *Consciousness and the Brain: a Scientific and Philosophical Inquiry*. New York, Plenum Press, 1976, pp. 125–153.
126. Shaffer, J.: The mind-body problem. In Edwards, P. (Ed.): *Encyclopedia of Philosophy*, New York, Macmillan, 1972, Vol. V, pp. 336–346.
127. Shakespeare, W.: *Hamlet* (Crawford, J. R., Ed.). New Haven, Yale University Press, 1917, 2 vols.
128. Sheargold, R. K.: *Hints on Receiving the Voice Phenomenon*. Maidenhead: by the author, 1973.
129. Sheargold, R. K.: The "Raudive voices." *The Journal of the Society for Psychical Research*, *48*:250–252, 1975.
130. Sidgwick, E. M. (Mrs. Henry Sidgwick) and Johnson, A.: Report on the census of hallucinations. *Proceedings of the Society for Psychical Research*, *10*:25–422, 1894.
131. Sidgwick, E. M. (Mrs. Henry Sidgwick): Discussion of the trance phenomena of Mrs. Piper. *Proceedings of the Society for Psychical Research*, *15*:16–38, 1900.
132. Sidgwick, E. M. (Mrs. Henry Sidgwick): A contribution to the study of the psychology of Mrs. Piper's trance phenomena. *Proceedings of the Society for Psychical Research*, *28*:1–652, 1915.
133. Sidgwick, E. M. (Mrs. Henry Sidgwick): An examination of book tests obtained in sittings with Mrs. Leonard. *Proceedings of the Society for Psychical Research*, *31*:241–400, 1921.
134. Sidgwick, E. M. (Mrs. Henry Sidgwick): Phantasms of the living. *Proceedings of the Society for Psychical Research*, *33*:23–429, 1923.
135. Smith, S.: *The Mediumship of Mrs. Leonard*. New Hyde Park, University Books, 1964.
136. Smith, S.: *The Enigma of Out-of-Body Travel*. New York, Garrett Publications, 1965.
137. Soal, S. G.: A report on some communications received through Mrs. Blanche Cooper. *Proceedings of the Society for Psychical Research*, *35*:471–594, 1926.

138. Stawell, F. M.: The ear of Dionysius: a discussion of the evidence. *Proceedings of the Society for Psychical Research,* 29:260–269, 1917.
139. Stevenson, I.: *Twenty Cases Suggestive of Reincarnation,* 2nd rev. ed. Charlottesville, University Press of Virginia, 1974.
140. Stevenson, I.: *Cases of the Reincarnation Type. Vol 1. Ten Cases in India.* Charlottesville, University Press of Virginia, 1975.
141. Stevenson, I.: *Cases of the Reincarnation Type. Vol. 2. Ten Cases in Sri Lanka.* Charlottesville, University of Virginia, 1977.
142. Stevenson, I.: Research into the evidence of man's survival after death. A historical and critical survey with a summary of recent developments. *The Journal of Nervous and Mental Disease,* 165:152–170, 1977.
143. Stevenson, I.: Xenoglossy: a review and report of a case. *Proceedings of the American Society for Psychical Research,* 31:1–268, 1978.
144. Stevenson, I.: *Cases of the Reincarnation Type. Vol 3. Fifteen Cases in Thailand, Lebanon, and Turkey.* Charlottesville, University Press of Virginia, 1978.
145. Tart, C. T.: A psychophysiological study of out-of-the-body experiences in a selected subject. *Journal of the American Society for Psychical Research,* 62:3–27, 1968.
146. Terrace, H.: *Nim,* New York, Knopf, 1979.
147. Thomas, C. D.: The modus operandi of trance-communication according to descriptions received through Mrs. Osborne Leonard. *Proceedings of the Society for Psychical Research,* 38:49–100, 1928.
148. Thomas, C. D.: A consideration of a series of proxy sittings. *Proceedings of the Society for Psychical Research,* 41:139–185, 1932–33.
149. Thomas, C. D.: A proxy case extending over eleven sittings with Mrs. Osborne Leonard. *Proceedings of the Society for Psychical Research,* 43:439–519, 1935.
150. Thomas, C. D.: A proxy experiment of significant success. *Proceedings of the Society for Psychical Research,* 45:257–306, 1939.
151. Thomas, C. D.: A new type of proxy case. *Journal of the American Society for Psychical Research,* 31:103–104 and 120–122, 1939.
152. Those amazing chimps. *Time,* March 10, 1980, p. 50.
153. Thouless, R. H.: *From Anecdote to Experiment in Psychical Research.* London, Routledge and Kegal Paul, 1972.
154. Tyrell, C. N. M.: *Apparitions,* 2nd ed. rev. London, Duckworth, 1953.
155. Van Eeden, F.: Account of sittings with Mrs. Thompson. *Proceedings of the Society for Psychical Research,* 17:81–84, 1901.
156. Wambach, H.: *Reliving Past Lives: The Evidence Under Hypnosis.* New York, Harper and Row, 1978.
157. Wambach, H.: *Life Before Life.* New York, Bantam Books, 1979.
158. Weingarten, S. M., Cherlow, D. G., and Holmgren, E.: The relationship of hallucinations to the depth structures of the temporal lobe. *Acta Neurochirurgica, Supplement* 24:199–216, 1977.
159. West, D. J.: A mass-observation questionnaire on hallucinations. *Journal of the Society for Psychical Research,* 34:187–196, 1948.
160. West, D. J.: The investigation of spontaneous cases. *Proceedings of the*

Society for Psychical Research, *48*:264–300, 1948.
161. West, D. J.: *Psychical Research Today*. London, Duckworth, 1954.
162. Wilkerson, Ralph: *Beyond and Back*. New York, Bantam Books, 1977.
163. Wittgenstein, Ludwig: *Tractatus Logico-philosophicus* (Pears, D. F., and McGuinness, B. F., Trans.). London, Routledge and Kegan Paul, 1961.
164. Wolman, Benjamin (Ed.): *International Encyclopedia of Psychiatry, Psychology, Psychoanalysis and Neurology*. New York, Van Nostrand Reinhold, 1977.
165. Wood, F. H.: *After Thirty Centuries*. London, Rider, 1935.
166. Wood, F. H.: *This Egyptian Miracle*, 2nd ed. London, Watkins, 1955.
167. Woodward, K. C.: Life after death. *Newsweek, 41*: July 12, 1976.
168. Woodward, K. L.: There is life after death. *McCall's, 103*:134–139, 1976.
169. Zorab, George: The survival hypothesis: an unsupported speculation? *Journal of the American Society for Psychical Research, 50*:248–253, 1956.

INDEX

A

"Abt Vogler," 108
Adenosine triphosphate, 37
Afterdeath survival (*see* Personal survival)
Afterlife, belief in, 142
Allison, L. W., 94n, 206
Alston, W., 27n, 207
American Sign Language, 186n
Annals of Sudurnes, 116, 117
Anoxia, cerebral, 139, 148, 151, 155
Apparitions, 127–130, 131, 156, 201, 202 (*see also* Near-death experiences *and* Hallucinations)
Aquinas, Thomas, 69, 70, 72n, 206
Archives, Iceland National, 117, 118
Armstrong, Daisy (*see* "Daisy Armstrong" case)
Assumptions
    death occurrence, as to, 11
    minds, as to, 6–8
    survivors, countability of, 10–11
    survivors, identity of, 8–9
Astral bodies
    characteristics, 74–75
    survival of, 13
Ayala, F. J., 38n, 39n, 40n, 207

B

Bahi, Robert, 21n, 206
Balfour, G. W., 90n, 114, 206
Barber, T. X., 193n, 206
Barrett, W. F., 135n, 206
Bash, John, viii, 80
Belief in afterlife, by Americans, 142
Bennett, E., 127n
Bernstein, M., 165, 206
"Biedermann, Gustav Adolph," 125
Björnsson, Hafsteinn (*see* Hafsteinn Björnsson)

Blavatsky, Madame (*see* Mediums)
"Bobby Newlove" case, 88–89
Bodies (*see* Interactions between mind and body)
Bogus communicators (*see* Mediumistic messages)
Book tests, 86–87
Brains
    consciousness and, 26–27
    hemispheres, severance of, 7–8
    mental activity and, 26–27, 29, 34–43
    transplants, 10–11, 20–21
"Bridey Murphy" case, 165–166
British Association for the Advancement of Science, 83
Broad, C. D., 39, 206
Brody, E. B., 179, 206
Browning, Robert, 108, 109, 110
Bundle theory (*see* Self)
Butcher, Henry, 104, 106, 111

C

Cambridge, England, 121
Campbell, Keith, 11n, 32n, 42n, 206
Carington, W., 98n, 206
Carrington, H., 104, 206
Cartesian dualism (*see* Dualism)
Cases, spontaneous, 128–129
Catholicism
    doctrine of immortality, 79–81
Cebes, vii, 200
Census of hallucinations, 135n
Cerebral anoxia (*see* Anoxia, cerebral)
Crawford, J. R., 127n
Cherlow, D. G., 156n, 212
Chess, kingless, 53
"Cheyne, Max," 122
Chimpanzees understanding language, 186n, 187n

Index

Christianity (*see* Catholicism)
Clairvoyance, 58–59, 105n
   explained, 58n
   knowledge through, 58–59
"Clark, Kathleen," 123
Cloning, survival by, 16–17
Combination-lock tests of survival, 105, 202
Communicators
   bogus or fictitious, 97–101
   defined, 85n
   drop-in (*see* Drop-in communicators)
Continental drift, 131
Consciousness (*see* Brains; Hypnosis; Minds; Survivors)
Control, defined, 85n
Cooke, Robert, 17, 18n, 19n, 206
Coombe-Tennant, Mrs. Winifred (*see* Mediums, Mrs. Willett)
Cooper, Mrs. (*see* Mediums)
Countability (*see* Minds and Survivors)
Crookall, R., 154, 155–156, 206
Cross-corresponding communications
   "Ear of Dionysius" case, 106, 111–112
   "Hope, Star, and Browning" case, 103, 107–111
   nature of, 102–104
   nonsurvivalist explanations of, 112–114
   random generation of, in experiment, 104
   skepticism in regard to, 104–105
   survival proof as, 104–107, 108–111, 112–114, 131, 201, 202
Cryobiology, 15–16
Cryptomnesia, 121–122
Curran, Pearl (*see* "Patience Worth" case)

D

"Daisy Armstrong" case, 89
Dalai Lama, 63–64
Dale, L. A., 127n, 206
Davis, Gordon (*see* "Gordon Davis" case)
Daydreams, guided, 193, 198
Death, when occurring, 11
Deathbed visions (*see* Near-death experiences)
Dennet, Daniel, 27, 52
Descartes, Rene, 30, 41
   self, view of, 44–49
Destruction hypothesis (*see* Near-death experiences)

Dionysius (*see* Cross-corresponding communications)
Disembodied personalities (*see* Spirits)
Disembodied survival
   concept of, whether intelligible, 27–28
   Epicurus on, 25
   evidence of, 83–90, 102–130, 135–164
   Flew on, 25, 44, 46, 49
   Geach on, 25, 53, 55
   Hobbes on, 25
   Hume on, 45
   Lucretius on, 25
   Penelhum on, 25, 49
   refutations of, 25–62
   resurrection and, 71–73
   Russell on, 5, 25, 26, 27
   theory of, 12
Disturbances (*see* Temporal lobe disturbances)
Dobzhansky, T., 38n, 39n, 40n, 207
Dodds, E. R., 94, 114, 206
Drift, continental, 131
Drop-in communicators, 115–126, 131, 201, 202
   defined, 115
   Gauld's "drop-ins," 121–126
   Runolfur Runolfsson ("Runki"), 115–120, 121
"Druce, Edward," 122
Dualism
   defined, 30
   materialism contrasted, 29–43
   objections to, 31–43
   personal survival, view of, 31
Ducasse, C. J., 66n, 67–68, 80n, 85, 207
Durham, North Carolina, 129

E

"Ear of Dionysius" case (*see* Cross-corresponding communications)
Eccles, John., 38, 39–41, 207
Edge, H. L., 91n, 207
Edwards, P., 25n, 27n, 42n, 207
Elastic messages (*see* Mediumistic messages, elastic)
Electronic voice phenomenon, 159–164, 201, 202, 203
Ellis, D. J., 160–164, 207
Energy, conservation of, 41

Engineering, genetic (*see* Genetic engineering)
Epicurus, 25
ESP
   card-calling tests of, 58, 59
   knowledge of the future, 199
   knowledge through, 57–62
   nonphysical, as, 57n
   "ordinary," 95
   retrocognition (*see* Retrocognition)
   Runolfur Runolfsson ("Runki") and, 116
   "super ESP" (*see* "Supertelepathy")
   see also Clairvoyance and Spirits
Evidence of personal survival
   religious, 79–81
   see also Disembodied survival; Out of body phenomena; Reincarnation; Personal survival
Experiences
   causative relationship between, 48, 51–52
   near-death (*see* Near-death experiences)
   out of body (*see* Out of body phenomena).
Experiments
   isolation, 147
   sensory-deprivation, 147
External world, 56

F

"Feda," 85, 86, 92, 98n
"Ferguson, John" (*see* "John Ferguson" case)
"Fletcher, Robert," 125
Flew, Antony, 25, 44, 46, 49, 53, 87, 88n, 99n, 113, 124, 128, 204
Forbes, Mrs. (*see* Mediums)
Ford, A., 135n–136n, 207
Freud, S., 153n

G

Gallup, George, 207
Gallup poll, 142
Garrett, E. J. (Mrs. Garrett), 207 (*see also* Mediums)
Gauld, Alan, 105n, 121, 122, 123, 124, 125, 126, 130, 207 (*see also* Drop-in communicators)
Geach, Peter, 25, 49, 53, 55, 80n, 207

Geels, D., 80n, 207
Genetic engineering, 16–19
Ghosts (*see* Apparitions)
Globus, G., 39n, 41n, 207
God, 30n, 38, 72, 80, 81
Gorakana, Sri Lanka, 167, 168, 169, 172, 174, 177
"Gordon Davis" case, 99, 101
Gospels, 80
Graham, B., 136n, 207
Green, C. E., 127n, 154, 156, 207
Greenwood, J. A., 210
Grosso, M., 55n, 207
Gurney, E., 127n, 208

H

Hafsteinn Björnsson, 115, 117, 118
Hallucinations
   anoxia, cerebral, and, 148
   autohypnosis and, 155
   autoscopic, 151, 153–154
   census of, 135n
   clarity of consciousness, 143–144
   drug-induced, 148, 151
   occurrence in general population, 135n
   out of body phenomena and, 156–158
   psychic, 129, 156n
   shared, 130
   survival-related (*see* Near-death experiences)
   vividness of, 148
   see also Near-death experiences
"Hamlet," 127
Hansel, C. E. M., 92n, 208
Haraldsson, E., 115, 118, 136, 137–138, 139–140, 141, 142–143, 144, 208, 209
Harary, S., 157n, 209
Harding, Hilda, 129
Hart, E. B., 154n, 208
Hart, H., 91n, 99n, 100n, 127–128, 129–130, 154, 156, 208
Hartwell, J., 157n, 209
Heim, A., 136n, 149n, 208
"Hentall, Eleanor," 123
Hick, John, 13–14, 55n, 70–71, 208
Hillside Strangler, Los Angeles, 185n
Hobbes, T., 25, 29, 208
Hodgson, R., 83, 84, 85, 104, 208

Holland, Mrs. (see Mediums)
Holmgren, E., 156n, 212
"Hope, Star, and Browning" case (see Cross-corresponding communications)
Hulme, A. J. H., 191
Hume, D., 44–49, 208
Hypnosis
  age-regression, 193n
  consciousness, unique state of, 193n
  group, 193
    past-life recall and, 192–199 (see also Xenoglossy)
  trances, physiological indicators of, 193n
Hyslop, James, 83, 104

I

Iceland, 116
Identity (see Personal identity)
Interaction between mind and body
  categorization of, 35–37
  Eccles on, 39–41
  locus of, 37–39
  physiology and, 37–39
  understanding nature of, 34–35
Isolation experiments (see Experiments)

J

Jacobson, Nils, 99, 136n, 183, 208
"Jacoby, Jensen" (see Xenoglossy)
James, William, 83, 84
James Miles case (see Miles, James)
Janis, J., 157n, 209
"Jayaratne, Sujith Lakmal" (see Reincarnation, Stevenson's studies, Sujith case)
"Jensen" case (see Xenoglossy)
Jesus, 80
"John Ferguson" case, 98
Johnson, Alice, 103
Journal of Nervous and Mental Disease, 166
Journal of the Society for Psychical Research, 127, 129, 157–158
Jowett, B., 208
Jurgenson, F., 159

K

Kletti, R., 136n, 149n, 209
Kreutziger, S. A., 150n
Kübler-Ross, E., 136n, 145, 208

L

Language
  aptitude test, 184, 187
  demonstration of comprehension, 186n
  word-reaction tests, 98n
Lawson, William, viii
Leadbeater, C. W., 136n, 208
"L.G.," 121
Leonard, Mrs. O. (see Mediums)
Le Shan, L., 96n, 208
Lieberman, R., 157n, 209
Life after death (see Personal survival)
Lodge, Oliver, 83, 89, 90n, 92, 93n, 114, 208
Los Angeles Hillside Strangler, 185n, 209
Lucretius, 25, 63, 69, 209

M

Mackenzie, A., 127n, 207
Marshall, L., 136n, 209
Materialism
  defined, 26–27, 29
  dualism contrasted, 29–43
  minds and brains, relationship between, 26–27, 29, 32, 33
  personal survival and, 27, 29
  Russell, B. and, 27n
Maxwell, G., 39n, 41n, 207, 211
McCreery, C., 127n, 154n
McElwain, H. M., 79n
McHarg, J. F., 139, 209
Mediumistic messages
  bogus communicators, 97–101
  cross-correspondences (see Cross-corresponding communications)
  book-tests, 86–87
  dramatization, evidentiary value of, 99–100, 101
  drop-in communicators (see Drop-in communicators)
  elastic, 91–94, 201

explanations of, as culturally conditioned, 101n
kinds of, 201
proxy sittings, 87–89, 201
scoring for correctness, 93
scripts, defined, 103n
"supertelepathy" explanation, 94–97
survivalist explanation, 94–97, 101
Willet scripts, 104
(see also Mediums)

Mediums
Blavatsky, Madame, 83
communications from spirits, 60
Cooper, Mrs., 98
Forbes, Mrs., 103n
Garrett, Mrs., 89–90n, 96n
Holland, Mrs., 103n
Leonard, Mrs., 85–90, 91, 92–96, 98n, 101, 131, 201, 203
Piper, Mrs., 83–85, 86, 89, 90, 91, 93–98, 101, 103, 107, 108, 109, 110, 131, 201, 203
Thompson, Mrs., 89–90n, 100, 103n
"ultimate," the, 82–101
Verrall, Miss, 103n, 107, 108, 109, 110
Verrall, Mrs., 103n, 107, 108, 109, 110, 112, 113
Willet, Mrs., 89–90n, 103n, 104, 111–112

Memories
experiences and, 48, 51–52, 68

Memory
personal identity and, 66–68
spirits', 51–52
unification of experiences and, 48

Messages
mediumistic (see Mediumistic messages)
sealed, as proof of survival, 105, 202

Miles, James, 98

Minds
abstract entities as likened to, 32–33, 35n
assumptions as to, 6–8
bodies (see Interaction between mind and body)
brains and, 26–27, 29, 34–43
consciousness and brain, 26–27
"conscious self," 39–41
conscious things as, 6–7, 10
countability, 6–8
material or physical, as (see Materialism)

nature of, 42–43 (see also Materialism and Dualism)
nonmaterial, as (see Dualism)
persons and, 7
sharing of, 31–33
spatial occupancy by, 30–33
see also Self and Spirit

Minnesota Multiphasic Personality Inventory, 184, 187
Modern Language Aptitude test, 184, 187
Monfort, Kirk, viii
Monroe, R., 154–155, 209
Moody, R. A., 136n, 145–149, 202, 204, 209
(see also Near-death experiences)
Moore, Bill, viii
Moore, Linda Ely, viii
Moore, Ralph J., viii
Moore, Sherry, viii
Morriss, R. L., 154, 157n, 209
Mt. Lavinia, Sri Lanka, 167, 172, 174
"Murphy, Bridey" (see "Bridey Murphy" case)
Murphy, Gardner, 107n, 209
Myers, F. W. H., 103, 107, 108, 109, 110, 111, 113, 127n, 208, 209

N

Nagel, T., 7n, 209
Near-death experiences
anoxia, cerebral, 148, 151
destruction hypothesis, 136, 139, 142
medical explanation of, 150–152, 202
Moody studies, 145–149
  anoxia, cerebral, 148
  descriptions, as uniform, 148
  dying, ideal experience of, 146
  informality of, 145–147
  nonparanormal explanations, 137–144, 147–148, 150–152
  out-of-body feature, 146, 148, 149
Osis-Haraldsson studies, 135–144, 204
  belief in afterlife, 142
  clarity of consciousness, 142–143, 144
  cultural differences, 141–142, 144
  desires, expectations, fears, 138, 140–141
  medical factors, 137, 139
  patients' moods, 137–138
Sabom studies, 149–151, 152

stress, 137–138, 139–140
    survival hypothesis, 136, 137, 139, 142
Newbold, R., 83
Newlove, Bobby (see "Bobby Newlove" case)
Norman, J., viii, 38n
Northumberland Fusiliers, 123
Noyes, R., 136n, 149n, 153n, 209

O

OBEs (see Out of body phenomena)
"One-horse dawn," 113
Osis-Haraldsson studies (see Near-death experiences)
Osis, K., 135, 136, 137–138, 139–140, 141, 142–143, 144, 149n, 201
Osty, E., 99
Out of body phenomena, 146, 148–149, 153–158, 201, 202
    anoxia, cerebral, and, 155
    apparitions and, 156
    described, 153
    electrically produced, 156n
    hallucinations and, 156–158
    literature concerning, 154n
    Moody and Osis results, compared, 149
    Moody studies and, 146, 148–149
    near-death experiences and, 146, 148–149, 153
    weight loss and, 157–158

P

Palmer, J., 157n, 209
Panati, C., 136n, 209
Pancha sila, 170
Parfit, Derek, 9n, 209
Parker, Richard, viii
Parsons, D., 92, 209
Pasetta, D., viii
"Patience Worth" case, 191n
"Pelham, George," 84, 85
Pellew, George (see "Pelham, George")
Penelhum, Terence, 25, 49, 209
Perrott-Warwick Studentship for Psychical Research, 160
Perry, John, 7n, 9n, 11n, 20, 52, 209, 210
Personal identity
    memory as necessary to, 66–88
    resurrection and, 69–73
Personality inventory test (see Minnesota Multiphasic Personality Inventory)
Personalities, secondary, 86n, 97–99
Personal survival
    assumptions as to, 6–11
    Descartes on, 45
    discarnate bundle of experiences as, 46–49
    discarnate subject of experiences as (see Spirit)
    evidence of (see Evidence of personal survival)
    corroborative as, 131–132, 202–203
    meaning of, 6
    mediumistic messages (see Mediumistic messages)
    question, what not, 5
    refutations of (see Refutations)
    spirit, as, 61–62
    theories of, 12–14
    (see also Disembodied survival; Reincarnation; Resurrection; Survival of an astral body)
Persons (see Minds; Self; Spirits)
Phillips, J. B., 136n, 210
"Philox," 111
Philoxenus, 111
"Phinuit," 97
Physical Society of London, 83
Piddington, J. G., 90n, 103, 107, 108, 109, 110, 210
"Pied Piper of Hamelin," 110
Piper, Mrs. (see Mediums)
Plato, viin, 200
Podmore, F., 90n, 127, 208, 210
Polyphemus, 111
Popper, K., 42n, 207
Pratt-Birge technique, 93
Pratt, J. G., 95n, 210
Price, H. H., 55n, 91, 96, 210
Prince, W. F., 127n, 210
Prior, A. N., 27n, 207
Properties, physical and nonphysical contrasted, 30–31
Proxy sittings, 87–89, 201
Puharich, A., 161

R

Radclyffe-Hall, M., 94n, 210
Randi, The Amazing, 84n, 210
Rao, K. R., 95n, 210
Raudive, K., 159–164, 203, 210
Raudive voices (see Electronic voice phenomenon)
Réallier case, 99
Refutations, 25–75
    "astral survival," of, 74–75
    disembodied survival, of, 25–62
    reincarnation, of, 63–68
    resurrection, of, 69–73
Reidentification
    spirits, of, 50–52, 62
    terms, effect of, 49–51
Reincarnation
    agency of induction, 190
    biology and, 178
    "Bridey Murphy" (see "Bridey Murphy" case)
    disembodiment involved, 63–64
    evidence of, 165–199
    fluctuations in population as precluding, 64–65
    heredity and environment, 65–66
    Lucretius on, 63
    memory and, 66–68
    past life recall, 194, 195–199, 201
        dates recalled, 197–198
        gender recalled, 196–197
        nature of, as nonspecific, 195
        refutations of, 63–68
        replication and, 70–71
        social class and race, of, 198
    Stevenson's studies, 166–179, 202
        nonparanormal explanation of, 179
        "Sujith" case, 167–178, 202
    theory of, 12–13
    "workshops," 192–199
    (see also Xenoglossy)
Replication (see Reincarnation and Resurrection)
Resurrection
    Aquinas on, 69, 70, 72n
    disembodied survival and, 71–73
    Hick on, 70–71
    identity and, 69–73
    Lucretius on, 69
    replication, contrasted with, 70–71
    self, person, or soul and, 71–73
    theory of, 13–14
Retrocognition, 183
Reykjavik, 117
Rhine, J. B., 210
Rhine, Louisa, 129, 130, 210
Richet, C., 114, 210
Richmond, K., 94n, 210
Riley, Nancy, viii
Roberts, C. S. B., 113n
Rogo, D. S., 153n, 210
Roll of Honor, London *Times*, 122
Roll, W. G., 157n, 209
Rorvik, D., 16n, 21n, 210
"Rosemary" case (see Xenoglossy)
Ross, G. R. T., 44n, 45n, 46n, 75n, 208
Royal Air Force, 124
"Runki" (see Drop-in communicators)
Runolfsson, Runolfur (see Drop-in communicators)
Russell, B., 5, 25–27, 210
Ryle, Gilbert, 35n, 210

S

Sabom, M., 149–151, 152, 202, 204, 211 (see also Near-death experiences)
Salter, H. de G. (Mrs. W. H. Salter), 89n, 92n, 94n, 211
Salter, W. H., 113, 127n, 211
Saltmarsh, H. F., 93
Sandgerdi, Iceland, 116
Savage, C. W., 40, 41, 211
Savodnik, I., 39n, 41n, 207, 211
Schmeidler, G., 93
Scientific survival
    possibilities, 15–22
    see also Cloning; Cryobiology; Genetic engineering; Transplantation biology
Scripts (see Mediumistic messages)
Self
    bundle-theory of, 45–49, 52
    capacities essential to existence as, 56–57
    Cartesian view of, 46, 47, 49
    "conscious-self," 39–41
    Descartes on, 44–45
    Hume on, 44–49
    subject of experiences as, 44–47, 49, 52

television program, likened to, 64
theories as to nature of, 44–49
see also Spirit and Spirits
Self-awareness
self-survival and, 56, 57, 61
Sensory-deprivation experiments (*see* Experiments)
Shaffer, J., 42n, 211
Shakespeare, W., 127, 211
Sheargold, R. K., 164, 211
Shroud, Turin (*see* Turin Shroud)
Sidgwick, E. M. (Mrs. Henry), 83, 86n, 87, 94, 97–98, 100, 127n, 211
Skepticism, cross-corresponding communications, 104–105
Smith, B. M., 210
Smith, K., viii
Smith, S., 154, 156, 211
Soal, S. G., 93, 98, 99, 100, 211
Society for Psychical Research, 82, 83, 87, 92, 103, 104, 112n, 121, 127, 129, 156
Society for Psychical Research, American, 157
Society for Psychical Research, Journal, 157–158
Socrates, vii, 200, 201
Soul (*see* Spirit and Minds)
Spirit
defined, 49
intelligibility of concept, 12, 14, 61–62
terms and reidentification, 49–52
Spirits
abilities of, 61
activities of, 54–56, 57–61
capacities essential to existence as a person, 56–57
communications through ESP, 60–61
ESP and, 54, 55, 57, 58–61, 62
existence as, 54–56
intelligibility of discourse about, 49–52
personalities of, 56–57
persons or selves, as not identical with, 53–62
reidentification of, 50–52, 62
Spontaneous cases, 82, 128–129
Flew on, 82
West on, 82
S.P.R. (*see* Society for Psychical Research)
Stawell, F. M., 104n, 111, 112, 212
Steiner, Chris, viii
"Stevens, Duncan," 124–125

Stevenson, I., 88n, 93, 115, 118, 152, 166–173, 177–179, 181–191, 208, 212
"Stockbridge, Harry," 123–124
"Street, Josephine," 122–123
Stuart, C. E., 210
Sudurnes peninsula, Iceland, 116
"Sujith" case (*see* Reincarnation)
"Supertelepathy," 94–97, 105n (*see also* Mediumistic messages)
Survival (*see* Personal survival and Scientific survival)
Survival hypothesis (*see* Near-death experiences)
Survivors
assumptions as to, 8–11
consciousness of, 10
countability of, 10–11
identity of, 8–9
persons and, relationship between, 8–10
Syracuse, N.Y., 111

T

Tapes, Raudive (*see* Electronic voice phenomenon)
Tart, C., 154, 155, 157, 212
Telepathy
explained, 58n
knowledge through, 59
see also ESP and "Supertelepathy"
Temporal lobe disturbances, 139
Terms, reidentification, effect as to, 49–51
Terrace, Herbert, 186n, 212
Thomas, C. D., 88, 94n, 212
Thomas, R. E., viii
Thompson, Mrs. (*see* Mediums)
Thouless, R. H., 95n, 136n, 212
Tiedeman, Kent, viii
Tigue, Virginia, 165 (*see also* "Bridey Murphy" case)
Times, London, 122, 125
Tissue, apparitional, 130
Tongues, gift of (*see* Xenoglossy)
Topeka Veterans Administration Hospital Research Department, 155
Transplantation biology, 19–21
Troubridge, U., 94n
Turin Shroud, 80–81n
Tyrell, C. N. M., 127n, 212

U

UFO, 130
Uncertainty principle, 163
Utskalar, Iceland, 116, 117

V

Van Eeden, F., 100, 212
Vassar, C., 157n, 209
Verrall, A. W., 104, 106, 107, 111, 113
Verrall, Miss (see Mediums)
Verrall, Mrs. (see Mediums)
Veterans Administration Medical Center, Decatur, Georgia, 149–150
Visions, near-death (see Near-death experiences)
Voice phenomenon (see Electronic voice phenomenon)

W

Wambach, H., 192–199, 212
Weingarten, S., M., 156n, 212
West, D. J., 82, 128, 129, 130n, 135n

Wheatley, J. M. O., 91n
White, Robert, 20, 21n
Wilkerson, Ralph, 5, 213
Willet, Mrs. (see Mediums)
Wittgenstein, L., 200, 213
Wolman, B., 105n, 193n, 213
Wood, F. H., 191, 213
Woodward, K. L., 136n, 213
Word-reaction tests (see Language)
Worth, Patience (see "Patience Worth" case)

X

Xenoglossy
  evidence of reincarnation, 182
  explained, 180
  "Jensen" case, 180–191, 202
  recitative, 182
  responsive, 182
  "Rosemary" case, 184, 191

Z

Zorab, George, 101n, 213

www.ingramcontent.com/pod-product-compliance
Lightning Source LLC
Chambersburg PA
CBHW032223080426
42735CB00008B/693